RANDALL M. MILLER is professor
history and director of Americ
studies at St. Joseph's University.
JON L. WAKELYN is professor of hi
tory at the Catholic University of
America. Professor Miller is the
author or editor of seven books,
including *A Warm and Zealous
Spirit": John H. Zubly and the American Revolution* (Mercer, 1982). Professor Wakelyn is the author of three
books, including *Southern Com-
monfolk in the Nineteenth Century*
(1980, 1982).

CATHOLICS IN THE OLD SOUTH

Essays on Church and Culture

CATHOLICS in the OLD SOUTH

ESSAYS ON CHURCH AND CULTURE

Edited by

RANDALL M. MILLER
and JON L. WAKELYN

MERCER UNIVERSITY PRESS
MACON, GEORGIA 31207

ISBN 0-86554-080-2

BX
1410
.C34
1983

Copyright © 1983
Mercer University Press
Macon GA 31207
All Rights Reserved.
Printed in the United States of America.

All books published by Mercer University Press are produced
on acid-free paper that exceeds the minimum standards set by the
National Historical Publications and Records Commission.

Library of Congress Cataloging in Publication Data

Catalogs in the Old South.

Includes bibliographical references and index.
1. Catholic Church—Southern States—Addresses,
essays, lectures. 2. Catholics—Southern States—
Addresses, essays, lectures. 3. Southern States—
Church History—Addresses, essays, lectures.
I. Wakelyn, Jon L.   II. Miller, Randall M.
BX1410.C34   1983   282'.75   83-7893
ISBN 0-86554-080-2

TABLE OF CONTENTS

DEDICATION

For our colleagues and students at
Saint Joseph's University
and
The Catholic University of America

ACKNOWLEDGMENTS

We are grateful to our colleagues and students who, over the past few years, have expressed interest in our various concerns about the South and Catholicism and who in many ways, have contributed ideas and suggestions about these and other subjects which have inspired and informed our own work. We are especially grateful to Saint Joseph's University and The Catholic University of America for providing generous institutional and financial support for this project. In appreciation, we dedicate this book to our colleagues and students at our host institutions.

R. M. M. & J. L. W.

Church and Society

INTRODUCTION

by Randall M. Miller

The field of Southern religion now enjoys extensive attention and intensive study—helped no doubt by the recent public prominence of a "born again" president and a political "moral majority" rising from Southern fundamentalist congregations. Southern religious scholarship was once the preserve of defensive partisans. No more. It now rests in the hands of serious historians, anthropologists, and sociologists across the country who are committed to understanding religion as the cultural template of Southern identity and society. The study of religion in the Old South has been particularly rich in this regard. John Boles, Dickson Bruce, Sam Hill, Brooks Holifield, Donald Mathews, and Albert Raboteau, among others, have written important books that chart the South's religious terrain and locate Southern experience in a national, comparative-historical context. The enthusiastic responses greeting their works have attracted many others to the field, making the writing of antebellum Southern religious history a vigorous and prosperous cottage industry, both in and out of the region.

For all its vitality and vision, however, the study of Southern religion remains partial, incomplete, and, in some ways, even provincial. Many good studies exist to describe individual denominations, single issues (revivals and race relations foremost among them), selected clergymen or congregations, or brief time periods, but only Hill and Mathews have attempted to pull together the various monographic threads into a comprehensive canvas of Southern religion. Nobody has undertaken to weave the stories of non-evangelical groups into that fabric. Non-Protestants, particularly, have received only polite attention, at best, from the leading students of Southern religion and culture. Indeed, almost all significant work on antebellum Southern religion fixes exclusively on the central evangelical Protestant thrust of Southern culture, implicitly suggesting that the dominant religious mode and theology were the only ones in the Old South.

Catholics especially have suffered from scholarly neglect. Part of the problem derives from historical facts: Catholics were few in number and Catholicism survived outside the mainstream of Southern religious culture. Part of the problem relates to the historians' perspective. Most students of Southern religion are themselves Southern Protestants in background whose interest in Southern religion flows from their personal evangelical Protestant matrix. And, let it be said, a big part of the problem rests with Catholics and Catholic scholarship generally. Despite a surprisingly large body of writing about Catholicism in the South, Catholics have failed to impress their views on Southern historical scholarship. No wonder. Much of this writing lies buried in obscure, local, and Catholic journals, unknown and inaccessible to most scholars; worse, too much of it is defensive, contentious, and parochial, hardly the stuff of scholarship. Also, the rich profusion of sophisticated work on *American* Catholicism in recent years has remained preoccupied with Catholic development as an immigrant religion in the Northern, urban setting where most Catholics in America have lived and where Catholic power and identity have counted. The combination of the narrow geographic range of good Catholic scholarship and the evangelical Protestant orientation of Southern religious scholarship, then, has left Southern Catholicism without benefit of modern historical analysis and insight.

This collection of original essays addresses that need. It represents a beginning—a series of topical and methodological approaches toward a fuller understanding of Catholicism in the Southern context and, thereby, of the South as well. It explores a Catholic culture within a Protestant regional culture, but in limited terms. The essays are inevitably selective in subject matter and emphasis. In many ways, they only sketch the broad outlines of the wide range of questions in need of inquiry. The collection, then, will not satisfy the need for a comprehensive, interpretive account of Catholicism in the Old South. No solid foundation of monographic literature on Southern Catholicism yet exists on which to build a synthesis. But whatever its limited interpretive and topical sweep, this book makes a pioneering effort to treat Southern Catholicism in functional and symbolic terms and to relate Catholicism to regional culture.*

Two parallel lines of inquiry run through this collection. One line traces the Church's evolution in the South, with particular attention to the external social and the internal cultural forces shaping its institutional contours. The other line measures the responses of several different Catholic groups to their religious and social environment, with particular attention to the social and cultural functions of religion and, to a lesser extent, to the development of Catholic folk cultures and a Catholic *mentalité*.

Like all religions, Catholicism performed both spiritual and social roles for its followers. It offered both worship and society. As a belief system, Catholicism helped its adherents to make sense of their world. Through rituals and symbols rooted in the sacramental center of Catholicism, communicants established spiritual and psychological links with their God. The Church also prescribed basic definitions of proper conduct and attitudes toward secular society. Catholicism, of course, was not (and is not) morality, but it did provide a moral compass to guide both public and private life. On a more mundane level, it provided a sense of belonging by binding individuals together with common values for common purposes. Participation together in worship; in educational, charitable, and devotional organizations; in parish construction and maintenance—all gave Catholics shared beliefs and experiences that formed the marrow of a distinctive religious culture.

All this required organization and direction. The Church was (is) an institution. Building the institutions of the Church was particularly

---

*Throughout this book, the Church refers to the Catholic Church. Readers who might find Catholic terms (e.g., religious—any person, clerical or lay, male or female, who is a member of a religious institute devoted to God; or pastoral—a letter that might relate to anything affecting the spiritual life of the diocese addressed by a bishop to the faithful and clergy of his diocese) unfamiliar should consult Donald Attwater, ed., *A Catholic Dictionary* (2nd. ed. rev., New York, 1949); or Albert J. Nevins, M.M., ed., *The Maryknoll Catholic Dictionary* (New York, 1965).

important to Catholics because the sacramental focus of Catholic religion required trained priests; its moral authority hinged on instruction in catechism and instruments of discipline; and its social unity grew from parish churches, schools, and associations. Building the institutions of the Church became the principal concern of Church leaders in the Old South, for they understood that without an institutional framework Catholicism could not exist. The politics and processes of the Church's institutional development are described in the first four essays in this collection.

Raymond Schmandt took on the difficult task of dredging up and sifting through the immense secondary literature on Catholic institutional development in order to present a descriptive overview of the Southern Church establishment. He makes the important point that the Southern Church was the font of American Catholicism from the late eighteenth through the early nineteenth centuries. How the Church in the South went, so seemingly all Catholicism would go. Nobody anticipated the waves of Catholic immigrants who later swept into Northern cities and who, almost by force of numbers alone, recast the Church to make it responsive to the religious, social, and political needs of a Northern, urban immigrant population. The cautious Southern Church gave way to a more militant American Church. Schmandt's diocese-by-diocese despcription of episcopal efforts to build churches and schools and to nuture Catholic intellectual life reveals the paucity of Church resources virtually everywhere in the South. The Church lacked the human and financial resources to complete its institutional framework, and, indeed, as several other essays show, the attempt to construct a Catholic Church unleashed cultural forces that threatened the very unity the Church was attempting to create.

In a more speculative piece, I used the cultural clashes within the Church to compare Southern and Northern Catholic experience. By examining the immigrant character of Southern Catholicism, I discovered that ethnicity played a social and political role in the Southern Church much like that in the North. The patterns of immigrant Catholic life seemed national in character—except, of course, for the presence of slavery in the South. The trustee controversy manifested the ethnic tensions within the Church. It also reflected the democratic, intensely localistic impulses of Southern society generally. The uneven, contested, and often shallow planting of Church authority left room for various strains of ethnic subcultures to grow in the Southern Church.

The Church, then, was no gestalt—no single, inclusive entity impos-ing one culture on the dispersed Catholic population. Several subcultures marked its Southern character, even as the American Church, coming into Irish hands by the 1850s, began to demand greater uniformity in social behavior and devotions. Contention within the Catholic fold, how-ever, sapped the Church's resources and made it vulnerable to both internal and external manipulation.

As Richard Duncan demonstrates in his essay, the Church recognized its minority status in an overwhelmingly Protestant society and assumed a low political and social profile for much of the antebellum period. Church leaders embraced Southern attitudes regarding slavery—a point illustrated by several authors in this book—and reminded detractors of Catholic contributions to American national development. The various Catholic subcultural groups transcended their intramural differences to unite on social policy because Catholic theology in the nineteenth century stressed personal salvation through the sacraments and disengaged from social reform by claiming no moral responsibility for the fate of the world.

In fact, as Sister Frances Jerome Woods illustrates in her chapter on women religious, individual Catholics translated their private concern for human suffering into corporate acts of mercy by establishing or joining congregations of religious to nurse the sick, feed the hungry, and comfort the orphaned and impoverished. Catholics were not insensitive to socie-ty's ills, but the Church's institutional responses were selective in the public causes it supported.

In that sense, Catholicism converged with the dominant evangelical Protestantism of the Old South. The Protestant establishment, too, taught the doctrine of the "spirituality of the church" and largely abstained from legislating social morality and structure by the 1850s. For that reason, perhaps, Catholics did not appear wholly alien in the South-ern world. Insomuch as Southern culture respected the family, ascriptive authority, and the ethic of honor, the Catholic Church did not enter a wholly alien society.

Southern Catholic and Protestant experience converged in other ways as well. The vast expanse of the South and the shortage of clergymen generally contributed to the institutional development of both Catholic and Protestant religious life. Whatever unity or orthodoxy a Southern evangelical ethic imposed on the region by the 1830s, permutations of social practices and church politics sprang up across the South. The Catholic Church's struggle with lay leaders over church finances and appointments of pastors never approached the congregational autonomy of evangelical Protestant churches, of course—the Church was too structured over centuries for that—but it did give Catholic and Protestant laymen a common language of democracy when discussing church affairs. On the frontier, especially, Southerners took what religion came their way. Baptists, Methodists, Presbyterians, Catholics, whatever, all gathered together to hear an itinerant preacher. Such common experiences blurred theology and polity enough to fuse the assembled worshipers into a Christian fellowship—at least for the moment. In addition, as Jon Wakelyn points out, Protestants and Catholics regularly met one another in the schoolhouse, the marketplace, and the courthouse. The absence of a developed public school system in much of the South made Catholic schools attractive to many Protestants. So too did the good reputations Catholics enjoyed as teachers. The mingling of Protestants and Catholics in schools forged the "old school" ties that helped to sustain the political and social hegemony of the merchant/planter classes in the Old South, irrespective of religious affiliation. Such mingling probably also dissipated anti-Catholic sentiments among Protestant elites.

Catholics also joined Protestants in proclaiming the rightness of slavery, the litmus test of Southernism. Indeed, the Catholic Church was a slaveholding church, inextricably bound up in managing slave property while, like Protestant churchmen, admonishing its followers to carry the Gospel into the quarters and to improve the physical conditions of bondage. Father R. Emmett Curran documents the painful dilemma of one Catholic religious order as it grappled with its obligation to bring slaves into Christian fellowship without disrupting its economic necessity to extract labor from them. The Jesuits of Maryland, as Curran shows, resolved their dilemma by selling the slaves southward in 1838, but not before tensions between American-born and European-born Jesuits over slave maintenance and disposal shook the Maryland Jesuit conscience and establishment. Throughout the South, however, the Church's complicity with slavery helped to stave off nativism and anti-Catholic attacks. It also compromised the Church's ministry to the slaves.

The Church's ministry to the slaves revealed its institutional weaknesses—the shortage of priests and overextended bishops, and its social priorities—support for the prevailing political and social arrangements that did not threaten Church development and teaching. As I suggest in a survey of black slaves and Catholicism, the Church's teaching and organization hardly reached the slaves, who were left largely to themselves to nurture their own Catholicism or to forsake the "mother church" altogether. The lack of effective Church control also allowed local planters to use the local churches for their own political and social purposes. Gary Mills provides a copious case study of a colored Creole family who made the local Catholic church into an instrument for preserving the tripartite caste system of Louisiana that gave them significant social and economic power. In building, supporting, and administering the local church the colored Creole Metoyer family controlled the ritual lives of their locality and demonstrated again that religion had many uses.

Southern Catholics subscribed to the region's standards of status and power. As Jon Wakelyn argues, Catholic elites, for example, acted very much like non-Catholic elites in their vocations, politics, and manners. Within the context of their subregions, they followed the ways to wealth in commerce, the professions, and planting marked out by their Protestant peers and demanded the political power and social prestige owing to their class. In like manner, as Richard Duncan suggests, Catholic settlers in the upper South moved along the social and economic paths of settlement in tandem with Protestant settlers. To be sure, both Catholics and Protestants struggled to make the land conform to their respective religious beliefs, but both Catholics and Protestants succumbed to nature, adjusting to the physical, social, and economic contours of the lands they occupied. That process of adaptation bore upon the character of Southern religions. It also established the rhythms of life that governed the region.

For all their similarities with the dominant evangelical Protestant culture, however, Catholics and Catholic culture were different. Their fundamental theology, their rituals, even the habiliments of their clergy clearly set the Catholics apart. In more subtle ways, the Catholic Church departed from Southern norms in providing opportunities for women, through participation in religious orders, to assume leadership roles and occupations denied them in secular society—a point Sister Frances Jerome Woods makes in her chapter. The Catholic Church was also an immigrant church. The South attracted far fewer immigrants in the antebellum period than did the North, a population pattern that reinforced the South's sense of distinctiveness. As an increasingly immigrant church in a proudly native-born, Protestant society, the Catholic Church suffered suspicion and, where Catholics crowded in great numbers, out-right hostility. Richard Duncan describes the transformation of the cautious Catholicism of the Carrolls in the upper South to a more militant Catholicism of Irish priests and prelates after Baltimore received a heavy influx of immigrants. That transformation ignited an Upper South nativism that revealed how much residual distrust of Catholics remained in Southern, indeed Protestant-American society. The character of immi-grant Catholics, especially the impoverished Irish working on the levees and transportation systems of the South—work that no fit native-born Southerner was willing to do—further estranged Catholics and Protes-tants. As Dennis Clark shows in his description of the immigrant Irish, the new Catholic immigrants remained a people apart from the region because nobody would have them. Finally, the Catholic population was increasingly an urban population in a society rooted in the soil. Insomuch as Southern urban interests diverged from Southern rural interests, Catholics moved away from the dominant Southern culture.

Insiders or outsiders—Southern Catholics wrestled with the some-times conflicting demands of their religious culture and their regional one. This tension underscored Catholic life in the Old South, and indeed in all the New Souths that followed. Southern Catholics never resolved the dilemma of their double identity, for both Catholic culture and Southern culture remained in constant flux. As there never was a single Southern Catholicism, no single inclusive Southernism ever existed to fix the social and cultural compass for all who lived in the region. However much the Old South developed a distinctive regional culture based on an agrarian political economy, slavery, and social conservatism, and tethered its diverse elements to an overall political unity and common social purpose by the 1850s, other Souths persisted, if only in muffled tones, to provide the cultural and social elasticity any society needs to survive. The interplay between the Church and Southern culture is then the subject of this book.

A CHURCH IN CULTURAL CAPTIVITY: SOME SPECULATIONS ON CATHOLIC IDENTITY IN THE OLD SOUTH[1]

by Randall M. Miller

As late as 1815 the Catholic Church in America remained largely an Anglo-American community with its one see, Baltimore, the Rome of the United States. The Church maintained a low political and social profile, conscious of its minority position in an avowedly Protestant nation and preoccupied, as it was, with ecclesiastical organization and consolidation. By 1860, however, a new *American* Catholic Church had emerged. The Anglo-American character of the older church receded as an onrush of Catholic immigrants, principally from Ireland, filled up church pews and offices. The immigrant freshet overwhelmed the older, genteel Anglo-American Church, but it also set in motion internal ethnic rivalries that would mark Catholic life for the rest of the century. The Church followed the Catholic immigrants flowing into the burgeoning

[1]Research for this essay was conducted with support from the American Council of Learned Societies, the American Philosophical Society, the Cushwa Center for the Study of American Catholicism (University of Notre Dame), and the Saint Joseph's University Board on Faculty Research. I would also like to thank Paula K. Benkart, Joseph Gower, and the participants in the Seminar on American Catholicism at the University of Notre Dame for their criticisms of earlier drafts of this essay.

cities, and in some cases rural counties, of America, and it rapidly built an ecclesiastical structure to serve the needs of the expanding Catholic population. By force of sheer numbers, immigration brought power and, in time, affluence to the Church, and it fostered a militancy and self-confidence in the Church that in some ways discouraged the new Catholic population from assimilating into American culture and society.

This new American Catholic Church aroused nativist fears of papal domination and foreign corruption. By heightening Catholic self-awareness, nativism reinforced the centripetal tendency among Catholics to view themselves as a people apart, even as they were trying in many ways to become a part of America. The Church responded to nativism in the 1840s and 1850s with an unyielding defense of Catholic values, particularly in the North where most Catholics resided and where most Catholic power rested. The Church's performance charted the movement of Catholics from the periphery of American consciousness in the early nineteenth century into the vortex of American politics by mid-century.

But the growth and spread of Catholic culture and the Church's self-confidence masked fissures within the Catholic social edifice. The Catholic Church of mid-century was not one people, but many. Different immigrant groups brought different cultures and values with them to America—and to the Church. The Catholic Church, the meetinghouse for faith and social action, was perhaps the one institution that immigrants readily recognized in their new world. Not surprisingly, they tried to shape the Church to fit their particular religious and cultural traditions and needs. The Church thus became both the point of convergence and divergence for the different cultural groups. Despite Irish numerical and clerical predominance in the Church by mid-century, no one group achieved total cultural mastery over it. Their common Catholicism drew different Catholic ethnic groups together, for whatever differences they had in private devotional practices, they subscribed to the same basic Catholic beliefs represented in the Mass. Their common Catholicism also set them off from the dominant Protestant American culture. But their ethnic loyalties also drove them apart. The Church's establishment of nationality parishes simply acknowledged the centrifugal forces at work inside Catholicism.[2]

---

[2]The literature on American Catholicism is enormous and growing. In the interests of brevity and the readers' patience, I have dispensed with all but the most essential citations. The basic survey of American Catholic history, which includes many insights on Southern

Although less buffeted by European immigration than its Northern counterpart, and less assertive in projecting a Catholic influence in society, the Catholic Church of the Old South exhibited similar contradictory tendencies of cultural fusion and fissure as it searched for a place in a Protestant world. But the Church in the Old South never fully conformed to the new American model rising in the North. The rural nature of Southern culture, the subregional variations of Catholicism from French Louisiana to the Anglo-American upper South, the poverty of priests and parishes, the light Catholic European immigration, the existence of an indigenous Catholic establishment before the American and immigrant advance, among other factors, all assured that a different brand of Catholic identity would develop in the South. More important perhaps, but difficult to document, the pervasive influence of slavery weighed on Southern Catholics and pushed them along a political and social path away from their Northern brethren.

In the antebellum era Southerners grappled with their own conflicting loyalties to region and nation. The sectional dispute over slavery quickened the South's closing ranks around its peculiar institution(s), which, when mixed with the literature of regionally self-conscious writers, bred a strident Southern nationalism. This prickly Southern self-consciousness easily slipped into a siege and then a paranoid mentality as Southerners discovered enemies from within as well as from without the region who threatened slavery and the Southern way of life. Black slaves chafed at their shackles, and the Southern proslavery apology notwithstanding, most Southerners knew this. White Southerners feared their slaves, even as they schemed to protect and extend slavery. In such a frame of mind, white Southerners discountenanced any breaches of Southern customs and manners. The Catholic Church, with its loyalties and structure reaching beyond the South, drew suspicious glances.

Church growth, is John Tracy Ellis's *American Catholicism* (2nd ed., Chicago, 1969). Also important is James Hennesey, *American Catholics: A History of the Roman Catholic Community in the United States* (New York, 1982). The theme of ambivalent Catholic identity and conflict with the American culture dominates the writing on the Church in the United States. Two good statements of this theme are Andrew Greeley, *The Catholic Experience* (Garden City NY, 1969 ed.); and Edward Wakin and Joseph F. Scheur, *The De-Romanization of the American Catholic Church* (New York, 1966). For an informed and provocative analysis of the character of the nineteenth-century Church see especially Jay P. Dolan, *The Immigrant Church: New York's Irish and German Catholics, 1815-1865* (Baltimore, 1975; pbk. ed., 1977); and Dolan, *Catholic Revivalism: The American Experience*, 1830-1900 (Notre Dame IN, 1978).

The Church, like the Protestant churches, yielded to social and political pressures and adopted a Southern stance on social issues. Almost in spite of itself, the Southern Church adapted to local conditions, with little appreciation of the consequences. The Church won social and political acceptance in the South by sanctifying the secular order of slavery and states' rights. Church leaders preached conciliation and consensus. The Church moved with its flock into the cotton and sugar fields and into the cotton ports and river towns; it promoted temperance and demanded obedience to Scripture and episcopal authority; and it urged good citizenship upon its members. It did not venture into the social and political arena, except to approve Southern positions.

The insidious influence of slavery crept into the Church. Catholic doctrine taught that slavery violated neither divine nor natural law, but it did deplore abuses and demand attention to the slaves' spiritual welfare. According to John Carroll in 1785, Catholic masters in Maryland abdicated their responsibilities to their slaves. He described the 3,000 or so black slaves held by Catholic masters as "very dull in faith and depraved in morals" because the masters kept them "constantly at work" and gave them no time for religion.[3]

Conditions for slaves of Catholic masters did not improve markedly in the nineteenth century. Consider the case of Brother Joseph Mobberly of the Society of Jesus. Mobberly ran a Jesuit-owned plantation in rural Maryland, along with another Jesuit and an overseer. Mobberly made much of the Catholic master's obligations to prepare the slaves for the sacraments and to encourage them in their devotional lives. He did not fare so well in his own experience with slaves. In his diary Mobberly confessed that the slaves did not trust him. No wonder. Mobberly's diary reveals a Jesuit master with a hardening heart. Mobberly grew exasperated over the slaves' repeated thefts, lackadaisical work, and running away. He lamented that the slaves everywhere in the South were "becoming more corrupt and more worthless" because lax discipline spoiled them. The slaves on the Jesuit plantation complained bitterly to Mobberly's superior about Mobberly's insensitivity, and Mobberly was relieved of his plantation duties in 1820. He was not a bad man. The vagaries and frustrations of managing "a troublesome property" simply eroded his

---

[3]Carroll quoted in John T. Gillard, *Colored Catholics in the United States* (Baltimore, 1941), p. 63.

good intentions and high ideals and made him sympathetic to the slave-holders' side of issues. Mobberly was not alone in this. Slavery, after all, had worked a similar effect on Thomas Jefferson.[4]

Private accommodations to the South's peculiar institution grew to public support for slavery. When several Southern critics charged the Catholic Church with abolitionist sympathies because of its opposition to the slave trade, Southern Catholic churchmen almost fell over themselves to correct such calumnies. Bishop John England of Charleston, the Church's most articulate and influential leader in the South, formulated the Southern Church's position on slavery. He reassured Southerners that Catholics were "determined" to prevent the "mischief" of antislavery interference in the South. England admitted that abuses existed in slavery, but he accepted the institution as compatible with state law, Church law, and divine law. Despite his private hope that slavery would end, England left the institution's fate in the hands of the legislature, not the Church. American Catholic thinking reserved the responsibility for man's civil welfare to the state. By labeling slavery a political issue, the churchmen of the South placed it outside the Church's province. They absolved themselves of any moral responsibility to pass judgment on the social world in which they lived. The Church, rather, was obligated to support the state. Whatever their personal wishes regarding slavery's future, Southern Catholic churchmen capitulated to the Southern pro-slavery apologists by retreating to the Church's conservative tradition.[5]

In January 1861, several months before his succession to the see of Savannah, French-born Augustin Verot provided the most detailed examination of the Catholics' proper relation to human bondage. In a sermon that was subsequently printed and widely distributed in the

---

[4]Brother Joseph Mobberly Diary (Georgetown University): 1:40-42. For other examples of European-born Catholic clergy acceptance of Southern attitudes on slavery and race, see Sister Dorothea Olga McCants, ed. and trans., *They Came to Louisiana: Letters of a Catholic Mission, 1854-1882* (Baton Rouge, 1970), pp. 39, 40, 168; and Giovanni Antonio Grassi, *Notizie varie sullo stato presente della repubblica degli Stati Uniti dell' America. . . .* (Rome, 1818), pp. 13-14, 111, 115-16 (copy at Rare Book Room, University of Notre Dame).

[5]Charleston *United States Catholic Miscellany*, 10 October 1840, 17 February 1841; John England, *Letters to the Hon. John Forsyth on the Subject of Domestic Slavery* (Baltimore, 1844). For an excellent discussion of the Catholic position on slavery, see Madeleine H. Rice, *American Catholic Opinion in the Slavery Controversy* (New York, 1944).

South, Verot argued that slavery was both a duty and a burden. By trying to define the Church's role in a slave society, Verot sought to gain Catholic clergy a claim to intellectual and social leadership in the South—something Protestant churchmen had been striving to do for a generation. Like Protestant ministers, Verot attacked the evils of the slave trade, but doted on the paternalistic idyll of Southern slavery, rooted in familial trust and loyalty. Verot stressed the reciprocal nature of bondage. Masters must feed, clothe, and shelter their slaves decently, he advised, and they must raise them in the true faith. He especially enjoined masters to keep slave families intact. In return, the slaves owed obedience and industry to such benevolent masters.[6]

In this, Verot mirrored the general Southern conception of slavery. Like their Protestant counterparts, Verot and other Catholic clergymen urged their followers to uphold the social order by ameliorating the conditions of bondage—hardly a subversive argument. The Catholic Church uttered the right shibboleth of Southern society.

The Church's acceptance of slavery evolved into support for Southern nationalism. During the sectional crisis, Southern Catholics stood with their region. Among prominent Catholic political figures in the South, twenty-one of twenty-three favored secession in 1860. The Church walked in the shadow of the secessionists. A few bishops whispered misgivings about unchecked Southern nationalism, and a few flinched when secession came. Most Southern Catholic churchmen, however, lined up with the Confederacy, for reasons of expediency if not of conviction. The Catholic bishops and priests blessed the flags of Confederate regiments and prayed for Southern victories. They joined their Protestant fellows before the altar of Southern rights, and later of the Lost Cause.[7]

---

[6]A[ugustin] Verot, *A Tract for the Times. Slavery and Abolitionism, Being the Substance of a Sermon Preached in the Church of St. Augustine* ... (Baltimore, 1861). On evangelical Protestants' approach to slavery, see especially Donald G. Mathews, *Religion in the Old South* (Chicago, 1977), pp. 136-84; and H. Shelton Smith, *In His Image, But ... Racism in Southern Religion, 1780-1910* (Durham NC, 1972), pp. 129-207. On Southern Protestant churchmen's and intellectuals' efforts to gain influence in public and social policy, see Drew Gilpin Faust, *A Sacred Circle: The Dilemma of the Intellectual in the Old South, 1840-1850* (Baltimore, 1977).

[7]On lay Catholic support for secession, see Jon L. Wakelyn, *Biographical Dictionary of the Confederacy* (Westport CT, 1977), pp. 25-26. On the bishops' endorsement of Southern rights policies see, for example, Bishop John Quinlan (of Mobile) to Bishop Patrick N. Lynch, 19 May 1861; and Bishop Lynch (of Charleston) to Archbishop John

The Catholic defense of slavery and support for Southern nationalism paid off when the Church faced the nativist upsurge of the 1850s. Nativists tried in vain to tar the Church with the brush of abolitionism. Indeed, no less a Southern statesman than Alexander Stephens of Georgia refuted such "libels" by reminding Southerners that alone of the churches in the United States the Catholic Church had "never warred against us or our peculiar institutions."[8] Governor Henry Wise of Virginia and other prominent Southern politicians chimed in to attack the anti-Catholic rantings of the Know-Nothings. The Catholic stance on slavery, like the Church's subsummation in Southern life generally, contributed much to the puny anti-Catholic thrust of Southern Know-Nothingism.

To be sure, many Southerners harbored dark suspicions of Catholic loyalty. The editor of the Tallahassee *Florida Sentinel*, in a state with only five Catholic churches in 1850, blamed the urban unrest in America generally on Irish-Catholic rowdyism and, during the Mexican War, wondered if Catholics would put the flag before their faith. Catholics in the South suffered from the negative images of Catholics in the North, for the Church did not rive along sectional lines over the slavery issue, as did the major Protestant denominations. The editor of the Charleston *Evening News*, for example, urged Southerners to check the Church's "political and property pretensions" in the region, but he admitted that native-born Southern Catholics were very likely safe on the right matters. Others were not so sure. As one Charleston man put it, "priestly habiliments 'doubtless' concealed the impurities of the devil." More typical was a Georgia woman who, while traveling in Europe, let her anti-Catholic fears gush forth in her diary. She attended High Mass in Milan and

---

Hughes, 6 January 1861, Lynch Papers (Archives of the Diocese of Charleston); and Lynch to Hughes, 4 August 1861, in the Baltimore *Catholic Mirror*, 6 September 1861. The Catholic role in the Civil War crisis is briefly related in Benjamin Blied, *Catholics and the Civil War* (Milwaukee, 1945), ch. 4; and Willard Wight, "The Churches and the Confederate Cause," Civil War History 6 (1960): 367-68, 371-73. For an example of a Catholic priest's excessive devotion to the Confederacy and the Lost Cause apotheosis, see Charles C. Boldrick, "Father Abram J. Ryan: The Poet-Priest of the Confederacy," *Filson Club History Quarterly* 46 (1972): 201-17; and Abram J. Ryan, *Poems: Patriotic, Religious, Miscellaneous* (New York 1896). On Catholic entrapment in the Lost Cause mystique, see Charles R. Wilson, *Baptized in Blood: The Religion of the Lost Cause,* 1865-1920 (Athens GA, 1980), pp. 34, 58-61.

[8]Stephens, quoted in Walter B. Posey, *Frontier Mission: A History of Religion West of the Southern Appalachians to 1861* (Lexington KY, 1966), p. 349.

thought the proceedings *"most amusing* and *funny."* She trembled to enter a Catholic church again, fearing some vague corruption of her soul would result. She condemned Rome, with its "30,000 priests," as "the most corrupt, profligate, and licentious place on the globe." For her, as for many Southerners ignorant of Catholicism, the Church contributed mightily to Europe's moral decay and threatened to do likewise in America.[9]

In many Southern minds, Catholic worship reeked of superstition and magic, and the Catholic hierarchy ran counter to American democratic principles. The large number of foreign-born priests in the South added to the suspicion that some sinister papal plot was afoot. The big fear, however, was that Catholicism, or rather Catholic immigrants, would bring disorder and corruption to the South—that the civil unrest and loose social structure of the North would seep into the South to bring down slavery and Southern society. Major election riots partly instigated by Irish Catholics in New Orleans, Louisville, and Memphis in the 1850s lent credence to such fears. These attitudes and anxieties fueled the Know-Nothing movement in parts of the South, but they did not direct it. The Catholics were too few and too scattered to pose much danger to Southern life. More important, as Avery Craven concludes, they were "too well integrated into Southern life to produce serious hostile reaction."[10]

---

[9]Tallahassee *Florida Sentinel*, 21 May 1844, 23 June 1846; Charleston *Evening News*, 15 October 1855; Diary of Joseph David Aiken, 1849 (typescript), p. 40 (Charleston Library Society); Kate Jones Diary, 22, 29 July 1851 (Southern Historical Collection, University of North Carolina).

[10]On the fear of Old World Catholic decadence infecting America and of modernization coming in Catholicism's wake, see, for example, New Orleans *Daily Crescent*, 21 March 1854. The *Crescent* is a mine of Know-Nothing thought in the only Southern city with a viable Catholic political and social threat. Avery Craven, *The Growth of Southern Nationalism* (Baton Rouge, 1953), pp. 238-39 (for the quote). On the weakness of the anti-Catholic element in Southern Know-Nothingism, see also W. Darrell Overdyke, *The Know-Nothing Party in the South* (Baton Rouge, 1950), and Clement Eaton, *The Freedom-of-Thought Struggle in the Old South* (rev. & enl. ed., New York, 1964), pp. 323-26. Southern images of Catholicism were largely borrowed from popular literature and reports of travel to Europe rather than from local experience. Apparently Southerners traveling in the North did not bother to find out about Catholicism there, indeed eschewed contact with Northern churches whenever possible: John Hope Franklin, *A Southern Odyssey: Travellers in the Antebellum North* (Baton Rouge, 1976), pp. 197-200.

There were some Southern people who found Catholicism appealing. George Fitzhugh, the eccentric but original proslavery writer, admired Catholicism because of its social discipline, authoritarianism, and respect for hierarchical order. Fitzhugh's anti-democratic thought found few takers in the South, but other Southern intellectuals discovered much to like in Catholicism. George Frederick Holmes, for example, read Catholic writers almost exclusively in the 1850s. For the Protestant "gentlemen theologians" of Southern towns and cities, Catholicism offered useful guides to the kind of rational orthodoxy they urged on their Protestant congregations. Indeed, Thomist scholasticism, which was a staple in the European seminaries training clergy who came to America, fit neatly into the gentlemen theologians' prescriptions for reasonable proofs of God's work and majesty. The Catholic insistence on authority appealed to men of a conservative social stripe. Levi Silliman Ives, the Episcopal bishop of North Carolina, converted to Catholicism partly for that reason.[11]

Lines of communication were open between Catholic and Protestant intellectuals and churchmen in the South, and those connections helped to dissipate anti-Catholic hostility. Bishop John England, who read widely in the classics, found congenial company in the local literary and philosophical society and mixed easily with the great men of estate and mind in Charleston. Catholic schools attracted Protestant as well as Catholic students because the priests and sisters had good reputations as teachers and because they were considered sound in their social views.[12]

Some Catholic churchmen and laity met anti-Catholic prejudice head-on. Bishop John England established the *United States Catholic Miscellany* in 1822 partly to combat the "misrepresentations and abuse" Catholics endured. Bishop Francis X. Gartland of Savannah entered the lists against nativism in 1851 by engaging a Baptist minister in a formal public debate which was judged by a panel composed of a Protestant, a

----

[11]Eugene Genovese, *The World the Slaveholders Made: Two Essays in Interpretation* (New York, 1969), pp. 191-93; Neil C. Gillespie, *The Collapse of Orthodoxy: The Intellectual Ordeal of George Frederick Holmes* (Charlottesville VA, 1972), pp. 45-47, 102-104; E. Brooks Holifield, *The Gentlemen Theologians: American Theology in Southern Culture 1795-1860* (Durham NC, 1978), pp. 101-109. Catholic and Protestant reformers occasionally joined hands to promote temperance in the South: see, for example, John Page Diary, vol. 1 (1836-1838), 19 February 1838 (Tulane University).

[12]On student life at a Catholic college—with examples of students sleeping through sermons but religiously attending debates on Know-Nothing politics—see the excellent Daniel Barlow Gorham Diaries, 1856-1859 (Louisiana State University).

Catholic, and a Jew. Throughout the 1850s, Ben Webb's Louisville *Catholic Advocate* pounded away at nativism and anti-Catholicism.[13]

Most Catholic clergy were more circumspect. Some were downright timid. In Alabama at the height of the Know-Nothing fever, for example, one priest refused to join Protestant ministers in saying prayers in the Alabama state legislature because, as a priest, he wanted "as little to do with public matters as possible."[14] This was an extreme position, of course, but it reflected Catholic temperament and tactics in the antebellum South.

Church leaders fixed their gaze on the institutional concerns of building churches and an ecclesiastical framework to support them, of recruiting and training priests and nuns, and of invigorating Catholic faith. The Church made no effort to evangelize among Protestants, and, indeed, it discouraged a few impressionable young men, like Jefferson Davis, who sought admittance into the faith. Unlike the Church in the North, the Southern Church, except in Maryland, did not push for Catholic access to public money for education. The Church looked inward. It had to do so. Internal problems aplenty demanded attention and kept the Southern Church from developing the self-confidence, strength, and militancy of the Church in the North.

A particularly vexing problem for the Church was lay-trusteeism. Lay trustees, or wardens, controlled the finances of individual churches, and in those states that prohibited the incorporation of religious bodies, they held title to church property. The practical need to establish churches among scattered Catholic settlers and the absence of an operating ecclesiastical structure in the interior of the country required lay initiative. Hard pressed to find priests and overwhelmed by pastoral duties themselves, as well as episcopal ones, the early American bishops were in no position to assume complete control of church affairs, nor did they necessarily want to do so. John Carroll, the first American bishop, endorsed the system of lay trustees without realizing its dangerous implications for episcopal authority. Laymen did not relinquish their

---

[13]England quoted in Peter Guilday, *Life and Times of John England, First Bishop of Charleston*, 2 vols. (New York, 1927), 2:457; Ray Allen Billington, *The Protestant Crusade, 1800-1860* (New York, 1938), pp. 256, 261.

[14]Faye Acton Axford, ed., *The Journals of Thomas Hubbard Hobbs...* (University AL, 1976), p. 175.

control over their churches readily, and, in fact, the wardens often used their temporal power to exert control over church discipline and composition. The trustees claimed the right to appoint and dismiss their own pastors. They invoked the American religious tradition of congregationalism and the American political tradition of localism in demanding that bishops comply with their wishes. European (especially Irish) precedents for lay control, European anticlericalism carried to America by Catholic immigrants, the lack of strong ecclesiastical discipline during the American Catholic Church's formative years, the mobility of Americans, and fractious priests unwilling to submit to authority anywhere also inflamed the lay trustee issue. The American bishops recoiled from lay pretensions, pointing out that under canon law the appointment and removal of pastors was vested solely in the bishops. In the early nineteenth century neither side yielded much ground, but the unsettled state of the Church's hierarchy gave the advantage to the trustees.

Until the 1840s, lay trustees in the South vigorously pushed their cause. In Charleston, Norfolk, and St. Augustine, and seemingly everywhere in Louisiana, ugly clashes between trustees and Church authorities occurred. Trustees staged public rallies, they issued denunciations of episcopal and papal "usurpations," they denied the bishops' candidates access to churches and maintenance, they threatened schisms, and they dragged Church authorities into court—all the while maintaining a firm grip on their particular churches. Some of the disputes lasted for years, and the bitterness of the struggles lingered for decades. In perhaps the most celebrated case of lay-trusteeism in the South, the wardens of St. Louis Cathedral in New Orleans rushed to the courts and the state legislature to interpose government between the Catholic prelate and Catholic people. In time, the bishops beat back these challenges, but the damage to the Church's prestige and unity retarded Catholic growth in the South, and the rancor fed the Protestant South's suspicions of Catholic autocracy. More important, the internal rumblings of lay-trusteeism exacerbated more serious faults within the Church.

The laity's assertion of authority also intimated a general contempt for priests. Some disputes quickly degenerated into personal assaults on unpopular priests. At St. Peter's Church in New Iberia, Louisiana, for example, parishioners interrupted the pastor's sermons and threatened his person. On one occasion, several church members set upon the priest with whips and sticks. In Monroe, Louisiana, boys threw stones at an unliked priest, and three Catholic toughs tried to drive him from town. The clash between the pastor and wardens at the parish church of St. John the Evangelist in Lafayette, Louisiana, which involved the priest's attempt to provide catechism for blacks among other disagreements with lay leaders, ended in the streets. A "ruffian" beat up the priest in full view of the townspeople, including the chairman of the board of lay trustees who supposedly stood by amused. The wardens preferred to have no priest rather than submit to the bishop's choice.[15] And so on. The message coming from Louisiana and elsewhere reverberated throughout the Church. In matters of government and social policy in the local churches, the lay leaders considered their churches to be their own preserves and not subject to encroachments and rulings of a distant episcopal power.

Bishops moved quickly to mollify angry wardens, but also to retrieve their power to appoint and dismiss parish priests, the nub of the lay-trustee issue. Whenever possible, they appointed suitable replacements for priests under fire from trustees, and they interceded personally to persuade wardens to accept their decisions. The bishops generally treated the lay leaders respectfully, but always without conveying any sense of agreement with the wardens' arguments. To answer repeated insults to priests and episcopal authority, bishops issued pastoral letters explaining the Church's side. In all their pronouncements the bishops strummed the same motif: that laymen did not have the right to usurp the Church's control over its clergy.[16]

Lay leaders required more than pastoral letters and personal visits to convince them to yield. Bishops interdicted rebellious congregations,

---

[15]New Orleans *Le Propagateur Catholique,* 24 June 1843; Roger Baudier, *The Catholic Church in Louisiana* (New Orleans, 1939), p. 407, 347-48; Minutes of Meetings of the Fabrique (Archives of St. Paul's Church, Mansura LA). See also Father Louis Alaux to Antoine Blanc, 22 May 1835, New Orleans Papers (University of Notre Dame).

[16]See, for example, *Le Propagateur Catholique,* 15 June 1844. For a typical response to recalcitrant priests and laymen, see Bishop Ignatius Reynolds (of Charleston) to "Seminary Faculty and Students," 19 August 1848, Reynolds Papers (Archives of the Diocese of Charleston), in which Reynolds admonished seminarians to respect episcopal authority and thundered against the *lese majeste* of trusteeism. On the Church hierarchy's attitudes toward trusteeism, see Peter Guilday, ed., *The National Pastorals of the American Hierarchy (1792-1919)* (Washington, 1923), pp. 33-35, 108-109. See also J. F. O'Neill to Patrick Lynch, 1 July 1847, Reynolds Papers, for the clergy's resignation concerning lay objections to any episcopal appointments.

denying them the sacraments. They pitted the episcopal party within each congregation against the trustees in efforts to seize effective control over church finances and governance, although such moves often intensified the disputes. They followed their lay opponents into the legislatures and courtrooms to contest lay presumptions.

Priests and bishops approached civil authority reluctantly, but inexorably, to uphold their claims, for they feared that in the United States courts and public opinion were unreliable safeguards for Church authority. They were often right. At Point Coupée, Louisiana, in 1843, for example, a priest brought suit against the wardens for refusing to pay his salary. The supreme court of Louisiana found for the trustees, stating that the local church board's charter granted the wardens sole control over the church's finances and property. In Florida, after the St. Augustine Church wardens closed the church to a priest whom they did not like, the priest sought a writ of mandamus to open the church. The Florida court sustained the wardens' right of patronage, and only the personal diplomacy of Bishop Michael Portier settled the dispute that had raged for over five years. In Louisiana in 1844 the Church fared better. In the important decision concerning the trustees of the St. Louis Cathedral of New Orleans versus the bishop, the state supreme court ruled that the civil courts had no jurisdiction in matters that were solely doctrinal or disciplinary within a church. Furthermore, the principle of patronage, which the wardens cited from the Spanish Code to support their case, had been abrogated after the American acquisition of Louisiana. In effect, the court stated that the wardens lacked the right to force the bishop to appoint a pastor of their choosing. But lacking the legal right to do so did not mean that the wardens lacked the power to have their way. Indeed, the wardens did not turn over title to church property to the bishop until 1883, and they exercised considerable influence over clerical behavior by holding on to church finances.[17]

By appealing to Caesar to resolve domestic problems, the Southern Catholic Church conceded its internal weakness. Even when Southern bishops finally established episcopal authority, they did not wholly subdue the principle of localism and lay authority. In New Orleans the

---

[17]*Le Propagateur Catholique*, 4 March 1843, 9 July 1844; for the Florida controversy, see a good summary in Michael Gannon, *The Cross in the Sand: The Early Catholic Church in Florida, 1513-1870* (Gainesville FL, 1965), pp. 138-47; on Louisiana, Baudier, *The Catholic Church*, pp. 254-58, 275-80, 309-11, 335-44.

Irish Catholic lay leaders who had aligned with the bishop in the case against the wardens of St. Louis Cathedral proclaimed their own freedom from any clerical overlords, even Irish ones, in matters of politics and society. Indeed, in 1853 their violent verbal assaults against the Church when the papal nuncio, Gaetano Bedini, declared his intention to visit New Orleans after his attempt to crush lay-trusteeism in New York, not only forced Bedini to cancel his trip to the South's supposed citadel of Catholicism, but also testified to the lay leaders' residual distrust of episcopal authority.[18]

In Norfolk and Charleston in the early nineteenth century the lay trustees cooperated with one another for a time. They adopted the common strategy of writing directly to Rome to supersede the bishop's authority and of threatening to create an independent Catholic church in America. The trustees wanted to confine clergy to spiritual matters. The Irish trustees in Charleston particularly invoked American republican ideology to counter episcopal authority. They complained that they had left Ireland for America to find civil and religious freedom only to discover that the American clergy were the enemies rather than the sentinels of such liberty. In both Norfolk and Charleston the wardens also preached localism. They challenged the right of a Baltimore prelate to interfere in Virginia or South Carolina concerns and enlisted American Revolutionary arguments to buttress their cause.[19]

In the end, the trustees got their way. They convinced Rome to establish separate dioceses for Virginia and South Carolina, even though,

---

[18]New Orleans *Daily Orleanian*, 22, 24 December 1853. The Know-Nothing paper, the New Orleans *Daily Crescent*, made much of Bedini's proposed visit and used it to fire anti-episcopal feelings. See, for example, *Daily Crescent*, 10 January 1854. The *marguilliers'* defeat was not a complete victory for the episcopacy over the laity. The Irish had aligned with the Church hierarchy largely because they had come to dominate, or expected to dominate, that hierarchy. They demanded and generally received episcopal support for their social and political interests, as well as for their religious ones. When episcopal authority retreated from such support, as in the question of open endorsement of Irish nationalism, the lay Irish leaders spit out venom about not being enslaved to episcopal authority. See, for example, *Daily Orleanian*, 8 April 1852.

[19]For samples of the trustees' documents, see John Tracy Ellis, ed., *Documents of American Catholic History* (Milwaukee, 1956), p. 225; *Documents Relative to the Present Distressed State of the Roman Catholic Church in the City of Charleston* ... (Charleston, 1818); and Guilday, *England*, 1:240-45. On trustees' use of American republican ideology, see Charleston Trustees to Archbishop Mar[é]chal, 8 December 1817, Maréchal Papers (Archives of the Archdiocese of Baltimore).

as in Virginia's case especially, the small number of Catholics did not justify separate dioceses. Part of the problem was Rome's almost complete ignorance of American conditions. By acceding to the demands of the Norfolk petitioners, Rome encouraged lay aggressiveness in America. Patrick Kelly, the first bishop of Richmond, appointed in 1820, pacified the Norfolk trustees for a time by siding with them. When he reconsidered his policy, the wardens revolted again and Kelly left Virginia forever in 1821. The Richmond (Virginia) bishopric stood vacant for the next twenty years—mute testimony to lay intransigence.[20]

Even in Charleston under the enlightened leadership of Bishop John England, lay power did not give way completely to episcopal authority. England removed the incubus of lay-trusteeism by incorporating lay leaders into his episcopal rule. In his program for Catholic development in his diocese, for example, he regularly consulted lay leaders and often deferred to their advice. England understood that in a republic lay support was critical to church growth and stability. Lay trustees, after all, constituted the chief means of fund-raising and influence peddling in each parish. Lay trustees were men of property and standing—those with time and money to devote to church affairs and, most important, with sufficient social prestige in the "deferential democracy" of the South to get elected to office. The pew renters, representing the local propertied classes, provided the church's regular income and so sought to control church finances and governance. Not surprisingly, they chose men like themselves to direct church affairs. And as men accustomed to rule in their local communities and as inheritors of the American republican tradition, they were not about to let "outsiders" have too great a hand in vital social institutions like the church.[21]

The lay leaders' tight grip on the local churches was in part a natural response to the facts of Catholic growth in the South. The expansion of

---

[20]The dispute in Norfolk is detailed in Peter Guilday, *The Church in Virginia (1815-1822)* (New York, 1924).

[21]For an appreciation of England's role in subsuming the laity in the church structure, see Greeley, *The Catholic Experience*, p. 82; and especially Patrick W. Carey, "John England and Irish American Catholicism, 1815-1842: A Study of Conflict" (doctoral dissertation, Fordham University, 1975), pp. 268-392. Pew renting was common among American Catholics as well as Protestants, even in the South. Some Catholic clergy opposed the system for the influence it gave to pew renters in the church. See, for example, John England, *Diurnal of the Right Rev. John England . . . 1820-1823* (Philadelphia, 1895), pp. 46-47.

the institutional church did not, at first, keep pace with the spread of Catholics across the South. In time, the Church established new dioceses that embraced both actual concentrations of Catholics and anticipated future Catholic settlement, but many Catholic settlers in the Carolinas, Georgia, upper Louisiana, Mississippi, Alabama, and Kentucky waited years for effective episcopal authority to assume some of the burdens of building churches, providing priests, and ministering to their physical and spiritual needs. The ambitious extension of dioceses in the South in the 1850s should not disguise the weakness of the episcopal contribution to actual church growth among the dispersed Southern population. Some sees remained vacant, and all bishops suffered a shortage of priests and money to make the Catholic institutional presence visible and significant.

Catholic settlement often preceded formal Catholic authority in the countryside. Away from Southern cities, laymen put up their own chapels and churches, arranged for priests to visit them, and organized Catholic community life. They acquired religious as well as temporal responsibilities. In the absence of priests, they catechized their own children, and in some instances their slaves as well, and they read prayers. The churches they built were literally their own, purchased with their savings and sweat. Not surprisingly, the lay church builders, through their elected church wardens, followed the Southern political maxim that those who owned and built the land should rule it. The trustees believed that their deeds to church property entitled them to something more than unblinking obedience to an arbitrary, and distant, episcopal power, and whatever priests might happen their way. They acted accordingly.

The crude log and clapboard structures the Catholic pioneers erected as churches attested to the frontier, voluntaristic character of their congregations, and, indeed, of the whole antebellum Southern Church. The cathedrals of Baltimore and New Orleans with their archdiocesan panoply of seminaries, colleges, and asylums cast shadows of Church majesty into the countryside, to be sure, but they did not reflect the state of Southern Catholic power until the 1850s, if then. As late as the mid-1830s, for example, Catholics in rural Maryland worshiped in "miserable wooden chapels." In Savannah, in 1859, the bishop, priests, and thirty orphans "huddled together" in a "shanty" through which "the wind whistled as through a basket," complained a missionary priest. When, in 1856, the Catholics of McEwen, Tennessee, decided to build a church, they simply copied the prevailing architectural style of most Southern Protestant and Catholic churches in the trans-Appalachian frontier. They built a log church. For most rural Catholics, private homes, tents, and rickety chapels often sufficed for religious purposes.[22]

The austere country churches hardly inspired awe among the parishioners. Many churches did not even have elevated altars for the priests. When church members made improvements, they did not always enhance the symbolic power of the clergy. The first internal improvement in the spartan St. Charles Church in Kentucky, for example, was the construction of benches for church members. At Point Coupée, in one of the richest parishes in Louisiana, the trustees withheld the priest's salary and money to purchase necessary items for worship, leaving the priest to celebrate Mass at an altar made of candle boxes.[23] The simple country churches symbolized the democratic tendencies of the early lay church builders as well as their poverty. They signaled the laity's reluctance to build beyond their means. Without generous lay contributions, the Catholic Church would have no symbols of power. The Southern Catholic Church had few replicas of its European or Northern magnificence, and Southern lay leaders apparently meant to keep it that way.

The Church was more than bricks and mortar, or timber and tabby as the case often was. The Church was a place where people gathered together. It served simultaneously as a religious and a social center. Distant Catholic families converged on the church on Sundays to exercise a common faith, but also to share information and one another's company. Nice Catholic girls met nice Catholic boys under the watchful, hopeful eyes of their parents. The local church in many ways was both a

---

[22]*Annales de L'Association de la Propagation de la Foi*, 5 (October 1832), 717; Fr. James Hasson to Fr. Woodcock, 10 January 1859, Missionary Letters (Archives of All Hallows Seminary, Ireland; copies in Ireland Papers, University of Notre Dame); Posey, *Frontier Mission*, p. 99; Matilda Charlotte (Jesse) Fraser Houstoun, *Hesperos, or Travels in the West*, 2 vols. (London, 1850), 2:108-109. An exception to the crude building habits of frontier Catholics was the German practice of putting up stone churches when possible. Germans came to stay wherever they settled and built churches that reflected their commitments to place and religion. The first stone church built in the interior of Missouri, for example, was built by German Catholic immigrants. See Charles van Ravenswaay, *The Arts and Architecture of German Settlements in Missouri: A Survey of a Vanishing Culture* (Columbia MO, 1977), p. 205. On the importance of the forms and area distribution of buildings, see Russel Gerlach, *Immigrants in the Ozarks: A Study in Ethnic Geography* (Columbia MO, 1976).

[23]J. Herman Schauinger, *Cathedrals in the Wilderness* (Milwaukee, 1952), p. 15; Fr. [Hubert] Thirion to Antoine Blanc, 4 April 1856, New Orleans Papers.

cause and a consequence of whatever group consciousness that developed among Catholic settlers.

Catholic church life in the antebellum South, as in the antebellum North, was never tidy. In the fluid social world of young America new immigrants and migrants pushed in on older communicants. They sought entrance to the local churches, and they also sought influence in them. Although immigration was greater and more conspicuous in the North, many Irish and German Catholic immigrants entered the Old South and stayed. In the port cities particularly they challenged native Anglo-American or French Creole Catholics for control of the churches. Indeed, the ethnic tensions in the Southern Church often colored the lay-trustee disputes.

Ethnic differences underscored almost all the bitter lay-trustee crises in the Old South. In the early nineteenth century, the French clergy, many of them learned, aristocratic exiles fleeing European libertarian democracy, combined with the Anglo-American Catholic establishment to try to vest control of the Church in American prelates because they feared the ignorant, déclassé Irish Catholics swarming into the Church in America. Baltimore Archbishop Ambrose Maréchal's many problems with lay trustees in Virginia and South Carolina derived from his animus toward the Irish as much as any other factor. The embattled Maréchal felt isolated, too, when Rome overruled his advice and appointed Irishmen to the Richmond and Charleston sees. He worried that, with a continuing influx of Irish immigrants, Irish bishops and priests would try to convert the fragile American Catholic Church into an Irish parish and thereby destroy the institution by inviting nativist attacks against it, by weakening its intellectual and social ties to the American Protestant establishment, and by introducing nationalistic tribalism into it. The cultural conflict ignited lay-trusteeism in Norfolk, for example, when the Irish parishioners objected to the appointment of a French priest for them. The trustees pressed for a separate diocese and shot off angry letters against the interference of a French bishop in local (read Irish) affairs.[24]

---

[24]Thomas T. McAvoy, C.S.C., made this point in his seminal argument, "The Formation of the Catholic Minority in the United States, 1820-1860," *Review of Politics* 10 (1948): 13-34. Part of Bishop England's success in subduing trusteeism in Charleston derived from his open support for Irish national interests. England was a regular speaker at the influential Hibernian Society in both Charleston and Savannah and rarely missed a chance to align himself with Irish sensibilities. See the *Tribute to the Memory of Bishop England by the Hibernian Society of Savannah, Georgia* (Savannah, 1842), p. 3; and

The importance of ethnicity in kindling lay-clergy acrimony should not obscure other causes of the lay-trustee issue. Localism, a deeply imbedded tradition of local control of social and political institutions, stemmed from the American colonial and Revolutionary experience. Reinforced by the white Southerners' almost pathological fear of external tampering with slavery, it no doubt contributed much to the controversy. So too in several cases did imperious, dogmatic clerics and lay leaders, abetted by arrant meddlers and ambitious men on both sides who used the issue to advance their own interests. Their behavior allowed little chance for communication and compromise. Ethnic homogeneity did not guarantee peace in the parishes. The anticlerical tirades and violence in rural Louisiana demonstrated that much. Ethnic diversity did not necessarily result in a rebellious laity. The stability of the Kentucky Catholic settlements showed that. Still, it is suggestive that the longest, nastiest lay-trustee disputes had an ethnic cast to them and that such crises subsided when one ethnic group, generally the Irish, achieved overwhelming numerical and clerical dominance in a diocese.

The case of New Orleans is instructive. Antebellum New Orleans was several cities in one. Its character evolved from colonial Spanish and French occupation, American annexation, and after 1830, from a significant foreign immigration. European immigrants largely accounted for the city's substantial white population growth in the late antebellum period, and they both shored up and eroded the city's Catholic establishment by increasing its number of communicants on the one hand, while introducing ethnic rivalries and onerous social service responsibilities on the other.

The older French and Spanish population, or Creoles, crowded into the original French quarter below Canal Street, where their stucco houses and Latin Catholicism bore witness to their cultural resistance to "Americanization." The newer American elements, who came to dominate the city's trade and tried to inject Anglo-American Protestant manners and morals into its culture, lived adjacent to the Creole section. The German and Irish immigrants filled up the marshlands surrounding the old city, but many Germans and Irish dispersed throughout New Orleans. French immigrants gravitated toward the congenial Creole quarter. Blacks, slave and free, and numerous other groups mingled in the several neighbor-

---

Minutes of the Hibernian Society, Charleston, 1827-1847, 18 April 1842 (South Carolina Historical Society).

hoods and added to the variegated colors and customs of the cosmopolitan port.[25]

Many German and Irish Catholic immigrants lived in shanties and tenements and suffered unspeakable misery. Recurrent epidemics, suffocating heat, and voracious insects compounded their suffering. The new immigrants often labored as day workers along the docks or toiled in other kinds of heavy work. Some few rose to a comfortable living, even wealth and prominence; others, like the skilled workers, plied their trades successfully enough to escape the uncertainties and poverty of life on the docks; but most immigrants apparently struggled as draymen, stevedores, riverboat men, construction workers, and the like. Despised for their poverty and ignorance by the Creole Catholics and American Protestants alike and afflicted by all the ills of an unhealthful physical and social climate, the immigrants drew together in their respective groups for sustenance and succor.[26]

They also moved toward their church. That was just the rub. The Church, the most important social institution for immigrants outside the family, was not wholly theirs, and for a time it was not even within their neighborhoods. German and Irish Catholic immigrants regarded the Church as the tie that bound them to their pasts. Lacking physical barriers to separate themselves from other groups in the city, the ethnic groups built social and cultural barriers to help preserve their cultural values and institutions. Immigrants who might have had little association with the Church in the Old World made it the fortress of their ethnic identity in the New World. Religion thus helped to define ethnic boundaries. In some ways, this process began in Europe and extended to America. But the American experience was not just a carry-over of European religious loyalties and practices. It was, rather, an ongoing synthesis of the peculiar mixes of Old World patterns and interests in different New World social

---

[25]For contemporary descriptions of the various districts, see, for example, A. O. Hall, *The Manhattaner in New Orleans* (New York, 1851), pp. 34-35; and C. S. Latrobe, *The Rambler in North America*, 2 vols. (London, 1836), 2:332-33. Irish and German immigrants entered New Orleans at the rate of 30,000 to 40,000 a year by 1850. Many moved up the river, but many remained at least for a time.

[26]On living conditions, see Roger Shugg, *Origins of Class Struggle in Louisiana* (Baton Rouge, 1939, pbk. ed., 1963), p. 40. Earl Niehaus, *The Irish in New Orleans, 1800-1860* (Baton Rouge, 1965), pp. 28-34, describes living conditions in detail and shows that the Irish were not concentrated in one ghetto, but were, rather, dispersed throughout the city in the back alleys and side streets. Still, Irish "districts" were apparently identifiable.

and cultural settings. The products of this ethno-religious interaction were as unpredictable as the weather.[27]

The universality of the Catholic Mass and ritual, devotions, and spiritual exercises made the Church a psychological as well as religious refuge for Catholic immigrants in a Protestant world. The centripetal force of Catholicism brought believers together physically in the Church and spiritually in the sacraments. The Eucharist then, as now, stood at the center of the Catholic liturgical service, indeed of Catholic religion. As anthropologist Anthony Wallace observes, ritual "is religion in action." It "accomplishes what religion sets out to do."[28] The liturgical service, with its established time, place, and ritual, fixed the religious orbit of worshipers everywhere in the Catholic universe. Transubstantiation occurred literally and figuratively at the Mass, transforming Catholic communicants of diverse social and cultural backgrounds into one corporate entity—the body and blood of Christ and the Catholic Church.

Centrifugal forces of culture, however, spun Catholics away from their sacramental center. German, Irish, and French Catholics did not always honor the same religious heroes or stress the same private devotions. They did not preach, or want preached, the same kind of sermons. Irish and German Catholics, for example, felt uncomfortable in St. Louis Cathedral in New Orleans because the priests spoke only in French. Each group wanted preaching in its own language. The immigrants wanted as priests their own countrymen—persons who shared common cultural and religious customs and values. They did not want to be foreigners in their own church.

The religious differences between Irish and German Catholic immigrants posed no permanent, insuperable obstacles to a sense of Catholic community among them because, differences in language and customs notwithstanding, Irish and German Catholic immigrants nurtured a similar piety. Irish and German Catholics subscribed to Tridentine Catholicism. Theirs was a parish-oriented faith that "emphasized the sacraments of baptism and confirmation, attending Mass, receiving com-

---

[27]The best discussion of the European and American interlacing of religion and ethnicity is Timothy L. Smith, "Religion and Ethnicity in America," *American Historical Review* 83 (1978): 1155-85.

[28]Anthony F. C. Wallace, *Religion: An Anthropological View* (New York, 1966), p. 102.

munion at least once a year, and annual confession of one's sins." For
them, the catechism was "the handbook of the faith." Tridentine Catholicism encouraged spiritual activism, which German and Irish Catholics
manifested in their devotions and religious confraternities.[29]

A "devotional revolution" underway in mid-nineteenth century Ireland, however, gave Irish immigrants a sharper sense of "peoplehood"
than the Germans, who came from several regions within Germany and
did not share all the same religious habits. According to Emmet Larkin,
through a complex interaction of social, economic, and political forces,
the Irish clergy consolidated their hold on the Irish Church during the
nineteenth century. They communicated their zeal and piety to their
congregations by emphasizing regular participation in the sacraments,
especially confession and communion. The priests encouraged the communicants in their devotional exercises, which were "mainly of Roman
origin and included the rosary, forty hours, perpetual adoration, novenas,
blessed altars, *Via Crucis*, benediction, vespers, devotion to the Sacred
Heart and to the Immaculate Conception, jubilees, triduums, pilgrimages,
shrines, processions, and retreats." Sodalities, confraternities, purgato-
rian societies, temperance and altar societies, among other religious
organizations, provided regular communal participation in the devotional exercises. The exercises appealed to all the senses in the Mass
"through music, singing, candles, vestments, and incense." Private devotions sustained public religious expressions "by the use of devotional
tools and aids: beads, scapulars, medals, missals, prayer books, catechisms, holy pictures, and *Agnus Dei*." All such practices and instruments
increased attendance at Mass, spiritual activism, and respect for Church
authority. The clergy ceased to administer the sacraments in private
dwellings, "profane places," and brought the whole of Catholic life and
identity into the church. By giving order and direction to Irish Catholic
religion, the Church became a vehicle for Irish nationalism. The Irish
Catholic immigrants of the 1850s carried their religious enthusiasm and
their enthusiastic religion (and nationalism) with them to America.[30]

Irish Catholics could not at first practice spiritual activism or develop
a sense of Catholic community in the latitudinarian Creole Church of

[29]Dolan, *Immigrant Church*, p. 7 and passim.

[30]Emmet Larkin, "The Devotional Revolution in Ireland, 1850-1875," *American
Historical Review* 77 (1972): 625-52 (pp. 644-45 for quotes).

New Orleans. The immigrants took matters into their own hands. In 1833, for example, several Irish businessmen bought town lots and built a "small frame church," St. Patrick's, for the city's Irish. The bishop, Leo de Neckere, acknowledged the Irish lay initiative and appointed Irish priests to serve the new church. As the Irish population spread in and around New Orleans, Irish Catholics demanded their own churches, even when a neighborhood parish church was available. At St. Mary's Assumption, a predominantly German church, Irish parishioners threatened schism in the 1840s until they got their own Irish church and pastor. By the mid-1850s Irish lay initiative led to the location of Irish parishes in Lafayette (a suburb), the Third Municipality, and the Second Municipality in back of the American sector of the city. In each parish the Irish set up social and charitable societies and schools, thereby reinforcing their attachment to their church. The more prosperous of the Irish settlers reached across parish lines in organizing the Catholic Institute, an association of businessmen and tradesmen who sponsored lectures on political and intellectual issues of current interest and, through the Institute's library and newspaper, promoted an Irish Catholic identity. For most Irish Catholics, however, the priest and the parish were the real glue bonding them with the Church; and the expansion of Irish parishes and the recruitment of Irish priests in New Orleans hardened Irish Catholic religious commitment.[31]

German Catholics in New Orleans often made do with parish churches like the one in Carrollton, where the priest ministered in German, French, and English to the multilingual congregation. Wherever German Catholics concentrated, however, they pressed for separate facilities. Germans insisted on catechism classes and preaching in German, and demanded German churches where they could locate German Catholic charitable, social, and religious activities. They converted dance halls, warehouses, and more humble buildings into rooms for services and instruction. In 1847, for example, many German Catholics living in the city were unable to attend services at the two "German" churches, both on the edge of New Orleans. They petitioned the bishop to give them a vacant building in the city, promising to provide repairs, vestments, and

---

[31]Baudier, *Catholic Church*, p. 369; Niehaus, *Irish in New Orleans*, pp. 104-109. The Institute's activities can be followed in its newspaper, the *Southern Standard*. The formation of the Institute also reflected divisions within the Irish "community" along class lines and lines of old against new residents of New Orleans.

all other necessities. In multiethnic churches Germans clung to whatever special privileges they had in order to maintain their autonomy. In 1858 the Germans in Lafayette turned away French worshipers from the ten o'clock Mass because the French were assigned the eight o'clock Mass and the Germans the one at ten o'clock. Germans insisted on clear ethnic boundaries within the church. At St. Mary's Church Germans protested the French and blacks having services in "their" church, not so much because of prejudice but because they feared that the presence of non-Germans in St. Mary's "might by degrees" turn it "into a French or English Church, and they might one day get dispossessed of it entirely," wrote one contemporary. They even demanded that a German father be made the superior of the Redemptorists serving them. The dearth of German priests, however, impeded German Catholic parish growth, and the dispersal of the Germans throughout New Orleans and its environs did not justify separate parishes.[32]

The Irish and German presence in the New Orleans Church aroused Creole opposition. The Creoles never fully accepted American annexation of Louisiana. They waged a long war of cultural and social exclusivism to preserve their Creole culture and to brace up their slipping political strength in lower Louisiana. To the Creoles, the Irish and Germans constituted a dire threat to Creole cultural and political influence because they swelled the numbers of non-Creoles in the city and the Church. The new immigrants drained the Church's resources, and by their clamor for separate parishes, they broke Catholic unity, a chief source of Creole power in the city. Their poverty embarrassed Catholic

---

[32]Baudier, *Catholic Church*, pp. 367-69; (?) Baumann to Antoine Blanc, 26 June 1847, New Orleans Papers; Blanc to John Purcell, 4 November 1847, Purcell Papers; (University of Notre Dame); Lafayette French Parishioners to Blanc, 17 December 1858, New Orleans Papers; George Ruland to Blanc, 17 June 1854, New Orleans Papers. The problem of finding a German church for the growing German population in the city became critical in 1851 when a fire destroyed one of the churches with a German worship service: Blanc to Purcell, 24 October 1851, Purcell Papers. In recruiting priests for his archdiocese, Archbishop Antoine Blanc sought priests who could speak several languages, but he did not want priests who spoke only German: Blanc to Purcell, 15 March 1859, Purcell Papers. Germans lacked their own asylums in New Orleans as well as their own churches, and they sent their orphans and poor to the Catholic asylums where the Irish and French predominated. This too caused resentments among the Germans. See, for example, Blanc to Purcell, 10 January 1853, Purcell Papers; and George Ruland to Blanc, 17 June 1854, New Orleans Papers. For a comparison of German and Irish Catholics in another Southern town (Vicksburg, Mississippi) see, for example, Fr. M. D. O'Reily to Blanc, 9 November 1841, New Orleans Papers.

society generally. Worse, Irish Catholics seemed destined to take over the Church hierarchy and to transform the Church into an arm of Irish nationalism and piety.

From 1805 on the Creole trustees, or *marguilliers*, of St. Louis Cathedral had contested the bishop's right to appoint and remove pastors. By the 1840s the growing episcopal sympathy for the new immigrants' needs and the staffing of Irish parishes had stiffened the Creole *marguilliers'* determination to keep control of "their" cathedral. The trustees lost the legal and political battles over the right of patronage, but the Church hierarchy, which became increasingly Irish during the crisis, lost Creole support for the principle of Catholic unity. Indeed, prominent Catholic Creole leaders, such as the historian Charles Gayarré and the poet Abbé Adrien Rouquette, for a time joined the Know-Nothing movement in Louisiana in order to stem the Irish immigrant tide. They sought to regain in secular politics some of the influence they had lost in Church politics. In the 1850s the Irish Catholics' public criticism of Creole religious laxity, antiauthoritarianism, and nativism staked off the distance separating the old and new Catholics of New Orleans.[33]

The Catholic Irish, or Germans or French, were not distinct homogeneous groups. Class tensions, Old World jealousies, settlement patterns, length of residence in New Orleans (and America), and ideology divided the groups from within. Because of selective migration, the South escaped much of the turmoil of Catholic intragroup tension, but differences between old and new Irish (or German or French) settlers, for example, no doubt colored the character of Catholic parish politics and piety. However, the lack of records of Catholic mutual aid societies, fraternities, and other social and religious organizations prevents any hard con-

---

[33]Archbishop Blanc noted that in New Orleans the Know-Nothings recruited "numbers" of "Creole young men" by their show of liberalism regarding Catholics: Blanc to John Purcell, 21 March 1854, Purcell Papers. Gayarré was particularly incensed by voting frauds, which he tied to Irish immigrants and lax naturalization laws. See, for example, his pamphlet, *Address to the People of the State on the Late Frauds ... on the 7th November, 1853 in the City of New Orleans* (New Orleans, 1853). Gayarré challenged the anti-Catholic bent of the Know-Nothing party, but lost in national councils, whereupon the heavily Creole Catholic Louisiana elements left the party. For Gayarré's protest against the religious clause of the Know-Nothing platform, see his pamphlet, *Address to the General Assembly of the Know-Kothing Party held in Philadelphia, May, 1854* (n.d., n.p., copy at Tulane University). On Rouquette, see D. R. Lebreton, *Chala-ima: The Life of Adrien-Emmanuel Rouquette* (Baton Rouge, 1947), pp. 187-98. On the *marguilliers*, see Baudier, *Catholic Church*, pp. 335-44 and passim.

clusions about the social and cultural configurations of the subgroup variations.

Residential concentration, shared lifestyles, and common work experiences also defined and reinforced ethnic identities. The residential diaspora of Germans and Irish in particular added to the mutations of ethnic identity within each group. Residential dispersion inhibited the growth of exclusively ethnic organizations necessary for the maintenance of what Milton Gordon terms "primary relationships" within the group, and it transferred to the Church functions of preserving group identity. As a result, ethnic identities may have been transformed into religious identities over time and brought the various subgroups together.[34]

The Irish and German Catholics had begun to move apart, but the Creole challenge and the episcopal support for ethnic parishes brought them together in the "new" Catholic Church of New Orleans. So, too, did their similar Tridentine Catholicism which was preached and practiced in the new parishes. Bishop Antoine Blanc, who finally prevailed over the *marguilliers* in 1844, courted the Irish particulary in his effort to secure episcopal authority. He understood that the Irish tradition of clerical authority, when grafted on to their disgust over Creole latitudinarianism and nativism, made the Irish his natural allies. Blanc's wisdom culminated in the growing support for his authority among Irish and even German parishioners and his growing sensitivity to Irish and German needs.[35] In New Orleans lay and clerical authority converged because the Irish conquered the Church, but lay leaders did not renounce all claims to independent action. The bishop's accommodations to Irish interests simply obviated the need for any but Creoles to summon their residual power.

By the 1850s, the Irish became the dominant element in the New

---

[34]On the importance of residential concentration, and common work experiences and class interests, see William L. Yancey, Eugene P. Ericksen, and Richard N. Juliani, "Emergent Ethnicity: A Review and Reformulation," *American Sociological Review* 41 (1976): 391-403; and especially Kathleen Neils Conzen, "Immigrants, Immigrant Neighborhoods, and Ethnic Identity: Historical Issues," *Journal of American History* 66 (1979): 603-15. On the residential habits of the Irish generally, see Lawrence J. McCaffrey, *The Irish Diaspora in America* (Bloomington IN, 1976).

[35]Antoine Blanc to Bishop John B. Purcell, 10 January 1844, Purcell Papers. On Irish support for Blanc's policies and Irish Catholic definitions of religious duties, see John Pryor, et al., for 1560 members of the St. Patrick's Total Abstinence Society, to Antoine Blanc, 10 November 1843, New Orleans Papers.

Orleans Church, comprising more than half the Catholic population in the city. The Irish Catholics' regular attendance at Mass and their participation in devotional exercises, along with their alliance with the episcopal power, gave them a powerful voice in Church affairs. This influence led to a proliferation of orphanages, benevolent associations, and free parochial schools in the late antebellum period that affected Catholic life in New Orleans more deeply and widely than the Ursulines' genteel private academy or the High Mass at the cathedral. Still, the Irish imprint on Gulf Catholicism did not completely erase other influences or conceal the internal ethnic and class distinctions within the Church.

There was also the matter of color. On the surface, the large black and colored Catholic population of New Orleans suffered little discrimination in the Church. They attended Mass and received communion in the same churches as the whites. They baptized their children there, and in many cases they even received instruction and the sacrament of marriage there. In fact, however, the Southern Catholic Church never warmly embraced its darkly complected communicants, and it moved with unbecoming caution in extending religious instruction and social services to them. In the countryside, the Church did almost nothing to confirm or nourish Catholicism among blacks, slave or free.[36]

The Church did not abjure its obligations to blacks; it simply ignored them. To be sure, two "black" sisterhoods emerged, and various individual clergy tried to catechize and otherwise instruct them. The Oblate Sisters of Providence, a congregation of black nuns, was founded in Baltimore in 1829. In New Orleans, the Ursuline nuns instructed blacks from the 1720s to 1824, and the Carmelites began a school for colored Creoles in the nineteenth century. Bishop Louis Du Bourg sought to continue this work through such organizations as the Christian Doctrine Society of New Orleans, and Bishop Antoine Blanc, in 1842, helped to organize the Congregation of the Sisters of the Holy Family, a community of colored sisters, to care for orphaned and aged blacks. Bishop John England launched a school for free black children in Charleston in 1835,

---

[36]On the Church's relations with blacks, see Randall M. Miller, "The Failed Mission: The Catholic Church and Black Catholics in the Old South," in Edward Magdol and Jon Wakelyn, eds., *The Southern Common People: Studies in Nineteenth-Century Social History* (Westport CT, 1980), pp. 37-54, reprinted in this book; and Albert J. Raboteau, *Slave Religion: The "Invisible Institution" in the Antebellum South* (New York, 1978), pp. 271-75.

and in St. Louis, in 1845, the Sisters of St. Joseph of Carondelet began teaching catechism and practical crafts to black girls. Such efforts, however, were too few and too easily abandoned. White opposition to the instruction of blacks forced England and the St. Louis nuns to close their schools soon after they opened them. The black religious orders remained understaffed and poorly supported throughout their ministry. The Church's uneven outreach to blacks was painfully apparent to those who were its intended recipients. As one black man in Louisiana observed in 1856, there were two kinds of convents in his state—the one for the rich had a high board fence that prevented people from seeing in, while the one for the blacks and poor had only an "open Paling fence."[37] That the founding of two poor "black" congregations, the interrupted work of the Ursulines, and the few cases of religious instruction for blacks constituted the main proof of the Church's mission to blacks spoke volumes on its social priorities.

The Church's principal problem was resources, not racism. The immigrant tide swamped the Church's few priests and meager finances, thus limiting its ability to reach out to all Catholics. Rural Catholics of all colors and conditions felt the pinch of resources keenly. It is perhaps significant that all the special efforts on behalf of blacks began before the great immigrant influx of the 1840s and 1850s and that the Church's special ministry to blacks lapsed during its struggle to meet the immigrants' needs.

Racial tension, however, figured in the halting ministry to blacks—at a time when evangelical Protestant churches embarked on their mission to the slaves. The Irish influence in the Church played a part in forming Catholic responses to black needs. The urban Irish clashed with the urban blacks, with whom they often competed for jobs in the trades and on the docks. The Irish steadily drove blacks from many occupations, a trend that heightened Irish-black differences everywhere in the urban South. Since the blacks of New Orleans dispersed throughout the city, they had to share church facilities with whites. Black Catholic and Irish Catholic worshipers could not easily avoid one another on the Sabbath, and the black-Irish tensions of the workplace no doubt intruded into the holy place.[38]

---

[37]Anton Reiff Journal, 1 February 1856, p. 29 (Louisiana State University).

[38]On Irish-black tension, see, for example, T. C. Grattan, *Civilized America.* . . . 2 vols. (London, 1859), 2:41-42; and Niehaus, *Irish in New Orleans*, pp. 49-54. Such tension was

The Irish influence within the Church also meant the dissemination of an Irish Catholic piety as the norm. While Tridentine Catholicism in many ways suited the Germans, the French-speaking and American colored and black Catholics did not share that tradition.

Priests were the vital link between people and the Church. The blacks, however, did not have their own priests. Irish, German, and French priests, recruited in Europe to serve the missionary American Church, preached and instructed their compatriots in their respective vernaculars. The American Church tried to train an American clergy to do likewise in the American idiom. Yet, although black Catholics understood either English or French, and sometimes both, by not having their own people as priests, they lacked access to a clergy sensitive to all their peculiar social and cultural needs.

The American Church did not call upon black lay preachers or create a black priesthood. Catholics viewed the priest as a sacral figure, not as a preacher of the Word. To officiate at Mass was the priest's primary duty, and this required training in liturgy and Latin. In Catholicism, then, laymen could not assume the role of priest simply by having grace, as they could in several evangelical Protestant groups. The shortage of priests everywhere in the antebellum South, however, dictated some accommodation to black needs. Several masters allowed trusted slaves to preach to their Catholic fellows. Bishop John England inveighed against the practice, fearing that such unlearned men would debase Catholic doctrine. Bishop William Henry Elder of Natchez, who encouraged missionary work among blacks, regarded blacks as "entirely animal in their inclinations" and "engrossed in their senses." To his and other churchmen's minds, the differences between the blacks' and the whites' moral code made the former poor stuff for the priesthood.[39]

When the need for black clergymen became strikingly evident after the Civil War, the Southern Catholic clergy still counseled against their recruitment. Black lay preachers were not actively suppressed by the

---

not inevitable; indeed, outside the city slaves might have viewed the Irish ditchdiggers and levee workers with sympathy. One report stated that slaves in St. Michael, Louisiana, were almost Fenians. See Fr. [Claude] Tholomier to Antoine Blanc, 18 April 1857, New Orleans Papers.

[39]Charleston *United States Catholic Miscellany*, 10 September 1831; Elder to the Society for the Propagation of the Faith, 1858, Elder Papers (Archives of the Diocese of Natchez-Jackson); Elder to John M. Odin, 13 May 1866, New Orleans Papers.

Church before the war, for there were too few of them scattered across the South for that. But they received no support from the Church and did not form the basis of a black Catholic priesthood after emancipation. The attitudes of the Irish bishops in the South mitigated against enlisting blacks as teachers, preachers, or priests. Without their own preachers, blacks would never wholly belong to the Southern "Irish" Church.

In New Orleans and the Gulf region generally, color, caste, and culture also divided colored Catholics among themselves. Light-skinned, middle- and upper-class, French-speaking free people of color occupied a middle ground between slave and free, black and white, in Gulf society. Below them were the poorer, darker, free blacks and the slaves. To be sure, some dark-skinned Protestant American free blacks possessed wealth and, concomitantly, social power equal to or greater than that of the free people of color, but they did not enjoy the privileged status that derived from the colored Creoles' long residence in Louisiana, their light skin, and their French culture. The free blacks also did not usually share the colored Creoles' Catholic faith.[40]

The wealthy free people of color had property in land, houses, and slaves. Property ownership offered hardy proof of their business skills, but more than that, of their acceptance of Southern standards of status. Property ownership put many colored Creoles at the apogee of "colored" society, but it did not insure their precarious elite position in a society committed to slavery and white rule. The free people of color may have resented their dependence on whites for protection and, in their busi- nesses, for patronage, but they understood the need to solidify those

---

[40]My account in the following paragraphs owes much to Donald E. Everett, "Free Persons of Color in New Orleans, 1803-1860" (doctoral dissertation, Tulane University, 1952); and David C. Rankin, "The Forgotten People: Free People of Color in New Orleans, 1850-1870" (doctoral dissertation, Johns Hopkins University, 1976); and Geral- dine M. McTigue, "Forms of Racial Interaction in Louisiana, 1860-1880" (doctoral dissertation, Yale University, 1975), chs. 1 and 2. On the persistence of colored Creole exclusiveness, see Arthé A. Anthony, "The Negro Creole Community in New Orleans, 1880-1920: An Oral History" (doctoral dissertation, University of California, Irvine, 1978). The complexity of New Orleans' "colored" social structure is well treated in John Blassingame, *Black New Orleans, 1860-1880* (Chicago, 1973), although Blassingame misses some of the significance of Catholic culture as a barrier between Creoles and American blacks. Differences among nonwhites—based on condition, status, color, and culture—were not peculiar to the Gulf region. The small number of "colored Catholics" in Charleston, for example, exhibited such divisions at one time. See Bishop England's description (1832) in Sebastian G. Messmer, ed., *The Works of the Right Reverend John England, First Bishop of Charleston*, 7 vols. (Cleveland, 1908), 4:319.

connections to survive as a "privileged" caste.

They ingratiated themselves to white society generally by catching runaway slaves and suppressing slave rebellions. The slaveholders among them developed reputations as hard masters. But most of all, they moved into the cultural and social orbit of Creole society by emulating French Creole customs and social behavior. They clung to their Creole Catholicism. The religion set them off from the outwardly more demonstrative Afro-Protestants who streamed into Louisiana. Catholicism gave colored Creoles and white Creoles a common religious language, a template from which a Creole cultural synthesis, brown and white, acquired its basic patterns. They rented pews in the French St. Louis Cathedral and joined the Creole quest for autonomy in the church of New Orleans. Through their faith, they forged alliances with a powerful white group and paced off clear boundaries between themselves and the city's slaves and free blacks.

The fragmented nature of New Orleans' colored population showed in many ways. The Catholic free people of color were often literate; many were comfortable or affluent. Blacks generally were unlettered and poor. Wealthy colored Creoles sent their children to France or to private schools in New Orleans where they became steeped in French literature and philosophy. French education built stronger bridges of language and custom with the white Creoles. The colored Creoles also established their own schools and social institutions, thereby walling themselves in further from the larger black and Protestant society. Even after the Civil War, the Catholic free people of color refused to attend Protestant-run freedmen's schools because they did not want to be identified with former slaves in any way. They remained anchored in their French and Catholic separateness, and still do. They blanched at any attempt to plunge them into the amorphous mass of blacks. In their verse and newspapers they celebrated their distinctive caste status, their French culture, and their Catholicism—their differences from the poor and enslaved blacks below them

The colored Creoles did not forget their social and cultural responsibilities to poorer people of color. In 1837, for example, Justine Fervin Couvent, a free woman of color, left property to establish a school for colored and black Catholic orphans. Wealthy colored Creoles underwrote the school's construction and operations.[41] But such acts of charity,

---

[41]Rodolphe Lucien Desdunes, *Our People and Our History*, ed. and trans. by Sister Dorothea Olga McCants (Baton Rouge, 1973), pp. 101-106.

practiced in a spirit of noblesse oblige, were not enough to close the gap between colored Creoles and their black wards. The wealthy Catholic free people of color did not wed their slaves (or free blacks either); they did not mingle with them socially; and they did not try to dictate their social and cultural behavior in all ways. They did not even want to sit with them in church. At St. Augustine Church in New Orleans, the wealthy colored Creoles bought half the pews and worshiped amid the white Creole families whose culture and favor they prized. The colored Creoles reserved the chairs on the aisles for their Catholic slaves.[42]

Their color, their caste, and their culture kept them apart from the blacks generally, and even from their own Catholic slaves, but it also separated them from the principal Church establishment once the New Orleans Church hierarchy passed into Irish hands. The colored Creoles' isolation from the larger black community led them away from supporting missions to the slaves and poor free blacks and so from enlarging the "colored" presence in the Church. Their French culture also prevented them from fixing the course of the New Orleans Church by the 1850s.

The diversity and dispersion of Catholics in the South, as in America generally, and the dizzying increase in people and institutions, especially in New Orleans and the North, taxed the organizational structure of the Church. Poor communications and localism combined with ethnic factors to sustain diversity in many areas of Church life, even in liturgical practice. Many bishops also clung to the independence they had in their own dioceses. The missionary status of the American Church, with no indigenous American traditions or hierarchy to direct its growth, further allowed a loose ecclesiastical structure and varied church practices to exist. To legislate uniform regulations for church life, the Church turned to councils of bishops. The councils of the antebellum era did not reconcile all differences within the Church, but they did pull bishops together in matters of religious services and obligations and of lay-clerical relations.[43]

---

[42]Baudier, *Catholic Church*, p. 365. See also Anton Reiff Journal, 3 February 1856, p. 30. By the end of the century, colored Catholic Creoles, who had erected many social and cultural barriers against blacks generally, often lived among Irish, Italian, and German Catholics in New Orleans, suggesting that religion served as a social bond of sorts. See Anthony, "The Negro Creole Community," pp. 150-52.

[43]On relations between bishops and religious orders and the bishops' desire to retain their autonomy, see, for example, Patrick N. Lynch to A.F. Hewit, 1 January 1858, Isaac Hecker Papers (Paulist Father Archives). On general Church legislation, see Guilday, ed., *National Pastorals*, pp. 17-186.

The bishops insisted that the ceremonies of baptism, marriage, and burial take place in the church. There the faithful Catholics would receive the sacraments from a priest, and there they would have their names recorded in the parish register. The construction of parish churches throughout New Orleans, and other Southern cities, and the multiplication of priests for the urban churches made all this possible in the 1850s, thereby enhancing the priests' authority and bringing order and unity to Church practice.

In trying to arrest declension and heal division, the Church also conducted parish missions, or revivals, particularly in the 1850s. The parish mission inspired conversions and rededications of faith among scores of Southern city dwellers. The preaching of Clarence Walworth at St. Joseph's Church in New Orleans, in 1854, confirmed a young James Gibbons in his decision to enter the priesthood. During his Savannah missions of 1856, Walworth convinced Irish Catholic immigrants to leave the grogshops for the cathedral.[44] The Catholic revivalists transmitted an individualistic piety and, by quickening religious intensity and devotion, strengthened the institutional Church. The parish mission espoused religious awakening but also individual moral discipline, especially temperance, frugality, and self-denial. The parish mission led to the growth of religious societies, the channels for renewed religious activism of those touched by the preaching. The revivals also brought different Catholics together in a common religious experience.[45]

By 1860 the Church had spread throughout New Orleans. Catholic parishes, schools, orphanages, hospitals, and confraternities ministered to the growing and diverse Catholic population. Particularly under the astute administration of Bishop Antoine Blanc, the New Orleans Church had increased its membership, as it expanded physically into all parts of the city. Parochial schools, colleges, and the diocesan seminary fostered Catholic learning and began to train a native clergy. Religious societies encouraged devotional and charitable activities. New churches and a handsome cathedral extended the range and splendor of Catholic service. A Catholic newspaper disseminated Church opinion and doctrine. School

---

[44]Ellen H. Walworth, *Life Sketches of Father Walworth* (Albany NY, 1907), pp. 130-31, 144-46. It is hard to know how long-lasting Walworth's success was. In 1857 Savannah had "but one efficient Priest" to build on Walworth's labors: John Barry to Patrick Lynch, 20 July 1857, Lynch Papers.

[45]On parish missions generally, see Dolan, *Catholic Revivalism*, passim.

books, catechisms, devotional aids, and sermons further promoted spiritual activism. They all increasingly presented a Tridentine Catholic piety intended to bring New Orleans Catholics together into a cohesive community.

But the Church's institutional expansion was uneven. The poorer parishes did not have the full complement of Catholic institutions, unless they fashioned them for themselves. Class, racial, and ethnic lines divided the Church within itself. The rapid growth of the Catholic establishment in the 1850s did not keep pace with the more aggressive Protestant expansion. Beset by internal divisions and poverty, the Catholic Church was unable to prevent the American Protestant social and political ascendancy in Louisiana, much less anywhere else in the South. The Catholic Church in New Orleans benefited from the bishops' efforts to enclose Catholics in a Catholic world of church and social institutions—efforts reinforced by the institutional Church through its legislation and councils and by the nativism of the 1850s. Still, the New Orleans Church remained a conglomeration of ethnic and elite parishes spliced together by a common theology more than any social, cultural, or economic cement. A common Catholic identity never fully congealed there or anywhere in antebellum Southern cities.

In the rural South—the true South—few resources for Catholic community existed. Spiritual activism was not possible where there were no religious societies, no churches, and no priests to guide a small Catholic population strewn across a vast area. Whatever their internal problems, the urban churches at least had the tools to achieve a measure of Catholic consensus and commitment. Catholics in the rural areas, however, limped through the nineteenth century in an appalling state of religious stagnation and declension. Catholic group consciousness emerged only in pockets of Catholic settlement, such as among the Creole free people of color and the Acadians (or Cajuns) of Louisiana who used their Catholicism and their French culture to ward off the Americanizing forces storming the Gulf region. But the Creole free people of color and the Cajuns were special cases, "forgotten people" out of the main currents of Southern and Catholic social experience.[46]

------

[46]For an excellent account of the free people of color, see Gary B. Mills, *The Forgotten People: Cane River's Creoles of Color* (Baton Rouge, 1977). There is no good account of Cajuns and Catholicism.

Everywhere else in the rural South, the story was one of no priests, no churches, and no money. In 1837, for example, when the diocese of Natchez was erected, only two priests, both on loan from New Orleans, operated in Mississippi. By 1860 their number had increased to a mere eighteen to cover the entire state. In Kentucky, in 1815, ten priests rode about the state visiting the widely scattered 10,000 or so Catholics. Catholics in Bardstown and Louisville enjoyed the full range of Catholic institutions by the 1830s, but rural Catholics in the state rarely saw a priest more than once or twice a year, if at all. The Catholics of Tuscaloosa, Alabama, relied on occasional visits by a priest from Mobile and met in a Masonic hall for many years. The Catholics of North Carolina did without any priests for years at a time. The number of priests serving the rural South remained small throughout the antebellum period. A flurry of church building and recruitment in the 1850s alleviated some of the problems, particularly in Louisiana and Kentucky, but the bishops of the South still issued their annual litanies of the paucity of physical and human resources for the dispersed rural population.

Parish missions, sometimes lasting for a week, intermittently brought Catholic preaching and piety into the Southern backcountry and perhaps saved scores of Catholics from giving up their faith altogether. In Kentucky Bishop Benedict J. Flaget set off a two-year spasm of revivals in 1826. Catholics left their farms and villages to converge on the revivals, where they listened to sermons, confessed their sins, and renewed their spiritual and communal Catholic identity. In the 1830s the Jesuits conducted missions which spread from Bardstown into Kentucky and Tennessee. Earlier, in Louisiana, Bishop Louis Du Bourg "spent himself preaching missions, giving instructions, preparing Confirmation classes, and hearing confessions." The priests conducted revivals anywhere they could find an audience—even in Protestant churches.[47]

Selfless, vigorous, and tireless, the Catholic revivalists, like their Protestant counterparts, rode across the country to shore up a flagging faith. The priests worked hard, but they could only do so much. The vast distances, the poor roads, the vicissitudes of Southern weather, and the countless Southern maladies all took their toll. As Jay Dolan has shown, the missions worked wonders in regenerating Catholic faith and piety,

[47]Martin J. Spalding, *Sketches of Early Catholic Missions of Kentucky* (Louisville, 1844), pp. 288-300; Dolan, *Catholic Revivalism*, p. 20; Baudier, *Catholic Church*, p. 284.

but they were not an integral part of Catholic America until the 1850s. Most missions were conducted in cities and towns anyway. Few priests ventured into the almost trackless woods of the rural South. The Catholic evangelists' march across the South waited for a later time, and its absence prevented the growth of Catholic group consciousness in the Old South.

Without priests and churches, even devout Catholics had trouble fulfilling their religious duties. In Pittsylvania County, Virginia, the Irish Catholic Egan family confessed to an eroding sense of spiritual wholeness because they lacked regular Catholic instruction; still, they maintained a "species of home religion" with family observances at Christmas, New Year's, Twelfth Night, weddings, anniversaries, and birthdays. James Bower, an Irish Catholic watchmaker living near Chester Court House, South Carolina, decided to leave the area because of the poor prospects for religion there. He tried to organize a Catholic church on a subscription basis so that a priest would remain in the area, but the project failed. Bower watched his family grow up without adequate religious training and, worse, filled up with dangerous ideas from "sectarian teachers" whom Bower hired in the absence of priests and nuns. In North Carolina the want of Catholic clergy forced William Gaston to arrange for a priest to travel from Charleston, South Carolina, to solemnize Gaston's marriage. Fearing a loss of faith because they were unable to meet their religious obligations, Gaston and several other Catholics nearby offered room, board, slaves, and horses to any priest who agreed to live among them. They waited years to find one.[48] Not all prospective Catholic bridegrooms were as patient as Gaston. Wealthy Catholics could afford to bring priests to them, or they could travel to towns where priests held services. Most rural Catholics lacked the time, means, or inclination for such heroic exertions. They slipped away from an active Catholicism.

---

[48]Postscript of Mrs. Egan in Bartholomew Egan to James C. Egan, 10 December 1845, Egan Family Collection (Northwestern State University of LA, Natchitoches); James Bower to Rev. Corcoran, 10 July 1854, Reynolds Papers; William Gaston to Archbishop John Carroll, 25 October 1805, Carroll Papers (Archives of the Archdiocese of Baltimore); and Gaston to Archbishop Ambrose Maréchal, 20 August 1819, Maréchal Papers. Conditions in North Carolina did not improve for the next thirty years. For an excellent contemporary account of the miserable state of Catholic life there, see Patrick Ryan to Patrick Lynch, 28 January 1856, Lynch Papers. For a good description of Catholic life and activity in the state, see also Stephen C. Worsley, " 'The Great Bug-Bear': Catholicism in Antebellum North Carolina" (unpublished manuscript, May 1982).

The religious ignorance and apathy of Southern rural Catholics aston-
ished observers. When the French Daughters of the Cross established
their school and convent in north-central Louisiana in 1856, they found
religion there in a sorry state. In a population of 10,000 Catholics, only
two to three hundred fulfilled their Easter duties. Only one man went to
confession.[49] A low rate of regular participation in Mass was not unusual
in rural antebellum America, but faithful Catholics were expected to
receive communion "at least once a year, generally at Easter time."[50] The
shortage of priests contributed to the miserable record of religious observance in rural Louisiana, and it reinforced a Southern habit of irregular
church attendance that would persist throughout the century. The
mother superior of the Daughters of the Cross mission put her finger on
another, more fundamental cause of religious neglect. The rural Catholics, she wrote, were "not idolators or heretics," rather they were "simply
indifferent." They listened to the Word, but did not abide by it. "The
people feared only sickness and death," she added, and they wanted a
priest only for baptism, marriage, and burial. The children preoccupied
themselves with pleasure and hardly knew how to make the sign of the
cross. Their parents were no better, and, indeed, they did not even worry
about their children making first communion. According to the sisters,
the Catholic planters just wanted to grow cotton, rice, and corn. They did
not bother with their Catholic religious duties, for they already worshiped
at their gin houses and cotton warehouses, the true cathedrals of the rural
South.[51]

This was not an isolated case. Religious neglect abounded in the
South. Missionaries reported widespread ignorance of basic Catholic
doctrine and practice everywhere in the South. Many Catholics did not
attend Mass, they did not baptize their children in churches, and they did
not receive the sacraments of penance and the Eucharist. In a word, they
did not meet any of their duties as Catholics. Some did not marry in the

---

[49]McCants, ed., *They Came to Louisiana*, p. 39.

[50]Dolan, *Immigrant Church*, p. 55.

[51]McCants, ed., *They Came to Louisiana*, pp. 39, 57, 66-67. Although widespread, this
indifference was not universal among French-speaking Catholics in rural Louisiana. For
letters of a devout Catholic family deeply concerned about Catholic education, good
relations with clergy, and observation of Catholic duties and feast days, and all suffused
with Catholic piety and passion, see the Honoré P. Morancy & Family Papers (Louisiana
State University).

Church, and too many married Protestants, from whom they adopted Protestant "errors" in the match. One missionary priest summed up the situation nicely, stating that Southern Catholics had nothing but "the name of Catholic and an empty shadow of their belief."[52] Some did not even have that. The Church had much work to do to make nominal Catholics into practicing ones.

The Old South moved to the cadences of the spoken word. Indeed, Southerners often measured a man's character as much by the way he said something as by what he said. Rural isolation, broken only by occasional meetings at the county seat and church, and the lack of formal schooling prescribed a system of personal religion and strong preaching much like the personal politicking of the region. Southerners took their religion and their politics straight. Preaching counted much in the Old South, and it counted in the Catholic South too. As advocates of a minority religion in a voluntaristic Protestant society, Catholics had to preach well to hold on to their communicants, and they had to preach up to the Southern standard to avoid ridicule. In the South the sermon was often the only opportunity the clergy had to instruct, to make sense out of doctrine. The Church recognized the pastoral value of preaching, and Southern Catholics demanded it. As one French nun remarked, Catholics in rural Louisiana attended church "more for the sermon than for assistance at Mass." Catholics, particularly the new immigrant Irish working inland, were "not a reading people" anyway. According to one determined priest in rural Georgia, few Catholics could do more than write their names, and even in the cities, where literacy was more widespread, most were "utterly unable to comprehend the theological, philosophical and political" arguments of Catholic publications like the *Miscellany*. The spoken word was the only reliable means of reaching the Catholic "common people."[53] Good preaching attracted otherwise indifferent Catholics to church. Bad preaching kept them away.

The Southern Church suffered too much bad preaching. In comparison with Protestant ministers, most Catholic priests came off badly. Some priests developed reputations that haunted the whole Church. The basic problem was not the content of the messages so much as it was the

---

[52]*Annales de l' Association de la Propagation de la Foi* 5 (July 1832): 605.

[53]McCants, ed., *They Came to Louisiana*, p. 57; S. F. Kirby to Ignatius Reynolds, 30 June 1847, Reynolds Papers.

delivery of them. Too many priests were unattuned to the techniques of revivalism. Worse, too many priests stumbled in the American idiom.

As a missionary church in the nineteenth century, the American Catholic Church relied on European religious orders to supply priests and missionaries. They came to America, to the South, ignorant of local customs and language. Worse, some looked upon "rustic" Americans as savages more needful of correction than instruction. The hard conditions of the country and the inadequate, erratic financial support from Church and laity discouraged recruitment and retention of clergy in the South. The Church worked with the tools at hand—often young, dedicated, but foreign missionaries who knew little of the country they would enter.

The priests' difficulties with local dialects and customs undermined their pastorates, as well as their preaching. Personal visitation afforded chances to seed interest in benevolent enterprises, to instruct, to discipline, and to explain doctrine. Personal visitation and counsel were important pastoral roles that foreign-born priests could not easily fulfill. The lack of priests and dispersed population made regular, frequent visits difficult in any case, but the foreign-born priests' ignorance of the nuances of Southern life made them poor counselors. To be sure, several priests compensated for their linguistic and cultural shortcomings by providing more than sacraments and sermons. A Father Cellini in rural Missouri, for example, functioned as a postman and physician, bringing news and, with God's grace, healing to grateful Catholics.[54] Church law, however, prohibited priests from engaging in secular occupations. Few priests supported themselves outside the benevolence of fellow clergy and relatives. Fresh out of seminary, the young missionaries knew little of medicine or other practical skills which might have added to their livings and ministered to their flocks. And they did not know the language. The language differences simply magnified the cultural distance, and in some cases distrust, between clergy and laity in the Old South.

Some Catholics did not even want the foreign-born priests around. In his pastoral letter of 1844, Bishop Antoine Blanc of New Orleans complained that many Catholics waited until sick people were unconscious before they called the priests for Extreme Unction. In rural Louisiana the

---

[54]"Documents from Our Archives," *St. Louis Catholic Historical Review* 3 (1931): 107-108. The "healing" of the priests cropped up occasionally in accounts of the rural South, particularly from French-speaking areas. See, for example, "Reminiscences of Adam Hall," Louisiana W.P.A. Narratives (Louisiana State University).

Daughters of the Cross discovered that it was "a rare thing" for Catholics "to call a priest before the death of a sick person" because they thought the priest's arrival would hasten the sick person's demise.[55] The priests were bad luck.

Southern priests and missionaries had no trouble honoring their vows of poverty. They subsisted on small allowances from bishops, gifts from relatives, and in the case of missionaries, meager subsidies from their host societies in Europe. Catholic clergy in the rural South barely had enough support for the coarsest clothes and food. They became beggars, lived frugally, and often despaired of survival.[56] Several Catholic congregations promised assistance, but delivered little. The trustees at the church in Natchez, for example, assured Bishop John Chanche that he would want for nothing. Six months after his arrival in Natchez, Chanche was still waiting "to see the first cent."[57] Southerners generally had no reputation as great givers, and Catholic Southerners were no different. The scarcity of money in the rural South also made regular contributions unlikely. Whatever the causes of the poor support, the priests' poverty made them unduly dependent on both the laity and their orders for support. The lay trustees meted out aid sparingly, a policy that hardly endeared laymen and churchmen to one another. The priests' poor estate also demeaned them in the eyes of their people, who must have resented their constant pleading for money.

Unsure of the language and of their support, and spread thinly over the country, the priests and missionaries did not become the arbiters of

---

[55] *Le Propagateur Catholique*, 15 June 1844; McCants, ed., *They Came to Louisiana*, p. 39.

[56] For example, see P. F. Parisot, *The Reminiscences of a Texas Missionary* (San Antonio, 1899), pp. 25-26; Baudier, *Catholic Church*, pp. 281-83; C. J. Croghan to Patrick Lynch, 19 May 1856, Lynch Papers. The rough manner of the rural folk also drove some "aristocratic" priests to despair, and even to flight. See, for example, J. O'Neill to John England, 20 February 1841, England Papers (Archives of the Diocese of Charleston).

[57] Chanche quoted in James Pillar, *The Catholic Church in Mississippi, 1837-1865* (New Orleans, 1964), p. 5. Trusteeism and ethnic divisions disrupted the Church's progress in Mississippi too. See, for example, Fr. J. Guillon to Antoine Blanc, 14 January 1853; and Fr. George Cooper to Blanc, 22 October 1856, New Orleans Papers. Religious women suffered privations as well, even with pledges of community support. On the difficulties of the women in maintaining orphanages and schools, see, for example, Sister M. Gonzaga, "Summary of the Foundation of St. Vincent's House, Donaldsonville, LA" (1844), in Donaldsonville History Papers (Tulane University); and McCants, ed., *They Came to Louisiana*, passim.

the rural Catholics' social and moral world. For that, lay Catholics looked to the catechism and religious books available to them, but most of all they looked to themselves.

Catholic planters had their children, and sometimes their slaves, baptized, and they made some attempts to send their people to religious services. Some invited priests to visit the plantations several times a year to celebrate Mass, and to baptize, wed, and bury white and black alike. Such occasions called for special preparations. A holiday spirit prevailed as free and slave anticipated the priest's arrival. The slaves particularly recalled these events. Rural Catholics looked forward to the priest's visit "for the treat" and for the break from the monotony of farm life. Too many Catholic masters, however, refused to allow their slaves to attend services away from the plantations, for they feared a loss of control would ensue if they let the slaves go off alone. Most Catholic planters apparently exerted no extra efforts to bring priests to their plantations. The personal records of black and white Catholics echo with the almost complete absence of any reference to priests· or their ministrations. The priests were not around enough to make a difference.[58]

Rural Catholics resorted to self-instruction and lay preaching to meet their religious needs, if they did not let their religion lapse completely. Planters sometimes employed black lay preachers to keep their slaves at home and satisfied, but the practice was not widespread. Making a virtue of necessity, Father Stephen T. Badin of Kentucky educated several slave women in the fundamentals of the faith "so that they, in turn, could teach the children and older Negroes."[59] Nobody followed his lead. Whatever regular guidance slaves, and whites too, received in Catholic doctrine came from the planters. They read the catechism and taught the Lord's Prayer. They directed the plantation folks' devotional lives. As a result, Catholic practice absorbed many personal idiosyncrasies. Without Church instruction and discipline, the rural Catholics failed to develop a tight, coherent Catholicism or Catholic group identity.

In one of her works, the Southern Catholic writer Flannery O'Connor has an aristocratic Southern lady remark: "If you know who you are, you can go anywhere." Southern Catholics were never quite sure who they were or where they were going. The Church in the Old South moved in

---

[58]See below, p. 34, for a fuller discussion of Catholicism and slavery.

[59]Posey, *Frontier Mission*, p. 194.

several directions because its people came from diverse places and, aside from a common quest for salvation, came to the Church for different reasons. The Southern Church did not produce a culture, for the Church was not (and is not) *a* culture. It embodied several cultures and served several societies, and still does.

As an immigrant institution in the cities, the Southern Church insulated newcomers from some Americanizing forces by conserving their Old World beliefs and religious practices and, as in New Orleans, by allowing immigrants a significant role in shaping Church policy. As a Southern institution, the Church marched to Dixie's tunes of slavery and Southern nationalism. Like the Protestant churches, the Catholic Church sought consensus and cooperation with the social order so that it could cultivate freely its inward spiritual plantation. There was no fundamental incompatibility between the demands of Southernism and Catholicism. As a religious institution, the Church spread its ecclesiastical reach and teaching by the 1850s to lay the foundation for Catholic solidarity, at least in the cities.

But none of these processes was completed by the eve of the Civil War. The Creoles and Cajuns of Louisiana and the Anglo-Americans of Maryland and Kentucky still put their cultural imprint on Southern Catholicism in the 1850s and kept the Church from becoming just an immigrant institution. Whatever its bending to Southern social and political winds, the Church did not give up its universality or sever its institutional and spiritual loyalties that transcended regional identity. Southern Catholics never escaped their double sense of being both Southern and Catholic. Unless they quit their faith and heritage altogether, which was never easy to do even in the straitened circumstances of the rural South, they struggled with the inner tension of being "both native and alien" at the same time, as Flannery O'Connor once put it. It is significant that Southern Catholics stayed Catholic by and large, even when support for their faith was woefully inadequate. They fell into religious neglect and ignorance, but they did not all become Protestants. And Protestantism was an imprimatur of true Southernism. Catholic identities emanated in concentric circles of culture, region, and church. Catholic group consciousness, or self-consciousness, was hastened by the external pressures of nativism and the internal growth of the Church establishment. But Southern Catholicism never matched the self-confident Catholicism of the antebellum North, and the direction of the *American* Church passed into Northern hands.

AN OVERVIEW OF INSTITUTIONAL ESTABLISHMENTS IN THE ANTEBELLUM SOUTHERN CHURCH[1]

by Raymond H. Schmandt*

The Catholic Church in the Old South grew out of two distinct roots, one English, the other Latin. The English sources produced the institutions and population of Maryland, Kentucky, and the District of Columbia; the Latin font created the religious atmosphere of the French and Spanish Catholic settlements along the Gulf Coast and the lower

---

*[*Editor's Note*: This essay contains little formal documentation because we commissioned Professor Schmandt to survey the large secondary literature on Southern Catholicism, especially unpublished theses and dissertations and articles in Catholic periodicals, in order to present a brief account of Catholic institutional establishments. The chapter is directed particularly to those readers who are unfamiliar with the nature of Catholic institutional development in the South.]

[1]Most material for this essay is drawn from the standard printed sources that are listed in the bibliography on the American Catholic Church: Edward R. Vollmar, *The Catholic Church in America: An Historical Bibliography* (2nd ed., New York, 1963). Also useful is John Tracy Ellis, *A Guide to American Catholic History* (Milwaukee, 1959). Citations will be given for the more recent literature, to indicate a direct quotation, or for some other overriding reason.

Mississippi Valley, areas that came under American sovereignty later than the English colonies. With the passing of time and under the impact of immigration the two traditions eventually blended, although they never entirely lost their separate identities. In the early American decades, however, the differences remained sharp and decisive, running much deeper even than the superficial marks of language and physical characteristics. However important these factors were, they represented only the external manifestations of two very diverse sets of social and political values that expressed themselves in disparate religious attitudes and practices.

In the English-speaking world, and hence among the Catholics of the upper South, the Church had been a minority religion with a history of survival explicable only in terms of vibrant faith and concerted effort. English and Irish Catholics consequently exhibited an ingrained, dynamic, independent spirit, and zeal in religious attitudes that endowed their faith with a firmly apologetic, activist character. The congregations that owed their beginnings to Spanish or French endeavor rested on an entirely different foundation: an established church relationship, government control and support making independence and personal initiative superfluous, and an acceptance of Catholicism as a cultural artifact, a routine aspect of life that elicited few heroic actions or made few strenuous demands.

These generalizations are not meant to deny the importance of geography, climate, or economic and social status as contributing factors in molding the particular forms that Southern Catholicism assumed, but rather to call attention to the more subtle influences that are easily overlooked. The fact is that the Catholic Church in the South was not a single entity in anything but its faith during the antebellum period. The similarities of structures, organizational patterns, and common problems of personnel and finance concealed very real attitudinal divergences.

The South as a whole was originally the dominant element in the American Church. Until the 1830s and 1840s, the majority of the bishops lived below the Mason-Dixon line, including the American primate, the archbishop of Baltimore. And for a significant time bishops of French origin—hence culturally aligned with the South regardless of their place of residence—outnumbered other ethnic groups among the hierarchy. By mid-nineteenth century the situation had changed, and the Church in the South had passed its peak. Patterns of immigration were the fundamental cause. Northern and Midwestern elements thereafter prevailed and gave the American Church its enduring image.

This essay is a broad, general survey of the Church in the antebellum South. It is meant only to introduce the names of some of the most prominent leaders of the Catholic communities, and to mention the most important institutional concerns. It surveys the establishment of the normal administrative structure and gives the names of the occupants of the various sees. It refers to such basic concerns as the recruitment of clergy, the seminary system, and the synodal gatherings needed to establish a foundation in canon law. Education demands attention as second in importance everywhere, and the beginnings of a distinctive Catholic intellectual life can be seen before mid-century. The role of the laity within this new body, the American Catholic Church, had to be defined by law and custom, and the resultant trustee controversies represented part of that development. Much of necessity remains unsaid. Such topics as ethnic considerations; social and economic status of the Catholics; work among the Indians and blacks, especially the slaves; the immigration and acculturation process; and cultural life in general—all are themes that must await other historians and other occasions.

The separation of the colonies from England compelled the Sacred Congregation for the Propagation of the Faith, the Roman body that, under the pope, controlled the American Church, to establish a normal diocesan organization. After a five-year transition as an independent mission, the new nation received its first diocese on 6 November 1789, when Pope Pius VI designated John Carroll to preside as bishop and fixed his see in Baltimore. The new diocese embraced the entire United States. It included about 35,000 Catholics, over half of whom lived in the South. Maryland contained by far the largest number. In 1795, this diocese expanded as a result of Spain's cession to the United States of its claims to most of Alabama and Mississippi, which were joined, ecclesiastically, to Baltimore. A decade later, amid some confusion about their proper status, the lands that the nation acquired by the Louisiana Purchase also became Baltimore's responsibility. This arrangement endured for ten years. On 8 April 1808, meanwhile, the whole vast area was raised to the rank of an archbishopric at the same time that the four infant suffragan dioceses of Bardstown, Philadelphia, New York, and Boston were removed from Carroll's care.

John Carroll, the first bishop, was a Marylander, a former Jesuit educated in France and Belgium, with a distinguished record of labor in his own state.[2] Having served for five years as Superior of the American Mission, he was a natural choice for the see of Baltimore in 1789. A unique feature of his elevation was the fact that he was selected by the American clergy rather than—what was the usual practice—simply being designated by Rome. Thereafter, however, Rome insisted on its unrestricted right to create dioceses and appoint bishops, although most of the time it listened to the recommendations of the American hierarchy before taking action, both in erecting new units of church government and in selecting the incumbents.

John Carroll's exemplary conduct of his office set high standards for his successors. His familial association with the nation's founding fathers endowed his person and his actions with the characteristics of a venerable statesman and public figure such as would have been quite wanting in a foreigner or a man of a different cultural background. Carroll sensed that the American Church, while a branch of the church universal, was nonetheless unique, as unprecedented as was the American political philosophy, and this uniqueness demanded innovative theological expression as well as novel or at least experimental techniques of government. Preserving the balance between the old and the new, or, rather, cautiously resisting the tendency of the old to overwhelm the new was the challenging task that he faced. An assortment of crises kept him fully occupied dealing with an often fractious clergy, placating his fellow ex-Jesuits, guiding and assisting newcomers, and encouraging educational undertakings. He died on 3 December 1815.

Baltimore's subsequent archbishops lacked the distinctive flair of John Carroll, yet each had his particular personality and talents to contribute in his leadership role.[3] Generally they pursued rather cautious

---

[2]On John Carroll, see the monumental publication edited by Thomas O'Brien Hanley, S.J., *The John Carroll Papers*, 3 vols. (Notre Dame IN, 1976). Two very important recent studies by James Hennesey are "The Vision of John Carroll," *Thought* 54 (1979): 322-33, and "An Eighteenth Century Bishop: John Carroll of Baltimore," *Archivum Historiae Pontificiae* 16 (1978): 171-204. Also useful for background is Hennesey's "Roman Catholicism: The Maryland Tradition," *Thought* 51 (1976): 282-95.

[3]Brief biographical data concerning all the prelates treated in this essay can be found in Joseph B. Code, *Dictionary of the American Hierarchy, 1789-1964* (New York, 1964); in the annual *Catholic Directory*; and, frequently, in the *New Catholic Encyclopedia*.

policies. Leonard Neale, Ambrose Maréchal, James Whitfield,[4] Samuel Eccleston,[5] and Francis Patrick Kenrick[6] in turn served the see. As it grew in strength of numbers and resources, sections of the Baltimore archdiocese separated to become independent jurisdictions in their own right.

The Latin cultural element entered the American Catholic Church through the French immigrant clergy, such as Archbishop Maréchal, who arrived at the Atlantic ports. Yet the main gateway for this particular ethnic strain was the Gulf Coast, and in Louisiana the second diocese in the United States, after Baltimore, was created. In 1793, not long before the Louisiana Purchase, the Holy See had detached the Spanish and French settlements from the see of Havana and had formed the diocese of Louisiana and the Floridas. Bishop Luis Peñalver y Cardenas was the first Ordinary until his transfer to Guatemala in 1801. His departure left Louisiana without a resident bishop for the next fourteen years, a period coinciding with the American acquisition, of which Roger Baudier said: "There is no darker page in the history of the Church in Louisiana."[7] At the moment of the transfer of sovereignty, according to Reverend Thomas Hassett, diocesan administrator in New Orleans, the whole far-flung diocese had only twenty-one scattered parishes, with twenty-six priests, all but four of whom had declared their intention of abandoning Louisiana when American control began. Most of these priests were French and Spanish with a few Irish among them. In addition, financial ruin faced the Church since most institutional expenses and salaries had formerly been paid by the royal governments, a practice that had to end in 1803.

---

[4]Matthew Leo Panczyk, "James Whitfield, Fourth Archbishop of Baltimore, the Episcopal Years: 1828-1834," *Records of the American Catholic Historical Society* 76 (1965): 27, quotes from one of Whitfield's letters to Bishop John England a passage that summarized well the view that he, and indeed most of the later Baltimore prelates, entertained about the type of policy to carry out: "For my part I am quite adverse to unnecessary agitation and excitement; experience seems to prove, that walking silently in the steps of my predecessor, doing what good Providence puts in our way and publishing it as little as possible has with God's blessings promoted Religion more and made it more respectable in the eyes of Protestants than if a noisy stirring course had been pursued." *Records* is cited hereinafter as *RACHS*.

[5]Columba E. Halsey, O.S.B., "The Life of Samuel Eccleston, Fifth Archbishop of Baltimore, 1801-1851," *RACHS* 76 (1965): 69-156.

[6]John P. Marschall, "Francis Patrick Kenrick, 1851-1863: The Baltimore Years" (doctoral dissertation, Catholic University of America, 1965).

[7]Roger Baudier, *The Catholic Church in Louisiana* (New Orleans, 1939), p. 249.

Rome officially assigned Louisiana to John Carroll, who governed through administrators.[8] In 1812 he appointed Louis William Du Bourg, a French Sulpician priest and a native of Santo Domingo educated in France, who had formerly been the president of both Georgetown College and St. Mary's College in Baltimore. It was a good appointment. After three years as Vicar Apostolic, Du Bourg became bishop of the diocese of Louisiana and the Floridas, with New Orleans as his chief city. He faced enormous problems. The arrogant Spanish Capuchin friar, Antonio de Sedella, defied him and enjoyed much popular support. Religion in general was a matter of little more than perfunctory concern to the Catholic populace. Ecclesiastical records are filled with evidence of a low level of morality; concubinage was an accepted way of life that especially victimized the free black population. Even the newspapers harassed the bishop constantly. As a result, Du Bourg preferred to spend as much time as possible in the upper portions of his diocese, where he did his most significant work. In 1826 he resigned.

Joseph Rosati, C.M., had been consecrated coadjutor to Du Bourg in 1824. An Italian with a background in education in the Vincentian seminary in Perry County, Missouri, Rosati was determined not to be saddled with New Orleans permanently. In 1826 Rome divided the diocese, with everything north of the state of Louisiana becoming the see of St. Louis under Rosati's jurisdiction. The bishopric of New Orleans, as the lower Louisiana jurisdiction was called hereafter, went in 1829 to Leo Raymond De Neckere, a Belgian Vincentian. De Neckere did not live long enough to make a mark for himself; the yellow fever epidemic of 1833 carried him off.

Continuing the practice of appointing French-speaking prelates in New Orleans, Rome next designated Antoine Blanc as the fourth bishop. Born in France, Blanc had come to the United States in 1817. At the time of his appointment in 1835, he found twenty-six churches in his diocese, now almost nothing more than the state of Louisiana, with twenty-four priests to serve them. Blanc was the first bishop to be fully devoted to that area alone, and he labored industriously and successfully, aided by an

---

[8]James J. Pillar, "Catholicism in the Lower South," in Lucius F. Ellsworth, ed., *The Americanization of the Gulf Coast, 1803-1850* (Pensacola, 1972), pp. 34-43; William B. Faherty, "The Personality and Influence of Louis William Valentine Du Bourg: Bishop of Louisiana and the Floridas (1776-1833)," in John F. McDermott, ed., *Frenchmen and French Ways in the Mississippi Valley* (Urbana IL, 1969), pp. 43-55.

annual subvention from the Society for the Propagation of the Faith in France which gave the bishop some financial security. Blanc's firm assertion of his authority finally eliminated the anti-episcopal opposition of the church wardens. He developed a diocesan seminary and encouraged other educational institutions. Even the religious climate improved markedly after the dread yellow fever epidemic of 1853 killed seven priests and 11,000 citizens within six months; the catastrophe remarkably stimulated the piety of the survivors. Rome acknowledged the progress in New Orleans in 1850 by raising it to the status of an archbishopric, with suffragan sees at Mobile, Natchez, Galveston, and, after 1853, Natchitoches.

St. Louis became a bishopric in 1826 and an archbishopric in 1847.[9] Insofar as it had been part of the Louisiana Territory, St. Louis fell under the jurisdiction of the archbishop of Baltimore from 1803 to 1815, and then of the diocese of Louisiana and the Floridas until 1826. Its pioneers had come from France and Spain, and the Latin atmosphere lasted into the 1840s. Its religious climate was much healthier than that of lower Louisiana, partly because missionary work among the Indians, a concern to the clergy of the Louisiana Territory, attracted some of the great leaders of the Catholic endeavors into St. Louis.[10]

Bishop Joseph Rosati, C.M., diocesan administrator since Du Bourg's departure, was the founding bishop of St. Louis.[11] His term of office lasted from 1826 to 25 September 1843. Of him, the historian of the archdiocese writes: "Rosati had all the characteristics a missionary bishop should have: organization, zeal, order, discipline, dedication. He was in love with his work and a loving associate of all his co-workers."[12] At the start of his episcopacy Rosati's diocese contained fourteen priests, fourteen parishes and missions, two seminaries, a college, and a boys' school. At the time of the first diocesan synod in 1839, the statistics read: eighty clergymen, forty-seven churches with resident pastors, five with occasional visitors,

---

[9]William Barnaby Faherty, *Dream by the River. Two Centuries of Saint Louis Catholicism, 1766-1967* (St. Louis, 1973).

[10]Peter J. Rahill, "The St. Louis Episcopacy of L. William Du Bourg," *RACHS* 77 (1966): 67-98. When the diocese was established, it embraced Arkansas, western Illinois, Missouri, and the vast northwest.

[11]Peter J. Rahill, "St. Louis Under Bishop Rosati," *Missouri Historical Review* 66 (1971-1972): 495-519.

[12]Faherty, *Dream by the River*, p. 61.

five chapels and sixty missions, plus over one hundred nuns of four different congregations.

Under St. Louis's second bishop and first archbishop (after 1847), Peter Richard Kenrick, whose career spanned a half century from 1843 to 1895, the archdiocese lost much but not all of its Southern identity. Having had a Frenchman and an Italian as its head, the see now had an Irishman. Kenrick, Rosati's own nominee, had associated with his brother, the bishop of Philadelphia, for a decade before moving west. His interests lay in the intellectual realm. Without neglecting his pastoral concerns, he was able to contribute to the broad cultural and intellectual life of his see. The influx of Irish and German Catholics grafted other valuable strains onto the original French stock. Just as the bigotry of the 1830s had been overcome, so was the Know-Nothing assault of the 1850s. Ecclesiastically, St. Louis served as the focal point for the Catholicism that radiated outward into the great expanse of the West, following the path of empire.

In addition to the three archdioceses—Baltimore, St. Louis, and New Orleans—twelve dioceses took shape in the South during the antebellum period: Bardstown (1808), Richmond (1820), Charleston (1820), Mobile (1829), Natchez (1837), Nashville (1837), Little Rock (1843), Galveston (1847), Savannah (1850), Wheeling (1850), Natchitoches (1853), and Covington (1853). The multiplication of sees gave evidence of the expansion of the Catholic population, although that growth was uneven and quite slow. Yet the formation of new sees spurred internal development in the Catholic communities and certainly entailed closer supervision of the faithful by a resident and near bishop. This in turn retarded the attrition that occurred wherever the faithful lacked regular clerical attention. One unfortunate effect of the multiplication of sees, however, was that it cut off outlying and poverty-stricken parts of the older ecclesiastical jurisdictions from the wealthier, more populous centers. This imposed severe strains on the inhabitants of the new dioceses who had then to support the various institutions that were a concomitant of an episcopal see. On the other hand, the intangible factor of local pride perhaps compensated for the financial pinch among the Catholic communities that no longer had to look across their borders for ecclesiastical leadership. In an age of strong states'-rights sentiment, this was a considerable asset.

Bardstown, Kentucky, was among the four bishoprics carved out of Bishop Carroll's territory in 1808. At that time, a sizable Catholic population, mainly drawn from Maryland, had concentrated in the north-central section of Kentucky around Bardstown, then a thriving town. A French missionary, the first priest ordained in the United States, Stephen T. Badin, had been working there since 1792. Another pioneer priest, the Belgian Charles Nerinckx, arrived in 1805. On their foundation the diocese of Bardstown rested, consisting in the beginning of the states of Kentucky, Tennessee, and Ohio, and the territories of Indiana, Illinois, and Michigan. Benedict J. Flaget, S.S., a Frenchman on the faculty of the Sulpician Seminary in Baltimore, became the first bishop in 1810.

Bardstown was already a flourishing Catholic community, with Dominican priests established at the convent of St. Rose since 1806 and three orders of nuns, two being entirely original American foundations: the Sisters of Loretto and the Sisters of Charity of Nazareth. Two coadjutors assisted Flaget at different times: John B. David and Guy I. Chabrat, both French, before his own death on 11 February 1850.[13] Bardstown's influence extended throughout the Midwest, along with Flaget's reputation for sanctity.

Meanwhile, changing patterns of settlement doomed Bardstown, and so the bishopric in 1841 was transferred to Louisville. By that time, only the state of Kentucky remained of the see's wide jurisdiction due to the creation of new dioceses on the periphery. Louisville had only one other antebellum prelate, Martin John Spalding, a native son of Bardstown. Educated in Rome, he became Flaget's coadjutor and, in 1850, his successor. Fourteen years later, Spalding was promoted to the archbishopric of Baltimore.

Three prelates presided over the antebellum dioceses of Richmond: Patrick Kelly, Richard V. Whelan, and John McGill. Created in 1820, the diocese embraced the entire state of Virginia. Few Catholics, however, resided in the state. In 1785, John Carroll had reckoned them as "not more than 200." Congregations developed at seven locations, the most important being Norfolk and Richmond. In 1820, there were probably no more than 1,000 Catholics within the diocese.

In the midst of the Norfolk trustee controversy, Rome established the diocese at the request of the dissidents and appointed as bishop the rector of an Irish seminary, Patrick Kelly. Archbishop Maréchal of Baltimore

---

[13]Bishop Flaget's reports to Rome are discussed at length in J. Herman Schauinger, *Cathedrals in the Wilderness* (Milwaukee, 1952), passim.

had not been consulted about the dismemberment of his jurisdiction, and from the start he worked to undo Rome's action. Bishop Kelly never saw his see city. He arrived at Norfolk on 19 January 1821, and stayed there until at his own request he was transferred back to Ireland on 28 January 1822.

After nineteen years, the Richmond see was revived under Bishop Richard V. Whelan. Born in Baltimore and educated first at Emmitsburg and then in France, he had ministered to the congregations of Virginia before being appointed bishop. The Catholic population remained small and scattered: even in Richmond they comprised a very small proportion of the citizenry. Arduous missionary journeys over long stretches of countryside occupied the bishop, who also tried but failed to maintain a diocesan seminary. The influx of Catholic laborers on the railroad construction crews in the northwest drew the bishop's attention to Wheeling in 1846, whither he transferred his residence. At his suggestion the seventh provincial council of Baltimore, three years later, recommended to Rome that a separate diocese be established there. Rome acceded to the proposal and created the diocese of Wheeling in 1850, with Richard Whelan as its first incumbent. He remained in Wheeling until his death on 7 July 1874.

Richmond, meanwhile, received John McGill as its third Catholic bishop. He came from Bardstown and had practiced law before entering the priesthood. A man of learning and eloquence, Bishop McGill's social presence won the respect of the non-Catholics of Richmond, even though the Know-Nothing bigotry of the 1850s found raucous expression in the gubernatorial election campaign of 1855. Cholera and yellow fever epidemics decimated the Catholic population, but increasing Irish and German immigration compensated for the losses. Although only a small minority, Richmond's Catholics, thanks to McGill's leadership, gained a degree of self-confidence and public respect that they had previously lacked in Virginia.

In 1820, Pope Pius VII created the diocese of Charleston, South Carolina, which encompassed both Carolinas and Georgia. The first incumbent was John England, of Cork, Ireland, the most imaginative and one of the most dynamic American prelates during the early nineteenth century. His own description of his see at the time of his arrival indicates its poverty in all respects, and hence the magnitude of the task before him:

When I arrived I found one small brick church in North Carolina, two frame churches and one log church in Georgia, being a total of four. The number of communicants was in South Carolina about 200, in Georgia 150, and in North Carolina 25, being in all about 375. The number of priests in South Carolina two, in Georgia one, in all three.[14]

In a life of constant activity Bishop England had to cope with refractory priests and determined lay trustees, the problem of recruitment of clergy, the establishment of educational and pastoral institutions, anti-Catholic prejudices, and a perennial shortage of funds. He instituted a novel system of annual diocesan conventions to involve the laity as actively as possible in the workings of the diocese. Frequently, too, he met with suspicion and even hostility on the part of Archbishop Maréchal of Baltimore, who went so far as to delate him to Rome. England's intelligence, culture, and oratorical skill won him the respect of the general populace, which redounded to the advantage of the entire Catholic community. Through his vigorous diocesan newspaper he disseminated his thoughts and influence throughout the whole American Catholic community. At his death on 11 April 1842, England left about 7,000 Catholics in his diocese, fourteen churches completed and some fifty parishes in the process of formation, twenty clergymen, and a rich variety of institutions of one kind or another.

Bishops William Clancy, Ignatius Reynolds, and Patrick N. Lynch were not able to carry on the ambitious, energetic programs of the founding prelate, in whose long shadow they gradually abandoned most of his projects. Yet Charleston's Catholicism had deep roots, and the England legacy in intellectual concerns nurtured James A. Corcoran, America's most prominent Catholic theologian of the mid-nineteenth century; his removal to Philadelphia after the war testified to the decline of Charleston's Catholic community.[15]

Alabama's Catholic history began with the Spaniards and Frenchmen who colonized the Gulf Coast. The ecclesiastical regime followed the secular government of the area in undergoing a number of permutations

---

[14]Peter Guilday, *The Life and Times of John England, First Bishop of Charleston (1786-1842)*, 2 vols. (New York, 1927), 1:506. The most recent work on England is Patrick W. Carey, *An Immigrant Bishop: John England's Adaptation of Irish Catholicism to American Republicanism* (New York, 1982).

[15]Sister M. M. Lowman, "James Andrew Corcoran: Editor, Theologian, Scholar (1820-1889)" (doctoral dissertation, St. Louis University, 1958).

before taking its final form.[16] At the beginning of American sovereignty the coastal section of Alabama fell within the jurisdiction of the bishop of Louisiana and the Floridas, while the interior was Baltimore's responsibility. After several experimental ventures, Rome, in 1825, formed the Vicariate Apostolic of Alabama and the Floridas, administered, after 1826, by Michael Portier, a French priest active in the Louisiana diocese. Then, in 1829, the vicariate itself became the diocese of Mobile, with Portier as its first bishop.[17] Appeals to his native land produced funds and clerical personnel. By virtue of this foreign help, along with his own unstinting efforts, Portier gradually developed an impressive diocesan institutional framework, but the number of Catholics in Alabama did not increase significantly.

Bishop Portier died on 14 May 1859. The prelate who succeeded him was John Quinlan, Irish-born president of the diocesan seminary in Cincinnati, Ohio. His congregation is said to have numbered about 10,000, at a time when the total population of Alabama reached 964,201, of whom 559,121 were free whites. That Catholics were an inconsequential fraction of the state's population can be seen by comparison with the statistics for other religious bodies in Alabama in 1860: nine parishes and nine mission stations under Quinlan (including the Pensacola part of his diocese) contrasted with 805 Baptist churches, 777 Methodist, 135 Presbyterian, and thirty-four Episcopal congregations.[18] Mere survival during the war years, and then gradual growth afterwards, was the story of the Mobile diocese under Bishop Quinlan, who lived until 9 March 1883.

By separation from New Orleans, Natchez, Mississippi, became a diocese in 1837.[19] Its extent embraced the entire state, with no permanent churches and only two priests, one of whom died shortly while the other left the diocese. About five or six hundred Catholics around the see city and smaller concentrations along the coast, with isolated families elsewhere, comprised the tiny Catholic proportion of the 400,000 population

---

[16]Pillar, "Catholicism in the Lower South," pp. 34-43. Michael Kenny, *Catholic Culture in Alabama* (New York, 1931).

[17]Guilday, *England*, 1: 590.

[18]The statistics cited in this paragraph are all taken from Oscar H. Lipscomb, "The Administration of John Quinlan, Second Bishop of Mobile, 1859-1883," *RACHS* 78 (1967): 21-24.

[19]James J. Pillar, *The Catholic Church in Mississippi, 1837-1865* (New Orleans,1964).

of the state. As with all the dioceses in the heart of the South, Natchez grew slowly. Moreover, the few Catholic residents lacked wealth and influence.

So pitiful a diocese, established by Rome on the recommendation of the American bishops, had trouble finding a bishop, but John J. Chanche, S.S., president of St. Mary's College, Baltimore, accepted the challenge in December, 1840. James J. Pillar, the historian of the diocese, has carefully chronicled Bishop Chanche's efforts in the fields of personnel and finances and Europe's responses to his appeals. The administration of Bishop James Oliver Van de Velde, S.J., Chanche's Belgian-born successor in 1852, was only a transitional period before William Henry Elder accepted responsibility for Natchez in 1857. He came from Mount St. Mary's College, Emmitsburg, but he had been educated in Rome and had also had pastoral experience to supplement his professorial training as background for his episcopal office.

Bishop Elder's episcopate concentrated on pastoral concerns of the most immediate sort, such as the welfare of the many transient Irish laborers working on the levees along the river and also the needs of the black population. Realism characterized his approach to the problems of his see. A low profile for his vulnerable community and a desire to accommodate to prevailing mores on social issues won him high regard and preserved the stability of his tiny flock. His defiance of the Union commanders when the war came to Mississippi illustrates how completely he identified with the social milieu within which he lived. He retained the bishopric of Natchez until 1880 when he moved to Cincinnati as archbishop of that see.

In 1837 the state of Tennessee was separated from the ecclesiastical jurisdiction of Bardstown and became the diocese of Nashville. One church, no resident clergy, and only some three hundred Catholics comprised the resources of the first bishop, Richard P. Miles, O.P., a Maryland native who had been raised in Kentucky. His fellow Dominicans, both men and women, were a major source of assistance for Bishop Miles, and the Dominican tradition in Nashville continued when James Whelan, another product of St. Rose Priory, succeeded to the episcopal see in 1860. Almost at once the problem of the war engulfed Whelan. At odds with his flock, Whelan resigned in 1863, the only bishop among the Southern prelates to do so.

As part of the Louisiana Territory, Arkansas came under the original jurisdiction of Bishop Louis William Du Bourg.[20] When the diocese of Louisiana was divided in 1826, Arkansas was assigned to St. Louis. The Catholic population consisted mainly of small French settlements along the rivers, some of which saw no priests for years at a time. Bishop Rosati dispatched missionaries, frequently from among the Vincentians in southeastern Missouri, to revive the faith and undertake the formation of congregations. Loretto nuns joined in the work. Success was limited, however, and it was felt that a separate diocese was needed. In 1843, when the Catholics numbered about 700, Rome established the see of Little Rock; it included the whole state of Arkansas plus the Indian territory occupied by the Cherokee and Choctaw tribes.

Reverend Andrew Byrne accepted the bishop's office. An Irishman who had been ordained by Bishop England of Charleston, he had worked there and in New York, where he was located when the call came to Little Rock. Byrne witnessed and encouraged an ethnic shift in the diocese, away from the previous French strain and in an Irish direction instead. Bishop Byrne also injected a new vigor into the life of Arkansas Catholics, but at the time of his death on 10 June 1862, scarcely a thousand communicants resided in the entire diocese, organized into eleven parishes served by nine priests.

Texas's independence in 1836, effectively terminating Mexican ecclesiastical as well as political control, raised the question of the status of the Catholics in the new republic and their religious future.[21] John Mary Odin, a Frenchman by birth and a member of the Congregation of the Mission, was the man who assumed the burden of rebuilding the area's Catholic life. In 1842, Rome gave it the transitional status of a vicarate apostolic with Odin as bishop. Five years later it became the diocese of Galveston. Odin saw the territory through the troubled years of the Mexican-American War and laid a sound foundation for the American

[20]Frederick G. Holweck, "The Arkansas Mission under Rosati," *St. Louis Catholic Historical Review* 1 (1918): 243-67; Holweck, "The Beginnings of the Church in Little Rock," *Catholic Historical Review* 6 (1920): 157ff.; Sister Mary Eulalia Herron, *The Sisters of Mercy in the United States, 1843-1928* (New York, 1929), ch. 5; Faherty, *Dream by the River*, p. 47 and passim.

[21]Sister Mary Benignus Sheridan, "Bishop Odin and the New Era of the Catholic Church in Texas, 1840-1860" (doctoral dissertation, St. Louis University, 1938); Ralph Bayard, *Lone-Star Vanguard: The Catholic Re-Occupation of Texas, 1838-1848* (St. Louis, 1945).

Catholic regime. When he resigned Galveston to accept the archbishopric of New Orleans in 1861, Texas had forty priests, fifty churches, several resident religious orders, one college, miscellaneous schools, and other institutions indicative of a flourishing Catholic life.[22]

Savannah, Georgia, became a diocese in 1850. It included all of Georgia and Florida up to but not including Pensacola, which remained attached to Mobile. Francis X. Gartland, a native of Ireland who had grown up in Philadelphia, accepted the Savannah see. He depended heavily on his Philadelphia friends, including Bishop Edward Barron, for assistance, but Gartland died of yellow fever on 20 September 1854. Another Irish immigrant, John Barry, succeeded him in 1857. Remembered by his subjects as "a man of extraordinary piety and holiness,"[23] and with his health broken by the missionary labor that had been his lot for most of his life, he died on 21 November 1859, while seeking volunteers in Paris, France. Savannah received its third bishop in the person of Augustin Verot, S.S., who came up from Florida in 1861.

Of Florida's Catholic past under the Spaniards, few traces survived at the time of its acquisition by the United States in 1821.[24] Bishop Du Bourg of Louisiana and the Floridas had given it little attention. Bishop England of Charleston, as Du Bourg's vicar, looked after the St. Augustine congregation, and he continued to do so after 1825 when Rome authorized the vicariate apostolic of Florida and Alabama under Bishop Michael Portier. But the task was beyond the resources of England and Portier. Florida languished until 1850, when it passed to Savannah, and then, to relieve the burden on the Georgian bishop, Rome made Florida into a vicariate apostolic in 1857. Augustin Verot, S.S., was consecrated bishop of the vicariate. He had come from Le Puy, France, and had lived in the United States since 1830, first as professor at St. Mary's College, Baltimore, and then as a pastor in the same region. In the normal course of events Verot could expect to become bishop of an independent diocese. The precarious condition of Savannah, however, and the equally tenuous

---

[22]Cited from Baudier, *Catholic Church in Louisiana*, p. 312.

[23]N. T. Maguire, "The Beginning and Progress of Catholicity in Washington, Wilkes Co., Georgia," *American Catholic Historical Researches* 11 (1894): 24.

[24]Michael V. Gannon, *The Cross in the Sand: The Early Catholic Church in Florida, 1513-1870* (Gainesville, 1965), pp. 100-18; Gannon, *Rebel Bishop* (Milwaukee, 1964), pp. 22-25.

status of Catholicism in Florida induced Rome to depart from the usual practice. While retaining the Florida vicariate, Verot was appointed to serve as Bishop Barry's successor in Savannah, effective on 16 July 1861. He was responsible for the spiritual care of about 8,000 Catholics in Georgia and perhaps 2,000 at most in Florida.

Another new unit of church government was created in the deep South in 1853 when Natchitoches became a separate suffragan see under New Orleans, to care for the Catholics in the northern sector of Louisiana. The first bishop, Augustus Martin, pastor of the single parish in Natchitoches, came originally from Rennes, France. Complete cultural accord prevailed between him and his communicants to such a degree that he was incapable of objective thought on social issues such as slavery. Bishop Martin's efforts to develop his diocese, however, suffered sad devastation when the Civil War came. He lived until 1875.

Farther to the north, Covington, Kentucky, also became a diocese in 1853. It was assigned to a Philadelphian, George A. Carroll, S.J. Educated at Mount St. Mary's and Georgetown, Carroll joined the Jesuits and moved to the Midwest. At St. Louis he had been president of the Jesuits' university, and in Cincinnati he engaged in educational and pastoral work. His diocese contained perhaps 7,000 Catholics, with twelve priests and thirteen churches, much better material to work with than what had fallen to the lot of bishops of Nashville, Natchez, and some of the other recently created Southern dioceses. Carroll presided over Covington until 25 September 1868.

By 1860, North Carolina was the only Southern state that was not either a diocese or a vicariate apostolic. Catholics lived there, but in numbers too small to justify or to support an independent establishment. The bishops of Charleston looked after them. North Carolina's Catholic history reached back to post-Revolutionary days, however. On 18 November 1818, Judge William Gaston of Newbern addressed a petition on behalf of himself and seventeen other Catholics asking the archbishop of Baltimore for a resident priest. Additional Catholics lived at Washington, Wilmington, and in lesser settlements, but there existed no single, strong Catholic center around which a bishopric could be established.

Rome's establishment of all these new dioceses achieved little more than the preparation of a table of organization, a plan of action. To implement this structure, personnel was needed. Every one of the new bishops faced the pressing problem of where to find clergy and nuns to help them achieve their twofold mission of ministering to the scattered Catholic communicants and recovering those who had drifted away. Only the sees on the fringes of the South ever enjoyed anything like an adequate supply of laborers. Two sources of help were available: the training of a local clergy through a seminary system, and recruitment from outside the diocese. Canon law preferred the former; more immediate results could be achieved through the latter. The bishops tried both.

From the Northern dioceses few priests other than sick men seeking a change of climate volunteered to come south. James Pillar has speculated that the reasons were the paucity of Catholics, the vast size of the parishes, inadequate finances, oppressive heat, and the constant danger from yellow fever epidemics, which time and again decimated the slim ranks of the clergy.[25] So, the prelates appealed to Europe. It became almost routine for newly installed bishops to tour Europe in search of volunteers for the American mission. Bishops born abroad enjoyed an advantage since they could begin in their native place and expect a warm welcome. The more persuasive the recruiter, the greater his success. Bishops Du Bourg, Portier, Verot, and Byrne, along with Fathers Charles Nerinckx and John Timon, C.M., particularly demonstrated ability in attracting enthusiastic volunteers.[26] Sometimes individual priests and nuns came to the Southern sees on their own initiative, as did groups of volunteers from religious orders. An exceptional case occurred in 1848 when Fr. Eutropius Proust led forty-three men (monks, brothers, novices, postulants, and familiars) from the monastery of Our Lady of Melleray near Nantes, France, to Bardstown, where Bishop Flaget helped them to locate at Gethsemani and found the first permanent American house of the Cistercians of the Strict Obedience. Groups of Jesuits also came from France to escape French anticlericalism in the early nineteenth century. Orders were especially useful to hard pressed American bishops since they provided continuity, handled their own internal discipline, and usually had at least some financial resources of their own.

Yet foreign clergy were sometimes a mixed blessing. Bishop England, for example, objected strongly to the vagabond Irish priests who

---

[25]Pillar, "Catholicism in the Lower South," p. 38.

[26]Bishop Du Bourg's travels in France and Italy during 1815-1817, for example, netted three groups of volunteers for Louisiana. A decade later he induced eleven Belgian Jesuits to come westward.

migrated into his diocese, often to the relief of their home see. While French-speaking clergy reinforced the ethnic character of the Gulf Coast congregations, their inability to communicate with English-speakers limited their usefulness and at times embarrassed their communicants, especially during the years of nativist activity.

Seminaries—that is, schools with a curriculum in philosophy and theology to prepare candidates for the priesthood—offered the only long-term solution to the personnel problem. Besides, the canons of the Council of Trent enjoined on bishops an obligation to provide such institutions in every diocese wherever possible. Consequently, every Southern diocese except Savannah, Wheeling, Covington, and Natchez established its own seminary in the antebellum period. Some of them lasted. Costs, lack of a faculty, and the small number of students presented problems that especially vexed the poorer dioceses. Southern prelates tried to overcome the difficulties by creating mixed institutions that combined a seminary curriculum for divinity students with a regular college or secondary school program in the hope that the combined income would prove adequate, especially if seminarians were used to teach the lower, secular classes.[27]

Once a body of clergy had been recruited, diocesan authorities had to concern themselves with matters of liturgical practice, discipline, and the uniformity of the regular religious ceremonies. Councils or synods were the usual procedure for preparing local legislation on such matters. As fellow partners of all the American bishops, the Southern prelates participated in the seven provincial councils of Baltimore between 1829 and 1849, and in the first plenary council, also at Baltimore, in 1852. These gatherings integrated the individual sees into a common legal structure and a uniform pattern of observances for the entire American Church. They thus prevented the Southern dioceses from developing separatist tendencies or peculiar practices in significant matters. Catholics always took pride in the universality and uniformity of their religion, and even on sociopolitical issues such as the abolitionist movement they tended not to differ much in North and South. Within the dioceses themselves, the local bishops summoned their clergy to councils or synods either to ratify or adopt enactments of the provincial councils of bishops or to deal with issues unique to the dioceses.

---

[27]The premier American seminary was Mount St. Mary's of Baltimore.

In addition to Baltimore, the Southern archbishoprics, New Orleans and St. Louis, convoked diocesan synods until attaining archiepiscopal status, after which they held provincial councils. The New Orleans synods and councils met in 1830, 1840, and 1844, and the provincial councils met in 1856 and 1860. The St. Louis diocesan synods convened in 1839 and 1850, and the provincial councils of St. Louis were held in 1855 and 1858. Synods met in other bishoprics as follows: Charleston (1831), Mobile (1835), Louisville (1850 and 1858), Galveston (1858), and Natchez (1858). The records of these meetings offer insights into the internal workings of the episcopal government and the multifarious expressions of Catholic life within these dioceses—liturgical, educational, and disciplinary.

General education, not just preparation for the priesthood, also required the bishops' attention. With public schooling virtually nonexistent in the antebellum South, churches had to provide this service. Catholics showed no inclination to shirk their duty, for education under Church auspices was universally regarded as the surest foundation for a Christian life and the quickest route for Catholic integration into the mainstream of American life.[28]

Lower education was the task of the nuns, and for girls the nuns provided everything since colleges admitted only men. Every bishop strove to attract the sisterhoods into his jurisdiction and to find means to support them. The presence of one or more of the female orders indicated a diocese's maturity and guaranteed its continued religious growth. In the long history of Catholicism in New Orleans, for example, the unpretentious, steadying influence of the Ursuline convent and its academy from 1727 onward was often the sole external expression of genuine religious life and the only harbinger of better days in the future.

Higher education was limited to men. Thirty-four Southern Catholic colleges—often, however, little more than high schools—came into

---

[28]Southern Protestants did not hesitate to take advantage of the educational facilities of the Catholics for the schooling of their children. Jefferson Davis attended a Catholic college in Kentucky, as did a number of other non-Catholics who attained prominence in later life. The genteel atmosphere of convent schools for girls apparently appealed to socially ambitious parents, Catholic or not. The Ursuline academy in New Orleans and Nazareth Academy in Kentucky, for example, had non-Catholics among their pupils on many occasions. And the Catholic administrators readily granted exemption to such youngsters from religious duties imposed on the Catholics. At the same time, though, the conversion of a non-Catholic pupil usually occasioned sincere if covert rejoicing.

being before 1861, either through the initiative of diocesan clergy and officials or of religious orders. Laymen were twice involved in the founding and control of Southern Catholic colleges. Throughout the United States during this period, eighty-six such institutions were founded, so that thirty-nine percent of the total were in the South. A large number of the Southern prelates in the antebellum period came out of an academic environment, either as administrators or professors, which fact predisposed them to promote the collegiate life in their new official capacity. Yet their financial resources remained very limited, as did their student enrollments. The failure rate was high and, in the end, with few exceptions only those colleges that were administered by religious orders survived more than a few decades. The decisive factor determining survival was always the growth or the stagnation of the local Catholic population.[29]

The diocesan colleges usually began in association with seminaries. Religious orders also hoped that the colleges would be the seedbed of vocations. This motivation was always present, but it was usually combined with genuinely intellectual concerns. The diocesan colleges suffered from staffing problems while the orders could more easily apportion their available manpower between pedagogical, pastoral, and missionary work. Laymen as teachers in the Catholic colleges were relatively rare and were employed only as a last resort. They were considered religiously less than satisfactory, and they had to be paid. As Nicholas Point, S.J., wrote to the Jesuit General when reporting in 1837 on the status of St. Charles College at Grand Coteau, Louisiana: "The price of Negroes and of professors is enormous."[30]

Haphazard beginnings and unnecessary duplication characterized Catholic collegiate endeavor. The diocese of Bardstown, Kentucky, illustrates the point. Between 1808 and 1821, three men's colleges opened in

---

[29]Edward J. Power, *A History of Catholic Higher Education in the United States* (Milwaukee, 1958), pp. 333-39, lists the Catholic colleges for men in chronological order of foundation. I would follow his lead but exclude Gethsemani College, still on the elementary level before 1861, and St. Stanislaus Seminary, White Sulphur, Kentucky, which was a seminary, not a college. On episcopal leadership in Catholic intellectual affairs, see the references to Southern bishops in Raymond H. Schmandt, ed., "Episcopal Support of Catholic Intellectual Activity—A Note on the Fourth Provincial Council of Baltimore," *The Catholic Historical Review* 64 (1978): 51-56.

[30]Quoted in Gilbert J. Garraghan, *The Jesuits of the Middle United States*, 3 vols. (New York, 1938), 3:136.

the diocese, all within fifty miles of the see city. A fourth college began in Louisville in 1849. Later, in 1860, a group of laymen undertook another college in Elizabethtown. Likewise, in the archdiocese of Baltimore several institutions competed for support and students. The earliest was Georgetown Academy, which owed its origins to John Carroll and the ex-Jesuits of Maryland. On paper Georgetown began in 1789, but it really opened its doors only in 1791 to a single student. In fact, the earliest institution offering real college-level work was Mount St. Mary's College of Baltimore, part of the Sulpician seminary complex. In 1816, the reconstituted Jesuits established Washington Seminary in the heart of the city. It closed in 1827, but reopened in 1848 as Gonzaga College. Another nearby Jesuit foundation, St. John's Literary Institute in Frederick City, Maryland, flourished with a collegiate course from 1828 to 1860. In 1852, the Jesuits began Loyola College of Baltimore. Colleges clustered around the more populous Catholic centers of the South, with similar patterns of redundancy.[31]

Perhaps more influential in developing Catholic intellectual life generally among laity were Catholic newspapers. Bishop John England pioneered with his weekly paper, the *U.S. Catholic Miscellany*, the first official Catholic journal in the country. The paper began in 1822, and except for interruptions in 1823 and 1826 when the bishop ran out of money, it continued regular weekly publication until 11 December 1861. The *Miscellany* was in England's mind primarily an apologetic venture. But is also served as England's forum; indeed, he wrote voluminously for it. The paper's wide news coverage and distribution gave it the character of a national paper and extended England's ideas far beyond the confines of his impoverished diocese.

Several other bishops enjoyed diocesan papers in which to advance their arguments. Such papers became the focal points for intra-Church issues and disseminated Catholic teaching to a scattered population. Bishop Antoine Blanc of New Orleans found the French paper, *Le Propagateur Catholique*, indispensable in settling the trustee issue. Its founder, Abbé Napoleon Joseph Perché, played a role in many exciting

---

[31]The Jesuits came to have the largest number of antebellum Southern colleges among the religious orders, yet their institutions could not attain a solid footing until they resolved a fundamental financial problem, a rule of the order that forbade them to charge tuition.

journalistic jousts, including the Know-Nothing episode, and attracted important Catholic writers to his pages, including Fr. Adrien Rouquette. Likewise, Benedict Webb used his Bardstown/Louisville *Catholic Advocate* to stir Catholic resistance to Know-Nothingism and nurture Kentucky's intellectual community. Although not part of the formal ecclesiastical structure, Catholic newspapers helped to forge Catholic opinions on political and social issues and, thereby, to strengthen the informal bonds of shared beliefs and concerns between Church leaders and lay readers.

The interior element within the ecclesiastical organization was the lay people, the reason for the whole elaborate structure. The laity gathered together into parishes, the places where they lived out their Christian lives. On the parish level the laity had a voice in their church, and it was there that occurred the clash between old and new views—the Old World and the New World theories of church governance—known as the trustee controversies. Despite the superficial issues that provoked them, these disputes represented an attempt by a progressive minority of Catholic laity to give their parish a novel form of popular involvement which they saw as conforming, better than the traditional patterns, to the American order of life and self-government. Trustee controversies erupted everywhere; in the South they occurred at Norfolk, Charleston, St. Augustine, and New Orleans.

During their pioneering days, congregations had commonly formed themselves into corporations to safeguard ownership of their property. Through elected boards of trustees, usually with the pastor, when there was one, as an *ex officio* member, the corporation exercised its responsibilities. Once a regular diocesan organization came into being, bringing with it closer hierarchical supervision, controversy arose over the limits of power: did the temporalities include the right to hire and remove pastors? Legally proper and correct, the parish corporations had long been the only element of continuity and stability in the missionary days of itinerant clergy, and the system had preserved communal property. But it had accustomed the members to handling their own affairs, and it brought into church governance the spirit of democracy and individualism that characterized American life at the time. Taking an intense pride in the unique American experiment in freedom and self-government, American Catholics yearned to extend that experience even into ecclesiastical areas. The opportunity was there to effect a rapprochement between the advanced principles of American thought and the time-tested discipline of the Roman Catholic Church.

Was the hierarchical structure of Catholicism adaptable to the egalitarian spirit of American democracy? That was always the fundamental question in the trustee controversies. But then a complicating factor arose. Many of the numerous immigrant clergy in the 1790s and later came as refugees from the radical democracy of the French Jacobins or the revolutionaries of Santo Domingo. To such individuals, democracy meant anarchy, persecution, and the destruction of Catholic values. These clergy could not share the aspirations of Carroll or of the American Catholics whom they were appointed to serve as parish priests. In addition, within any particular parish, as at Norfolk or Charleston, as soon as the basic ideological incompatibility between priest and people became evident, other irritants easily arose, especially the language problem of the French-speaking clergy serving congregations that were becoming increasingly Irish.

Hence, although the trustee controversies were precipitated by disputes about property and money, the essential issues went much deeper. As the arguments waxed in intensity, indiscriminate accusations of heresy, depravity, or ill will disgraced both sides. And on both sides personal interest came into the picture, too, to override principles.

Previous historians have dealt in detail with these squabbles; indeed, the literature is extensive. Earlier studies, however, have always come from the pens of conservative clerical historians whose work has been marked by a lack of objectivity and an unsympathetic attitude toward the trustees' point of view. Frequently, these writers took the position they did because of the fact that they came out of a European ecclesiological situation that had become badly corrupted during the Age of Absolutism. Only since the Second Vatican Council's reinterpretation of the role of the laity in the Church, of the concept of collegiality, and of a new political orientation for Catholicism, has it become possible to understand something of the trustees' mentality. They were, in many ways, men ahead of their time. Yet personal issues always intruded on principles, and unique features existed in every case. John England of Charleston seems to have been the only contemporary prelate who sensed the real meaning of trusteeism, and he was quite willing to embrace it in his constitution for his diocese. In short, this is an issue that calls for new investigation, and historical revisionism may well produce surprising results.[32]

For two generations some of the best Southern Catholic minds strove to Americanize their church, to create a symbiosis whereby all could live together in peace. Accommodation to prevailing social customs has always been the Church's most successful missionary practice, until such time as it attains enough strength to impose its own distinct ideology on secular society. This was the essential significance of the willingness to accept the practice of slavery on the part of John England, Augustin Verot, and Augustus Martin. They understood that the Church could not compromise with its environment on doctrinal issues, so they hastened to demonstrate compromise on social and political issues instead. They succeeded all too well. Thoroughly acclimated, and all too aware of their pitifully small numbers, the Southern Catholic prelates and people were unable to stand outside of their ambiance and pass judgment on themselves. That would have required a superhuman effort, and only saints can rise to such heights of self-analysis.

In structure and organization, the Southern dioceses did not differ a bit from their Northern counterparts, nor did their ecclesiologies diverge. Social circumstances and secular political philosophies differentiated North from South in general, and the Catholic congregations also, but there was no ground for speaking of two separate Catholic ecclesiastical bodies. Unity of faith overrode all other considerations. Even the original cultural patterns—the Latin deep South and the English-speaking North—had become blurred and superficial. The really basic difference lay in this: that the Northern Catholic community was expanding rapidly in an increasingly urban environment, while the Southern community experienced little growth and remained largely wedded to a more rural situation. Leadership in American Catholic affairs, consequently, along with the direction of Catholic interests, had already passed out of Southern hands, so that the Church in the South was becoming a backwater, a stagnant, neglected, and unprogressive institution. This it was destined to remain for the next several generations. But then, such was the lot of the whole Southern way of life in general, and there was no reason to think that ecclesiastical developments would be different.

---

[32]For the older literature, see Vollmar, *Catholic Church in America*. As an example of a brilliant new interpretation of one of the trustee controversies, see Patrick W. Carey, "John F. O. Fernandez: Enlightened Lay Catholic Reformer, 1815-1820," *The Review of Politics* 43 (1981): 112-29. See also the same author's "Two Episcopal Views of Lay-Clerical Conflicts: 1785-1860," *RACHS* 87 (1976): 85-98.

CATHOLICS AND THE CHURCH IN THE ANTEBELLUM UPPER SOUTH

by Richard R. Duncan

The roots of the antebellum Catholic Church, especially in the border states, were deeply embedded in the colonial experience. The Maryland tradition, drawing heavily upon its English origins, formed an important Anglo-American foundation upon which the Church rested. The English and colonial imprint shaped a cautious and conservative institution. Taking note of the dominant Protestant nature of the United States, it was essential for Catholics to become identified with and not to be viewed as antagonistic to the American spirit. For Catholics in the upper South not only was it important to be perceived as Americans but equally crucial, with the rise of sectionalism, for them to be regarded as Southerners as well.

The more tolerant winds of the Enlightenment, the upheaval of the American Revolution, and the French alliance temporarily muted the anti-Catholic impulse and led to the repeal of colonial restraints on the development of the Church. Consisting of less than one percent of the population, concentrated mainly in Maryland and Pennsylvania, Catholics were hardly a significant religious factor in the formation of the new nation. However, this relative obscurity allowed the Church precious time to begin the process of building a basic structure for future growth.

Acutely aware of their colonial disabilities, American Catholics had long embraced the concept of religious liberty and ardently supported the principle of separation of church and state. For American Catholics the idea was rooted in the Maryland tradition of the Calverts.[1] The fulfillment of that dream came with the Revolutionary movement. Catholics, although not necessarily and explicitly interpreting the Revolution as a means of securing religious liberty, supported the cause. Charles Carroll of Carrollton, one of the most articulate voices in reflecting Catholic opinion, provided visible involvement in the Revolution. Support for the Revolutionary movement in Maryland and Virginia won Catholics recognition and increased acceptance for their patriotism.

Recognizing their enhanced position, Catholics sought to consolidate their gains. John Carroll, fearing a continuing dominant position for the Episcopal Church in Maryland, worked with dissident Protestant groups in 1785 to defeat the Clergy Bill which would have provided a tax for the support of Christian ministers. In commenting to Charles Plowden Carroll, he wrote that "We have all smarted heretofore under the lash of an established church and shall therefore be on our guard against every approach towards it."[2] Later another Carroll, Daniel, serving in the Constitutional Convention, not only strongly supported the Constitution's ratification in Maryland but also worked for the addition of the First Amendment.[3] Much of the newfound optimism of Catholics was symbolized in the "Address from the Roman Catholics" to George Washington. Congratulating him on his election to the presidency, they were moved to write: "By example, as well as by vigilance, you extend the influence of laws on the manners of our fellow-citizens. You encourage respect for religion."[4]

For Catholics, American independence was important, but of far greater significance was the establishment of the principle of equality

---

[1]Matthew Page Andrews, "Separation of Church and State in Maryland," *Catholic Historical Review* 21 (July 1935) : 164-76; M. Ritta, "Catholicism in Colonial Maryland," *Records of American Catholic Historical Society* 51 (1940): 65-83; and Celestine Joseph Nuesse, *The Social Thought of American Catholics: 1634-1829* (Washington, 1945), p. 47.

[2]Thomas O'Brien Hanley, ed., *The John Carroll Papers*, 3 vols. (Notre Dame IN, 1976), 1:166-69; Archives of the Maryland Province of the Society of Jesus, box 57 (Georgetown University).

[3]Neusse, *Social Thought*, p. 83; John Tracy Ellis, *Perspectives in American Catholicism* (Baltimore, 1963), pp. 2-3.

[4]Hanley, ed., *Carroll Papers*, 1:410-11.

before the law. In contrast to their English counterparts, American Catholics could view their future optimistically.[5] Yet, fearing potential hostility to the establishment of a bishopric, Church leaders cautiously approached the problems of creating a church structure. As early as the Preliminary Treaty of Paris they realized that, with the severance of ties to England, American missions could no longer be considered under the jurisdiction of the Vicar Apostolic of London. Early in 1783 they began negotiations for the appointment of an American ecclesiastic. The French, attempting to test American political reaction, consulted minister Benjamin Franklin, who saw no obstacles. He not only indicated that the government had no jurisdiction over religion, but that he felt that Americans would not object to the establishment of a diocese under a French bishop. When asked his opinion of John Carroll, he heartily recommended the Marylander.[6]

Meanwhile Carroll and others had already begun the process of creating an organization. Assembling at Whitemarsh, Maryland, they laid the basis for unity in their approach to Rome. In a petition to the Propaganda de Fide they stressed the necessity for a "Superior of Missions," feeling it unwise to recommend the appointment of a bishop. They were also determined to prevent the appointment of a "Roman" for fear of raising the foreign domination issue.[7] Rome agreed but passed over the elderly John Lewis for a younger and more vigorous man. Initially, John Carroll was appointed as Prefect Apostolic. When no adverse reaction greeted the establishment of an Episcopal diocese, another petition was sent in 1788 requesting permission for the American clergy to elect a bishop for the United States. Granting the request, Rome endorsed their choice by elevating Carroll to the bishopric.[8] Carroll's approval by Rome also gave an implicit recognition of the Anglo-

---

[5]Thomas T. McAvoy, "The Formation of the Catholic Minority in the United States 1820-1860," *The Review of Politics* 10 (1948): 16.

[6]Ritta, "Catholicism in Colonial Maryland," p. 76. Along with Carroll, Franklin was a member of the Commission to Canada and came to know Carroll well. Peter Guilday, *The Life and Times of John Carroll*, 2 vols. (New York, 1922), 1:93-104.

[7]Hanley, ed., *Carroll Papers*, 1:166-69. For a discussion of the history of the Propaganda de Fide, see Joseph A. Griffin, "The Sacred Congregation De Propaganda Fide: Its Foundation and Historical Antecedents," *Records of the American Catholic Historical Society* 41 (1930): 289-325.

[8]John Tracy Ellis, ed., *Documents of American Catholic History* (Milwaukee, 1956), pp. 167-71.

American base of the Church and acceptance of its American character.[9]

Carroll, a member of the Society of Jesus before its suppression and of an important aristocratic Maryland family, was an outstanding choice. He had served the Revolutionary cause as a member of a congressional commission sent to Canada in an attempt to persuade French Canadians to join the Revolutionary Americans. Consequently, for the newly established diocese Carroll's Revolutionary and family prestige became important assets of respectability.

Carroll's initial problem was to unite and harmonize the various scattered communities in the United States. For the nucleus of his clergy he drew heavily on his associates, the former Jesuits, who now turned their energies to building a diocesan structure. The establishment of discipline was essential in bringing unruly elements into conformity with correct practices, for there was a fear of what impact American schismatic tendencies might have on the Church. Convening a synod in 1791, Carroll created a framework that dictated the form of the seven Baltimore councils from 1829 to 1849. He also carefully framed a prayer to be said at Sunday Masses and on feast days for those in civil authority and for the welfare of the republic. The prayer, embodying piety, also underscored Catholic civil allegiance.[10]

Carroll was aware of and sensitive to American conditions in his approach. He sought to establish good relations with Protestants and warned Catholics against isolating themselves from others. Catholics did intermingle and, in cases of necessity, used Protestant churches for services. Kentucky Protestants even contributed money to build a number of churches. At Bardstown, Protestants donated nearly $10,000 for the construction of the cathedral and served on the board to supervise its construction. In addition, non-Catholics gave land for various motives, to

---

[9]Thomas T. McAvoy, "The Catholic Minority in the United States, 1789-1821," *Historical Records and Studies*, vol. 39/40 (New York, 1952), pp. 33-50; Neusse, *Social Thought*, pp. 102-103. The Church faced a new experience with the establishment of the Baltimore diocese. For the first time it had to create an organization 3,000 miles away in a democratic republic that was basically Protestant and based on the idea of separation of church and state. Ellis, *Perspectives*, pp. 54-55.

[10]Ellis, ed., *Documents*, pp. 178-79; Peter Guilday, *A History of the Councils of Baltimore* (New York, 1932), p. 73; McAvoy, "Catholic Minority," p. 37; and Thomas T. McAvoy, *A History of the Catholic Church in the United States* (Notre Dame IN, 1969), pp. 66-67.

help the Church grow in western areas.[11]

In reaching out to Protestants, Catholic schools stressed open enrollment. The proposal establishing Georgetown College set forth the proposition that "Agreeably to the liberal Principle of our Constitution, the Seminary will be open to Students of every religious profession."[12] St. Joseph's College at Bardstown publicly announced that "No religious controversy is suffered to be introduced . . . nor are the religious principles of the Students interfered with." The Loretto Female Academy indicated that "The institution is Catholic; but . . . it carefully abstains from any encroachment on principles of others."[13] The Jesuits at St. Mary's in Kentucky attempted to allay Protestant fears by adopting a regulation that no student, unless of legal age, could be baptized without the consent of his parents.[14]

Bishop Carroll also preferred to minimize theological clashes with Protestants. He was reluctant to engage in controversies for fear of disturbing "the harmony now subsisting amongst all Christianity in this country, so blessed with civil and religious liberty."[15] Yet he was concerned with protecting the integrity of the Church. In the Synod of 1791 he warned the clergy against adopting those American practices which were not in keeping with Catholic discipline. Even though Catholics occasionally used Protestant churches by necessity, Carroll was most reluctant to exchange the privilege.[16] Normally, Carroll refused to engage in public controversy, but he was fully capable of doing so. In defending

---

[11]Joseph Agonito, "Ecumenical Stirrings: Catholic-Protestant Relations during the Episcopacy of John Carroll," *Church History* 45 (1976): 358-73; Ellis, ed., *Documents*, p. 219; Columba Fox, *The Life of the Right Reverend John Baptist Mary David (1761-1841)* (New York, 1925), pp. 83-84; and *Catholic Advocate*, 3 September 1842.

[12]John M. Daley, *Georgetown University: Origin and Early Years* (Washington, 1957), pp. 34-35; Ellis, ed., *Documents*, pp. 171-73.

[13]*Catholic Advocate*, 26 February 1842. On one occasion, when the Sisters of Charity met with opposition in an early attempt to establish a school, a local editor quickly responded in his columns: "They make no attempt at Proselytism; and the only religious influence they exert is that of their individual piety and exemplary conduct." Anna Blanche McGill, *The Sisters of Charity of Nazareth, Kentucky* (New York, 1917), pp. 108-109.

[14]Francis X. Curran, "The Jesuits in Kentucky 1831-1846," *Mid America* 35 (1953): 231.

[15]Hanley, ed., *Carroll Papers*, 1:82-141; Ellis, ed., *Documents*, pp. 149-51.

[16]Agonito, "Ecumenical Stirrings," p. 360.

the Church Carroll claimed for Catholics the liberties that they had helped to win in the Revolution.[17]

To put an American imprint on the Church was certainly one of Carroll's chief objectives. In context with this, and in the hope of minimizing friction, Carroll persuaded Rome to allow a modification in the consecration oath by omitting the promise "to seek out and oppose heretics."[18] But far more important to the bishop was his desire to build a native American clergy. Carroll placed a high priority on establishing a seminary to train future priests. Fortunately the coming of the Sulpicians, fleeing from the anticlerical attacks of the French Revolution, aided him in this goal. The Sulpicians established St. Mary's Seminary in Baltimore; later they organized Mount St. Mary's at Emmitsburg. Not only were the Sulpicians extremely important in shaping and forming the character of the early clergy through their seminaries, but they also reinforced the Anglo-American/French imprint on the early American Church.[19]

Carroll's successors were in accord with his desire for an American clergy. The Anglo-American proclivity was underscored with Bishops Leonard Neale and Samuel Eccleston, native Marylanders, and James Whitfield, English-born. Bishop Ambrose Maréchal, a former Suplician, taking note of the large foreign missionary nature of the clergy, pledged that he would "certainly leave nothing undone that will help me build up an entirely native clergy . . . [for] American priests, who are acquainted with the customs and characteristics of their fellow citizens, are, however, of all, the most dear to them." Ultimately, with the increasing Irish immigration, tensions between the Anglo-American group and the Irish led to sharp differences. The Irish, preferring priests of their own ethnic background, clashed with the Sulpicians and charged them with wanting

---

[17]McAvoy, "Catholic Minority," pp. 36-37.

[18]McAvoy, *History*, p. 81; Bernetta M. Brislen, "The Episcopacy of Archbishop Leonard Neale: The Second Metropolitan of Baltimore" (master's thesis, Catholic University of America, 1943), p. 19.

[19]McAvoy, *History*, p. 71. When Carroll was in England for his consecration, Father Nagot, Assistant Superior of St. Sulpice, visited him there and indicated a willingness of the Order to come to the United States to establish a seminary. Their learning and cultivation were greatly respected, making them readily acceptable to upper-class Americans. McAvoy, "Formation." p. 17; Columba E. Halsey, "The Life of Samuel Eccleston, Fifth Archbishop of Baltimore, 1801-1851" (master's thesis, Catholic University of America, 1963), pp. 33-35. For a treatment of the Sulpicians, see Charles G. Herbermann, "The Sulpicians in the United States," *Catholic Records and Studies* 8 (1915): 7-82.

to dominate the American Church. Maréchal denied any such intention. Pointing to the Irish appointments that he had made, the Archbishop countercharged by accusing Irish priests of being disturbers of the Church's peace.[20]

Increasing ethnic rivalries compounded an already difficult legal problem for the Baltimore diocese. The Church, lacking legal status in the United States, had to devise makeshift means to protect Church property. One method, the trustee system, contained serious potential dangers. And, unfortunately, trusteeism became the focal point for the emerging ethnic rivalry and produced a serious challenge to episcopal authority at Norfolk, Virginia.

Actually the trustee issue was a product of a number of factors. American democratic practices and the impact of the Episcopal vestry system helped to shape lay thinking. In many areas parishioners had already erected churches before the coming of the clergy. Laymen as a result expected to exercise considerable authority in parish management. Coupled with the demand for priests of their own ethnic background, some parishes dangerously began to assert the right of patronage. Weakness, inherent in the emerging Church's administrative structure, compounded by negligence and a lack of legal understanding, also opened the possibilities for challenges to episcopal authority.[21]

The roots of trusteeism actually extended back to the 1770s. The former Jesuits of Maryland, in an attempt to secure their property, had by necessity incorporated themselves as the Roman Catholic Clergymen of Maryland in 1792. Essentially the system did not run counter to Catholic discipline, and Bishop Carroll, taking note of the American situation, condoned it, although he quickly indicated that laymen had no spiritual authority. Unfortunately, Carroll was never able, despite suspensions, interdictions, and excommunications, to control fully the situation, and he left the legacy to his heirs. Soon trustees were claiming the right of *jus patronatus*, a right which the Church firmly denied.[22]

---

[20]Ellis, ed., *Documents*, pp. 215-17.

[21]Patrick J. Dignan, *A History of the Legal Incorporation of Catholic Church Property in the United States (1784-1932)* (New York, 1935), pp. 71-72, 142-44; McAvoy, *History*, pp. 93-94; Neusse, *Social Thought*, pp. 175-76; Peter Guilday, *The Catholic Church in Virginia (1815-1822)* (New York, 1924), pp. 5-6; Ellis, ed., *Documents*, pp. 218-19.

[22]Hanley, ed., *Carroll Papers*, 2:190; Guilday, *Church in Virginia*, pp. 6-8; Dignan, *History of Legal Incorporation*, pp. 57-58. Fear of ecclesiastical interference with their

In Maryland the problem was resolved by deeding property in the bishop's name, but considerable controversy arose in Kentucky. Catholics in Scott County drew up a republican constitution for their parish. Carroll, strongly disapproving, counseled Father Stephen Badin "to stem the proud torrent of such libertinism."[23] He advised Badin to use a simple fee conveyance vested in his name after posting bond to the church's trustees. Badin was then to name Carroll as his heir in his will. Trouble, however, arose when Benedict Flaget became bishop of the newly created Bardstown diocese and asked Badin to transfer the property to his name. Badin refused without certain conditions being granted. Even Bishop Carroll was not successful in mediating the dispute, and ultimately the Propaganda became aware of the controversy. Finally Badin's return to France in 1819 ended the crisis.[24] Ultimately the state legislature provided provision for trustees to hold church property, and Bishop Flaget merely appointed certain members of a congregation to serve in that capacity for the temporal management of the parish only. The bishop held the deed in trust for the congregation. He, in turn, had to transfer it to his successor by will.[25]

The most serious crisis came in Norfolk, Virginia, a challenge that Church officials in Rome feared might lead to the creation of an "Independent Catholic Church." For the bishops of Baltimore the Norfolk controversy became an agonizing source of embarrassment and scandal. In reaction to the old Anglican establishment, Virginia law prevented the incorporation of a religious denomination, and thus the Church's prop-

---

property became a reality under Archbishop Maréchal, and the dispute between the Jesuits and the Archbishop went to Rome for settlement. See R. Emmett Curran, "From Mission to Province: 1805-1833," in *The Maryland Jesuits 1634-1833* (Baltimore, 1976), pp. 55-56.

[23]Mary Ramona Mattingly, *The Catholic Church on the Kentucky Frontier (1785-1812)* (Washington, 1936), pp. 119-20, 139-40; M. J. Spalding, *Sketches of the Life, Times and Character of the Rt. Rev. Benedict Joseph Flaget, First Bishop of Louisville* (Louisville, 1852), p. 101. Bishop Carroll had a difficult situation in Baltimore involving German Catholics who wanted their own church. Carroll refused permission. The controversy ultimately ended up in court, which upheld the Bishop. Gerald C. Treacy, "Evils of Trusteeism," *Historical Records and Studies*, vol. 8 (New York, 1915), pp. 145-46.

[24]"Bishop Flaget's Report of the Diocese of Bardstown to Pius VII, April 10, 1815," *Catholic Historical Review* 11 (1915): 313-15.

[25]Spalding, *Sketches of Bishop Flaget*, pp. 247-48; Dignan, *History of Legal Incorporation*, p. 60.

erty was held by unincorporated trustees for the Roman Catholic Society of the Borough of Norfolk.[26] Peace, however, had been maintained until the death of Fr. Michael Lacy in 1815. In replacing him, Archbishop Leonard Neale, who had succeeded Bishop Carroll in that same year, selected James Lucas, a French priest, to fill the post. Unfortunately, the parish was largely Irish. The trustees greeted the appointment coldly and told Lucas that they had the right to reject an unsuitable priest. In a letter to Neale the trustees formally presented their claim. The confrontation soon became sharp and, much to the embarrassment of Neale and the Church, a public scandal. Dr. J. F. Oliveira Fernandez, leader of the group, in a letter to Archbishop Maréchal, who succeeded Neale in 1819, now demanded the creation of a bishopric for Virginia as well. In the meantime a similar situation in Charleston, South Carolina, had also become serious. The growing controversy, the appeals to the Propaganda, and the fear that the two congregations might join together, frightened Rome over the widening schism.

Geographic distance, problems of communication, intrigue in Rome, and the lack of complete information from the American hierarchy caused the Propaganda to compound the problem by making several unwise decisions. With fuller information Rome did partially reverse itself, but for fear that the Norfolk and Charleston congregations might unite under the Utrecht plan, Rome decided to divide the Maryland diocese. Out of deference to Maréchal the decision on the Virginia diocese was delayed until it could hear from him. The Archbishop strongly opposed the plan. Maréchal, believing that the dangers of schism were more imaginary than real, objected on the grounds that such a diocese could not financially support itself. He also indicated that division would be a blow to episcopal authority in the United States. Despite Maréchal's objections, Rome, fearing the consequences of schism, proceeded and named Patrick Kelly of the diocese of Ossory, Ireland, as bishop of the Richmond diocese in 1820.[27]

---

[26]Dignan, *History of Legal Incorporation*, pp. 60, 102.

[27]Guilday, *Church in Virginia*, chs. 1-4; McAvoy, *History*, pp. 94-108; Ronin John Murtha, "The Life of the Most Reverend Ambrose Maréchal, Third Archbishop of Baltimore, 1768-1828" (doctoral dissertation, Catholic University of America, 1965), pp. 56-57, 216-17; James Henry Bailey, "A History of the Diocese of Richmond from its Establishment, 1820, to the Episcopate of Bishop Gibbons, 1872" (doctoral dissertation, Georgetown University, 1952), pp. 9-22. The creation of the Virginia diocese, according

Kelly's appointment failed to end the turmoil. In Norfolk, Kelly, much to the chagrin of the Lucas supporters, sided with the schismatics. Fr. Lucas was forced to leave, but Kelly subsequently had his quarrel with the trustees who were now led by Fr. Carbry. The intensity of the struggle soon involved the civil authorities. Ultimately Carbry left Norfolk and Bishop Kelly was transferred to another diocese. With the see vacant, the Richmond diocese was temporarily placed under Maréchal's administration. Later the second Provincial Council requested the suppression of the diocese, but Rome refused. Finally at the request of Archbishop Eccleston it was restored, and Fr. Richard Whelan was consecrated as its second bishop on 21 March 1841.[28]

The scandal of trusteeism was more a cause of embarrassment than a real threat to the Church in Virginia. Anti-Catholic nativists, not understanding the controversy and already suspicious of the Church, used the conflict to attack Catholics as being anti-democratic and un-American. Despite its resolution in Virginia, the issue remained to haunt Southern Catholics elsewhere. But by the 1820s the Church in countering such charges had developed a number of defenses in identifying itself with American culture. Several themes were to be used repeatedly. Events commemorating the landing of the Catholic pilgrims at St. Mary's, Maryland, underscored Catholic presence in America from virtually the beginning of English colonization. The Calvert tradition of religious liberty and Catholic support of the Revolutionary cause were cited with great pride. Names such as Charles Carroll of Carrollton and George Washington, who had replied to the "Address from the Roman Catholics" with "I presume that your fellow-citizens will not forget the patriotic part which you took in the accomplishment of their Revolution, and the

---

to Professor Thomas McAvoy, did seriously threaten the respect for episcopal authority, one of the major characteristics of the Church in the United States. Fortunately for the Church, trusteeism had been reduced to a minor irritant by the time of the Church's great growth. McAvoy, "Catholic Minority," pp. 42-43 and "Formation," p. 14.

[28]Bailey, "History of Diocese of Richmond," pp. 22-29, 51-52; Guilday, *History of Councils,* pp. 109-110. Finally, in the wake of the Hogan controversy in Philadelphia, Pope Pius VII issued his *Non sine magno* on 24 August 1822, denouncing the pretensions of trustees to authority contrary to the laws of the Church. The Propaganda, in turn, issued guidelines for the use of the American bishops and clergy. Dignan, *History of Legal Incorporation,* pp. 117-21.

establishment of their government," fortified the tie with American nationality.[29]

For Catholics in Maryland, Kentucky, and Virginia, the emergence of sectionalism made it equally essential for them to be identified with Southern culture as well. The Catholic position on slavery made the blending of the Church with Southern life easier for Catholics, in some respects, than for a number of Protestant denominations. The Church, in principle, did not condemn slavery nor did it consider it a sin. Theologically it accepted the equality of all men before God, but in translating that concept socially the concern was for moral and spiritual equality. Slavery and serfdom were not challenged as social institutions, and the Church rationalized its approach in context with the idea of original sin. Yet, acceptance did not mean the denial of the slave as a person, and therefore Catholic thought contained obligations and duties for both the master and slave. The Church did not seek, beyond the requirement of Christian morality, to reform society. Accepting society as it found it, with the exception of the slave trade, the Church did not see the "peculiar institution" as being contrary to natural law.[30]

Southern Catholics used both the Old and New Testaments to justify their positions. They maintained that there was no condemnation of the institution in the teachings of Christ. Pointing out that the apostles had not condemned slavery, they cited St. Paul's counseling of slaves to obey their masters. Since no fundamental tenet of Catholicism was at issue, the ecclesiastical hierarchy, fearing the political ramifications of the issue, avoided discussion on the question. In their national councils they maintained silence. They preferred to approach it on a local basis.[31]

The Church's position was given scholarly articulation in 1840 by Bishop Francis P. Kenrick of Philadelphia, the future archbishop of Baltimore. In his *Theologia Moralis* he took a very cautious and conserva-

---

[29]Ellis, ed., *Documents*, pp. 175-76; *Catholic Advocate*, 28 May 1842, 20 April 1844, and 21 February 1846; "President Pierce and Maryland Toleration," *Metropolitan* 1 (1853): 554-55, and 3 (1855): 380-82.

[30]See "The Catholic Church and the Question of Slavery," *Metropolitan* 3 (1855): 265-73; Madeleine Hooke Rice, *American Catholic Opinion in the Slavery Controversy* (New York, 1944); Maria Genoino Caravaglios, *The American Catholic Church and the Negro Problem in the XVIII-XIX Centuries* (Rome, 1974); Joseph Delfmann Brokhage, *Francis Patrick Kenrick's Opinion on Slavery* (Washington, 1955); and Neusse, *Social Thought*.

[31]Brokhage, *Kenrick's Opinion*, pp. 41-42.

tive approach and reiterated the traditional teachings of the Church. Despite his regret over the continued existence of slavery, he placed the emphasis on respect for law. He wrote:

> That nothing should be attempted against the laws, nor anything said or done to free the slaves or to make them bear unwillingly. But the prudence and the charity of the sacred ministers should appear in their effecting that the slaves, imbued with Christian morals, render service to their master, venerating God, the supreme Master of all.[32]

Upper South Catholics were wary about any identification with the abolitionists. Immediatism and the radicalism that it represented were anathema to them. As a result, Archbishop Kenrick in his *Theologia Moralis*, as well as other churchmen, unwittingly contributed to the proslavery arguments of the South. Although Kenrick saw slavery as a social evil, he feared that the approach of the radicals would produce anarchy. Like many Southerners, Kenrick opposed immediate emancipation for fear that the black was unprepared to take his place in a hostile society. The disregard for property rights also horrified men like Kenrick.[33]

The hierarchy struck out at the abolitionists by inference. They exhorted laymen to use "strict integrity . . . in the fulfillment of all engagements . . . your obedience to the laws, your respect for the public functionaries." The 1852 pastoral of the Plenary Council was even more pointed. Catholics were counseled to "Show your attachment to the institutions of our beloved country by prompt compliance with all requirements . . . for the maintenance of public order and private rights."[34] The Baltimore *Metropolitan*, stressing the Church's conservative approach, asserted ". . . that as the Catholic Church alone by gradual and gentle steps abolished slavery in Europe, so she alone can abolish it in America."[35] The *Catholic Telegraph*, serving Kentucky readers as well as

[32]John Peter Marschall, "Francis Patrick Kenrick, 1851-1863: The Baltimore Years" (doctoral dissertation, Catholic University of America, 1965), p. 332; Rice, *Catholic Opinion*, pp. 70-71, 80-90.

[33]Marschall, "Kenrick," pp. 333, 336; Brokhage, *Kenrick's Opinion*, pp. 140-41, 163-64.

[34]Peter Guilday, ed., *The National Pastorals of the American Hierarchy (1792-1919)* (Washington, 1923), pp. 154, 192; Brokhage, *Kenrick's Opinion*, p. 42; and Rice, *Catholic Opinion*, pp. 63-64.

[35]*Metropolitan* 3 (1855): 266.

Cincinnatians, reflected a similar view and wrote that "For though disliking slavery, the Church—the only agent capable of emancipating labor from bondage—is opposed to any violent and revolutionary remedy for the evil."[36]

In keeping with their stress on respect for law, Catholics supported the Compromise of 1850 and the enforcement of the Fugitive Slave Act. In observing the presence of a number of anti-Catholic ministers among those demonstrating in Boston for the fugitive Anthony Burns, Catholics sharpened their hostility to the abolitionists.[37] Later, in 1857, the *Metropolitan* underscored its orthodoxy by defending Chief Justice Roger B. Taney in his Dred Scott decision against a Catholic reviewer.[38]

Accepting the nature of slavery as a social evil, a number of prominent Catholics looked to the colonization movement as a solution. Luke Tierman of Baltimore was among the founders of the Maryland State Colonization Society. Bishop Kenrick, responding to the urgings of Gregory XVI to support such projects, offered to supply priests for the American Colonization Society. Kenrick hoped that this might encourage manumissions with the prospect of sending freedmen to Liberia. Receiving no response, he then turned to the more receptive Maryland State Colonization Society. Ultimately, Kenrick's vicar-general, Fr. Edward Barron, and Fr. John Kelly of New York went to Cape Palmas as missionaries.[39]

In the public mind the Church's position was further fortified by actual Catholic practice. The Jesuits had had a long history of owning and using slaves on their plantations in Maryland. In 1831, the Jesuit Superior General estimated that the order owned 400 slaves, which made the Jesuits one of the largest slaveowners in the country at the time. It was not until 1838 that the Maryland Jesuits, facing severe financial exigencies,

---

[36]Mary Cecilia Palusak, "The Opinion of the Catholic Telegraph on Contemporary Affairs and Politics, 1831-1871" (master's thesis, Catholic University of America, 1940), p. 87. For the *Catholic Advocate*, underlying its objections to the abolitionists, was also its fear of governmental interference in areas potentially of a more religious nature. Rice, *Catholic Opinion*, pp. 73-74.

[37]Robert Francis Hueston, *The Catholic Press and Nativism: 1840-1860* (New York, 1976), p. 210.

[38]*Metropolitan* 5 (1857): 701. Taney was a prominent Catholic layman and served as legal counsel in the Provincial Council of 1829.

[39]Marschall, "Kenrick," pp. 334, 336; Brokhage, *Kenrick's Opinion*, pp. 163-64; Penelope Campbell, *Maryland in Africa* (Urbana IL, 1971), pp. 139-40.

sold them.[40] Other orders, such as the Capuchins and Ursuline nuns, also used the system, but the visibility of such clergymen as Fr. Badin, an early missionary to Kentucky, and Bishops Carroll and Flaget as slaveowners underscored for many the acceptability of the institution.[41]

Yet the Church was not insensitive to the religious life of both the slave and free black. The Church remained committed to its missionary zeal of spreading the Gospel. In its teachings and practices there was a concern to make the system as benign as possible and to prevent slaves from being deprived of their religious training and outlets.[42] Missionary work among the slaves and even free blacks, however, was fraught with difficulties and potential danger. The slave system assumed that slaves reflected the faith of their masters, and Protestants, generally unsympathetic and suspicious of Catholicism, presented a serious barrier. The Church, therefore, confined missionary activities to Catholic slaveowners who were often as neglectful of their responsibilities as their Protestant counterparts.[43]

The foundation built by Catholics in Maryland, Virginia, and Kentucky, in accommodating themselves to those factors that brought about the emergence of the South, and their continuing efforts to identify themselves as Americans served the Church well when its rapid growth brought about an increasing nativist reaction. At the end of the American Revolution Catholics had attracted little attention. In 1785, Bishop Carroll estimated that there were 15,800 Catholics in Maryland but no more that 200 in Virginia.[44] Increased immigration quickly changed this, as well as the ethnic composition of the Church. Ultimately, it also ended the dominance of the old Anglo-American group. The influx of Santo

[40]Peter C. Finn, "The Slaves of the Jesuits in Maryland" (master's thesis, Georgetown University, 1974). When the Jesuits sold their slaves, they sold them as chattels for life (p. 90).

[41]Rice, *Catholic Opinion*, p. 46. Bishop Carroll was uneasy about slavery. In his last will and testament he indicated that "my black servant Charles, to be however manumitted within twelve months after my decease ... and I charge on my personal estate or wardrobe the sum of fifty dollars . . . in testimony of his faithful services." Hanley, ed., *Carroll Papers*, 3:371.

[42]John T. Gillard, *The Catholic Church and the American Negro* (Baltimore, 1929), p. 15; Breslin, "Neale," pp. 50-51.

[43]Rice, *Catholic Opinion*, pp. 58-60; Gillard, *Catholic Church and Negro*, pp. 11-14.

[44]Ellis, ed., *Documents*, pp. 151-54.

Domingans in the 1790s heralded the beginning of what later became a greater impact with the coming of the Germans and especially the Irish.

Immigration and its radically changed nature produced both joy in the growth of the Church and despair in the corresponding rise of anti-Catholic attacks. The new Catholic immigrants, especially the Irish priests, contrasted sharply with the Anglo-American/French group. Ultimately, by the 1850s, the sheer volume of this new immigration also spelled a shift in leadership. In contrast with the Anglo-American acceptance of an inferior and minority position, the Irish brought a new militancy and aggressiveness to the Church. Yet, in the upper South much of the legacy of caution and conservatism, even under the Irish-born Archbishop Francis P. Kenrick, persisted and continued to serve the Church well within its Southern context. But even there, as in the case of the public school issue, a new assertiveness began to surface.

Although the North felt the great brunt of the new Catholic immigration, the urban areas of the upper South, to a lesser degree, also witnessed its impact. By 1830, Baltimore, as a port of entry and gateway to Western lands, experienced a pronounced upswing in the arrival of the Irish and especially Catholic Germans.[45] By the end of the decade of the 1840s, the city's population was twenty percent foreign-born. Baltimore's population soared from 80,625 in 1830 to 169,054 twenty years later. Urban expansion, plus a rapidly expanding industrial base which in a decade had increased its value of products by 400 percent, brought about dramatic economic changes. Communities in western Maryland, such as Frederick and Frostburg, also experienced sharp population increases. Cumberland in the decade of the 1840s increased 150 percent.[46]

Even Virginia received some of the influx. Demand for laborers to work on various internal improvement projects, such as the James River canal, the Blue Ridge Railroad, and the Baltimore and Ohio Railroad, brought a number of immigrants into the state.[47] Yet, out of a population of 1,421,661 in 1850, Virginia's foreign-born were estimated at only

---

[45]James V. Crotty, "Baltimore Immigration, 1790-1830: With Special Reference to Its German, Irish and French Phases" (master's thesis, Catholic University of America, 1951), pp. 20-21.

[46]Jean H. Baker, *Ambivalent Americans: The Know-Nothing Party in Maryland* (Baltimore, 1977), pp. 7, 15-17; Marcus Lee Hansen, *The Atlantic Migration, 1607-1860* (New York, 1961), p. 192.

[47]Klaus Wust, *The Virginia Germans* (Charlottesville VA, 1969), pp. 205-206.

22,953. Of that number, 11,643 were Irish and 5,511 Germans. At the height of Know-Nothingism the state's native population has been estimated at 97.81 percent, while in Richmond, an urban center, in contrast the foreign-born constituted 21 to 23 percent.[48]

Many immigrants arriving in Baltimore actually pushed westward along the Baltimore and Ohio Railroad and spilled over into the Ohio Valley. The farmlands of Kentucky and especially the river cities of Louisville and Covington served as magnets for the Germans. Joined there by the Irish and other immigrants, Catholic presence in the state grew rapidly between 1845 and 1860. In 1845, Kentucky had an estimated 30,000 Catholics; by 1852, the number had increased to 40,000, and to 56,000 in 1856, and by the Civil War to 80,000.[49] Louisville, by 1860, was over a third foreign-born.[50]

Unlike during the 1780s when there were few Catholics in the United States, by the 1850s the Church had in many areas become quite visible, both in property and numbers. In Maryland the Church had a greater property evaluation than any other denomination.[51] The great tide of immigrants in the late 1840s and 1850s further enhanced anxieties and fears of perceived threats by Catholics to American life. Since many of the immigrants were Catholic, nativists more often than not joined opposition to them with the old anti-Catholic impulse into a crusade to reform America. For the nativist, Catholics and immigrants became synonymous and interchangeable by definition.

The muted anti-Catholic impulse of the Revolutionary generation increasingly gave way in the 1820s to attacks on the Church. A number of factors helped to prompt the rise of religious tensions. Increased Irish immigration; the trustee controversy and its misperception by the Protestant community; reaction to religious liberalism and Protestant

---

[48]M. Xavier Dehner, "The Know-Nothing Party in Virginia: 1852-1860" (master's thesis, Catholic University of America, 1942), p. 5; Clement Eaton, *A History of the Old South* (New York, 1975), p. 280.

[49]Agnes Geraldine McGann, *Nativism in Kentucky to 1860* (Washington, 1944), p. 57.

[50]Clement Eaton, *The Freedom-of-Thought Struggle in the Old South* (New York, 1964), p. 238. Not only had Louisville become a center of immigrants in Kentucky but the Catholic center as well. Thomas W. Spalding indicates that by 1852 a third of the diocese was concentrated in that city. Spalding, *Martin John Spalding: American Churchman* (Washington, 1973), p. 59.

[51]Baker, *Ambivalent Americans*, p. 18.

revivalism—especially in the West; Catholic missionary zeal released by Pope Leo XII's Jubilee; the English Catholic Emancipation bill; the establishment of Catholic newspapers; and the holding of the first Provincial Council in 1829; all sharpened Protestant awareness of the increasing Catholic presence in the United States.[52] The American hierarchy grew alarmed over the attacks. At the Second Provincial Council Archbishop Whitfield and his prelates made a symbolic visit to the home of Charles Carroll of Carrollton, signer of the Declaration of Independence, to underscore their devotion and loyalty to American ideas.[53] In reacting to nativist attacks, the prelates counseled against the retaliation of rendering "evil for evil" but urged their parishioners "to discharge, honestly, faithfully and with affectionate attachment, your duties to the government . . . so that we may . . . sustain that edifice of rational liberty in which we find such excellent protection."[54]

Verbal confrontations multiplied, while the nativist press lashed out at the loyalty of Catholics, questioned the religious tenets and practices of the Church, and charged it with being undemocratic. The frenzy in some areas led to mob violence. The attack on the Ursuline convent in Boston sent shock waves through the Catholic community. Despite the horror of leading Protestants over such outrages, popular sentiment was not nearly so repentant. Later, in the summer of 1839, tension in Baltimore reached an explosive point, and a rumored attack on the Carmelite convent alarmed Archbishop Eccleston. Publicly expressing his appreciation to the mayor for protecting the convent, Eccleston also indicated his surprise that such threats could occur in a city that "reminds us of the Catholic founder of Maryland, one of the earliest and truest friends of civil and religious liberty."[55] Following the outbreak of serious rioting in Philadelphia, Church officials braced for the worst. Bishop Eccleston

---

[52]Ray Allen Billington, *The Protestant Crusade, 1800-1860* (Chicago, 1964), pp. 32-48; Neusse, *Social Thought*, p. 173.

[53]Guilday, *History of Councils*, p. 101.

[54]Guilday, *National Pastorals*, p. 78.

[55]*Catholic Advocate*, 12 October 1839. On 18 August 1839, a deranged nun, Olivia Neale, leaped from a window and sought refuge in a neighbor's house. The news spread quickly. The Rev. Robert Jefferson Breckinridge, a noted anti-Catholic lecturer and editor, further inflamed passions by his use of the incident. Rioting broke out as a result. Halsey, "Life of Eccleston," pp. 82-83.

canceled a visitation to Emmitsburg,[56] while the Louisville *Catholic Advocate*, in reporting accounts of the incident, reprinted Washington's comments on the Catholic contribution to the Revolution.[57]

The nativist upsurge eventually turned to political action to combat the putative power of Catholics. Nativists, angered over the results of the 1844 elections and charges of Democratic manipulation of immigrant voters, moved to organize an American Republican party. In contrast to the party elsewhere, in Maryland there was a denial that it was anti-Catholic. But in fielding candidates in 1845, and lacking such specific grievances, the newly named Native American party suffered a decisive defeat.[58] However, the crisis and war with Mexico temporarily diverted public attention, and the *Catholic Advocate* with relief wrote that "The violent and truculent faction which made so much noise a few years ago . . . has had impressed on its forehead the brand of public execration."[59]

War with Mexico, a Catholic country, potentially offered an embarrassing situation. Although generating additional questions and suspicions over loyalty, little damage was done, and actually Catholics gained greater respect. At the outset of the war Catholic journals either remained mute or supported the national cause. They generally avoided discussing questions of causation. Catholics in the army, consisting of an estimated third, won compliments for their service, which in turn added to the patriotic credits. Respect paid by the government in providing for army chaplains served as additional evidence of official approval.[60]

Yet, the marked economic and social transformations of the late 1840s and the following decade created serious societal strains. Symptomatic of underlying changes was the disintegration of the old second party system and the emergence of a period of political flux. In the

---

[56]Halsey, "Life of Eccleston," pp. 95-96.

[57]*Catholic Advocate*, 22 June 1844.

[58]James J. Combs, "The Know Nothing Party and the Unionist Movement in Maryland" (bachelor's thesis, Harvard College, 1963: copy on deposit at Maryland Historical Society), pp. 4-8.

[59]*Catholic Advocate*, 2 January 1847.

[60]Hueston, *Catholic Press and Nativism*, pp. 114-15; Blanche Marie McEnriry, *American Catholics in the War with Mexico* (Washington, 1937), pp. 31-32. There were rumors and charges concerning mass desertions of Irish Catholics in the army for refusing to fight against Mexico. Nativists cited the so-called San Patrico Battalion and especially John Reilly as evidence of such perfidy.

ensuing turmoil immigrants and Catholics became targets in the lashing out of frustration. The fears of those who felt that the American way of life was threatened paved the way for a political party opposed to both.[61]

Unwittingly, Catholic actions abetted the upsurge of nativism. Heightened Catholic revivalism in the 1850s undoubtedly sharpened antagonism in the Protestant community towards the Church. But more openly symbolic of growing Catholic militancy was the public school issue. Already a sensitive issue that had caused confrontation in New York in the 1840s, it erupted into Maryland in 1852. In that year Martin J. Kerney, a Catholic legislator, introduced a bill to allow parochial schools to receive public funds, thereby precipitating a storm of controversy in Baltimore. Even Archbishop Kenrick became involved and was sharply attacked in the press. The *Catholic Mirror* denounced the school system as unconstitutional, protested its support as unjust taxation, and claimed "the right to educate our own children in schools of our own choice." The paper maintained that "by requiring children should be educated without *any* religious principles," it violated religious liberty.[62] Protestants, in interpreting Catholic efforts to receive tax monies, viewed such protests as being assaults on the public school system. Ultimately, the Kerney bill died in committee, but not without having created a furor.

The unexpected visit to the United States by the Apostolic Nuncio, Gaetano Bedini, in the following year further intensified anti-Catholic tensions. Riots and demonstrations broke out in the wake of his travels in Cincinnati, Baltimore, and the District of Columbia. By 1855, the Know-Nothing movement had emerged in a virulent form in Maryland, Virginia, and Kentucky, as elsewhere. The American party platform of that year

---

[61]The Church in 1850, however, was not the vulnerable one that it was in 1790. Years of cultivating an American identity, underscored by patriotism, served it well in the new crisis. The acceptance of the Southern way of life and the Church's stress on its conservative approach to society fit well within the Southern context. With a population in the dioceses of Baltimore, Richmond, Wheeling, and Louisville estimated at 181,500, Catholics were not without allies. Democrats, drawing heavy support from both groups, realized fully the importance of Catholic votes for their party. From *Catholic Almanac* of 1854, in *Catholic Mirror*, 1 January 1854. Even though the figures are probably inaccurate, they do give some indication of the size of the Catholic community. Churchmen themselves, except on issues such as schools which involved a fundamental Catholic concern, studiously avoided involvement in politics.

[62]*Catholic Mirror*, 16, 23 April 1853. For Catholic revivalism, see Jay P. Dolan, *Catholic Revivalism: The American Experience, 1830-1900* (Notre Dame IN, 1978), who sees the "take-off" period for Catholic revivalism as the decade of the 1850s (p. 49).

called for "Resistance to the aggressive policy and corrupting tendencies of the Roman Catholic Church . . . by the advancement to all political stations . . . of those only who do not hold civil allegiance . . . to any foreign power."[63]

Yet, the anti-Catholic thrust of the movement in the upper South was less than clear. In Kentucky a third of the Know-Nothing grand council favored admitting Catholics,[64] while in Maryland, despite the party's specific demands for naturalization reform and barring Catholics from public office, its position on Catholicism itself was ambiguous. Attempts to differentiate between political aspects and the rights of religious liberty were unsuccessful.[65] Uneasy with an anti-Catholic position, Virginia Know-Nothings, meeting in Winchester in 1855, failed to include the words "Roman Catholic" in their platform. By inference they did condemn parties that accepted the proposition "that any foreign power, religious or political, has the right to control the conscience or direct the conduct of a freeman." In rejecting religious tests both the Virginia and Maryland Know-Nothing councils allowed Catholics to be admitted provided that they renounced any temporal allegiance to Rome. The central issue for them remained the question of loyalty.[66]

Catholic spokesmen quickly went through the litany of proving their devotion and loyalty to the United States. Citing past contributions to their country, they adamantly denied any temporal allegiance to the Pope and greeted Orestes Brownson's assertion of papal supremacy in spiritual and temporal matters with horror. Archbishop Kenrick in his *Vindication of the Catholic Church* strongly dissented from Brownson.[67] In a pastoral letter Kenrick counseled patience in adversity and reminded his parishioners: "To the Federal and State governments you owe allegiance

---

[63]"Platform of the American Party," *Metropolitan* 3 (1855): 406-13; Michael F. Holt, "The Antimasonic and Know-Nothing Parties," in Arthur M. Schlesinger, Jr., ed., *History of U.S. Political Parties*, 2 vols. (New York, 1973), 1:703.

[64]McGann, *Nativism in Kentucky*, p. 79.

[65]Baker, *Ambivalent Americans*, pp. 40-47.

[66]Philip Morrison Rice, "The Know-Nothing Party in Virginia: 1854-1856," *Virginia Magazine of History and Biography* 55 (1947): 64-65, 69-70; Holt, "Antimasonic and Know-Nothing Parties," pp. 610-11.

[67]Marschall, "Kenrick," pp. 223-25. There was an outcry among the American bishops, especially Martin J. Spalding of Louisville, and pressure was applied to Kenrick to remove his endorsement of Brownson's *Review*. Reluctantly, Kenrick succumbed to the pressure. Ibid., pp. 226-27.

in all that regards the civil order."[68] During the 1855 Virginia gubernatorial campaign Bishop McGill was asked what Catholics would do if the
Pope invaded Virginia. The bishop replied that "all Catholic citizens, no
matter where born, who enjoy the benefits and franchises of the Constitution, would be conscientiously bound, like native born citizens, to defend
the flag, rights and liberties of the Republic and repel such invasion."[69]
Bishop Martin J. Spalding of Louisville even more actively combatted
Know-Nothing charges. He used both the pulpit and pen to defend the
Church. In his *The Church, Culture and Liberty* he asserted that "on every
battlefield of our country . . . Catholics have freely bled, by the side of their
Protestant fellow citizens, for the honor and triumph of our country."[70]

The eruption of nativism and its political successes in 1854 had caught
many by surprise, but it was in the following year that its tide ran the
strongest. The fiery rhetoric evoked bloody rioting and disturbances in
Louisville and Baltimore and swept urban and state elections in Maryland
and Kentucky. Only in Virginia's very important gubernatorial election
did the American party suffer a serious defeat. Nativists in gaining
control over the Maryland legislature raised expectations of implement-
ing aspects of their platform into law, but such hopes were quickly
dashed. Their only accomplishment was to elect a United States senator.
Petitions calling for an investigation of nunneries fared poorly. A biparti-
san committee recommended no action in cases of abuse since sufficient
legal recourse already existed.[71]

Disillusionment with their accomplishments was not to be a telling
asset for the Americans. Party success in securing Maryland's electoral
vote in 1856 for Millard Fillmore, the American party candidate, was
anticlimactic against a background of disintegration. In viewing the
results of the Presidential election, the editor of the *Metropolitan*
reflected Catholic relief in exclaiming: "We rejoice at the result, not as
Catholics, but as citizens."[72]

---

[68]*Metropolitan* 3 (1855): 311-15.

[69]Dehner, "Know-Nothing Party in Virginia," pp. 43-44.

[70]Philip Wayne Kennedy, "The Know-Nothing Movement in Kentucky: Role of M. J.
Spalding, Catholic Bishop of Louisville," *The Filson Club History Quarterly* 38 (1964):
27-30.

[71]Richard R. Duncan, "Era of the Civil War," in Richard Walsh and William Lloyd
Fox, eds., *Maryland: A History 1632-1974* (Baltimore, 1974), p. 316.

[72]*Metropolitan* 4 (1856): 707.

For Catholics the crisis had passed. But, unfortunately, for Catholic and Protestant Americans of the upper South alike, a far more menacing threat to their security had emerged. The increasing sectional confrontation in the late 1850s between North and South overshadowed nativism and reduced it to relative insignificance. Catholics, reflecting a heritage of eight decades, were alarmed at the divisiveness of the sectional issue and its threat to the Union. The *Metropolitan* expressed it well for many: "As men, grateful for the benefits and protection we have received in the Union, we are resolved to cherish and defend it."[73] Yet, recognizing their Southern roots and identity, they sympathized with the South in the controversy. When secession and war became a reality, Catholics along with their Protestant counterparts in the border states were to experience agonizing division of loyalties.

---

[73]"Thoughts and Suggestions on the Catholic Question in America—No. 2," *Metropolitan* 5 (1857): 140.

CONGREGATIONS OF RELIGIOUS WOMEN IN THE OLD SOUTH

by Sister Frances Jerome Woods, C.D.P.*

From the earliest centuries of the Church, men and women have responded to the call to follow Christ. Groups of such persons with shared ideals came together and "religious" life—as this form of living came to be known—evolved. This life was a vowed consecration of poverty, celibacy, and obedience, lived in community and recognized by the Church. The vow of celibacy was a means of freeing the religious from the cares, responsibilities, and close attachments of married life. Poverty and obedience were means of freeing the religious from inordinate attachments to material things and to their own wills.

In responding to God's call, religious, then as now, try to experience God's love in such a way that this love tends to become the integrating center of life, and the consciousness of this love makes everything else

*I am indebted to Sister Janet Griffin for securing initial data from the Special Archives Project of the Leadership Conference of Women Religious in Salina, Kansas, for collecting library materials, and for valuable discussions on the data. I am also grateful to Sister Anna Marie Kaeberle who typed the final draft, and to several of my sisters in religion who provided helpful criticism. The research was supported in part by a mini-grant from the Hearst Foundation to Our Lady of the Lake University.

TABLE 1

Religious Congregations of Women Serving in the South, 1727-1868

Congregation	Year of Beginning Service in South	Place and Date of Origin	Place of American Foundation	Places and Dates of Major Southern Establishments, Other than Place of Foundation
Ursulines	1727	Rouen, France 1612	New Orleans LA	Galveston TX, 1847 St. Louis MO, 1848
Visitandines	1799	Annecy, France 1610	Georgetown DC	Wheeling WV, 1848
Daughters of Charity	1809	Emmitsburg MD 1809	Emmitsburg MD	Baltimore MD, 1821 New Orleans LA, 1830
Lorettos	1812	St. Charles KY 1812	Loretto KY	Perry Co. MO, 1823
Charity of Nazareth	1812	Thomas Co. KY 1812	Nazareth KY	
Madames of the Sacred Heart	1818	Paris, France 1800	Florissant MO	Grand Coteau LA, 1821 New Orleans LA, 1825
Dominicans	1822	Bethany KY 1822	Bethany KY	St. Catharine KY, 1823 Memphis TN, 1851

Oblates of Providence	1829	Baltimore MD 1829	Baltimore MD	
Our Lady of Mercy	1829	Charleston SC 1829	Charleston SC	Savannah GA, 1845
Mount Carmel	1833	Tours, France 1824	Plattenville LA	New Orleans LA, 1838 Lafayette LA, 1846
Holy Family	1842	New Orleans LA 1842	New Orleans LA	
Good Shepherd	1843	Caen, France 1641	Louisville KY	St. Louis MO, 1849
Mercy	1845	Dublin, Ireland 1831	Pittsburgh PA	Vicksburg MS, 1860
School Sisters of Notre Dame	1847	Mattaincourt, France 1597	Baltimore MD	New Orleans LA, 1856
Marianites of the Holy Cross	1848	Le Mans, France 1841	Lebanon KY	New Orleans LA, 1849 Opelousas LA, 1856
Incarnate Word and Blessed Sacrament	1853	Roanne, France 1625	Brownsville TX	Victoria TX, 1867
St. Joseph of Medaille	1855	Le Puy, France 1650	Bay St. Louis MS	New Orleans LA, 1856 Baton Rouge LA, 1868
Daughters of the Cross	1855	Paris, France 1641	Cocoville LA	Shreveport LA, 1860

(Source: Questionnaire responses from Special Archival Project, Leadership Conference of Women Religious, Salina, Kansas, 1980; Elinor Tong Dehey, *Religious Orders of Women in the United States*, rev. ed. [Hammond, 1930], pp. 363, 402.)

relative. The authenticity of the vocation finds its measure not so much in words as in deeds, that is, by a following of Christ's self-sacrificing love in the service and salvation of others. Through their consecration and commitment, religious are free to respond, out of love of God and of neighbor, to the needs of others—whatever these needs might be at any particular time.

Although all of the religious women shared in a common call to follow Christ and to serve the Church, they belonged to a number of different congregations, founded in different places, to meet a variety of specific needs. Members were generally called sisters, and those bearing major responsibilities were called superiors, and often addressed as Mother. In all, nineteen congregations gave service in the Old South. Table 1 (above) lists them by name in order of the date they began to serve in the South, and gives an overview of their place of origin and their principal establishments.

Two prevailing trends are perceptible from this overview. First, over half of the foundations had their origins in France. Since Louisiana was settled by the French, and had a large French-speaking population, most of the sisters of French origin came to Louisiana. The second trend is the concentration of native-origin congregations in either Maryland—the only one of the original colonies settled predominantly by Catholics—or in nearby Kentucky.

For new congregations to receive official recognition by the Church, the sponsorship of a priest was necessary. This priest not only helped the women secure approval, but he also served their spiritual needs and gave them direction, both of which were very important for their survival as an approved group of religious women. The earliest groups were required to be set apart from the world, or "enclosed," a restriction on their manner of witnessing their love and on evangelizing. Enclosure also reflected the place of women in a society.

Religious foundations were known by different names, depending upon the life-style. The older foundations were called "orders." An order composed of men, such as the Dominicans, often had a concomitant order of women whose way of life was modeled after that of the men, except that it was more enclosed. To circumvent the laws on enclosure, new foundations were called congregations, companies, or Third Orders Regular, known as tertiaries. Among the first of these foundations was one whose members were to visit the sick, the Visitation Sisters. But with

Church approval, the Visitation Sisters changed their mission to that of education in a monastic setting.[1]

The "Company" of the Ursulines, the first sisters to come to the South, was founded by St. Angela Merici to reform society through the family and the family through its women. They sought to diffuse Christian teaching into the homes and to give virtuous example to the world.[2] In 1727, when the Ursulines came to New Orleans, the city had more than its share of adventurers, prostitutes, and ex-convicts. Frenchmen lived in open concubinage, rarely attended religious services, and gave little monetary support to the Church.[3] Under these conditions, the sisters were expected to give witness to their faith by their presence and good example. They were also under contract with the Company of the Indies to set up and operate a hospital.[4]

Like St. Angela Merici, St. Vincent de Paul decided that his Daughters of Charity should go everywhere, caring for the sick in their own homes. He told his Daughters: "Your convent will be the house of the sick, your cell a hired room, your chapel the parish church, your cloister the streets of the city or the wards of the hospitals, your enclosure obedience, your grating the fear of God."[5] The Daughters carried out this mandate; during the Civil War, for example, they nursed on floating hospital ships and transports, in the tents and field as well as in permanent hospitals, in isolated camps reserved for contagious cases, and in military prisons.[6]

The norm of enclosure which had governed the life-styles of religious women from their beginnings continued as a source of conflict for the sisters in the United States. Thus, when the first Dominican Sisters were being trained in Kentucky, their director had them rise in the middle of the night to pray, after the model of the cloistered European sisters. Then the Dominican Sisters rose with the sun to pray again, to work in the fields, and to study.[7] The Madames of the Sacred Heart, who received

---

[1]Gerard Huyghe, "What Do We Mean by Religious?" *Religious Orders in the Modern World: A Symposium* (Westminster, 1966), p.7.

[2]Ibid.

[3]John Tracy Ellis, *Catholics in Colonial America* (Baltimore, 1965), p. 250.

[4]Roger Baudier, *The Catholic Church in Louisiana* (New Orleans, 1939), p. 63.

[5]Kathleen Elgin, *Nun—A Gallery of Sisters* (New York, 1964), p. 44.

[6]Ellen Ryan Jolly, *Nuns of the Battlefield*, 4th ed. (Providence, 1930), pp. 58-59.

[7]Sister Monica Kiefer, *Dominican Sisters, St. Mary of the Springs: A History* (Columbus, undated), p. 3.

property in Grand Coteau, Louisiana, from a wealthy widow who wished to live with them without becoming a member, had to work out a compromise with the benefactor, letting her live in the convent as a guest, but outside the cloister.[8]

The religious women of the pre-Civil War era could not afford what must have appeared to them the luxury of enclosure. Those who came from the relative comfort of French convents found the frontier especially demanding. Even the Madames of the Sacred Heart, who served the more affluent, thought that the hardships they experienced were extraordinary. In 1821, Mother Philippine Duchesne drew a parallel between her own situation in Missouri and that of the Jesuits in Siberia. She wrote: "If some of those from Siberia are looking for a mission field with the same type of work and the same climate during a good part of the year, they might come to our section of this globe. It takes souls of that quality to persevere out here; and if they went to a mission among the savages, they could even hope for martyrdom, either at the hands of the Indians themselves or with still more certainty at the hands of the lawless men who trade with them."[9]

To Mother Duchesne, gathering wood and harvesting crops were unaccustomed chores. In 1819, she wrote: "As we have no servant, we have frequently to gather wood in the forest. . . . When we have a visitor, we burn up our whole provision of fuel in a single day." Mother Duchesne also commented about the food, saying: "When the children go for a walk, they often bring back wild fruits and farm provisions, but we sometimes lack meat and often have only corn meal for making bread; and even this is expensive."[10]

Sister Hyacinth of the Daughters of the Cross wrote to France from northern Louisiana in 1856, "Labor here is most expensive and the workmen do not do a good job. One of my heaviest crosses was seeing our Sisters do such hard work. . . . We were carpenters, painters, upholsters [sic], gardeners, etc. The needs bring out our talents as well as accomplish the task."[11]

---

[8]Margaret Williams, R.S.C.J., *Second Sowing: The Life of Mary Aloysia Hardey* (New York, 1942), p. 81.

[9]As quoted in Louise Callan, R.S.C.J., *Philippine Duchesne: Frontier Missionary of the Sacred Heart* (Westminster, 1957), p. 334.

[10]Ibid., p. 313.

[11]Sister Dorothea McCants, trans. and ed., *They Came to Louisiana: Letters of a Catholic Mission, 1854-1882* (Baton Rouge, 1970), p. 38.

The Kentucky Dominicans, at the time of their founding, in 1822, did not only the work of women, but also the "hard, backbreaking work of frontier men." The pioneer sisters, thrown on their own resources, "labored in the fields; planted a kitchen garden in front of their cabin; gathered brush and rolled stumps and logs to clear the land for plowing and planted the food crops." They practiced unusual farming methods. One sister "guided the plow along the furrows into which another dropped the seed corn, while a third followed with a hoe and covered the seeds." Sometimes the "horse was so tired that a sister with an ear of corn in her hand had to walk before the poor beast to coax it along."[12]

The chronicles of the Loretto Sisters in Kentucky, the first winter after their establishment, in 1813, relate similar hardships. The Loretto Sisters hauled their own burdens in the field, and did their own digging, hammering, and sawing. They relied on remuneration from spinning and weaving to carry them through the winter.[13]

Other difficulties experienced by congregations who came in the 1850s to states adjacent to Louisiana are found in the archives of the Sisters of St. Joseph in Bay St. Louis, Mississippi. They taught in a one-room cabin four miles from their convent. The school had numerous crevices from which reptiles would emerge, coming down the walls and along the plank flooring, causing general excitement. After school, the Sisters walked home through a densely wooded forest where serpents would unexpectedly drop from the trees. After a rain, the footpaths became muddy ravines, necessitating the removal of shoes and stockings to cross them. In addition to this kind of trouble, they often depended upon the charity of their neighbors for food.[14]

The Sisters of the Incarnate Word and Blessed Sacrament, who came to Brownsville, Texas, primarily to counteract the proselytization efforts of the local Biblical Society, were so poor that they were unable to afford the food and medicine they needed for the fevers and ailments they experienced in a strange climate. Instead of problems with snakes, they had to contend with audacious rats that tried to carry off their bread. They came up with the idea of taking turns moving the bread by means of pulling a string tied to a rocking chair, "which luxury was magnanimously

---

[12]*Commemorative Booklet for American Bicentennial* (St. Catharine, 1976), p. 15.

[13]Anna C. Minogue, *Annals of the Century* (New York, 1912), p. 45.

[14]Eugenie Veglia, S.J., "The Sisters of Saint Joseph in Louisiana" (bachelor's thesis, Loyola University of New Orleans, 1936), pp. 26-28.

presented to them by the priest who had torn his only soutane as he sat on their proffered box."[15]

Many of the sisters' hardships grew out of the inadequate financial support congregations received from Church sources or their mother-houses; lack of such support seemed a constant concern. Almost as soon as the Madames of the Sacred Heart arrived in 1819, for example, Mother Duchesne wrote to France about the money problems.[16] By 1869, the Daughters of the Cross had become such an impossible financial burden on their French motherhouse that the American group was left to survive on its own resources.[17] Under the circumstances, the issue of enclosure would certainly be secondary to survival.

Starting a religious house was difficult in itself; however, nurturing it could be even more difficult. European-based congregations could usually ask their place of origin for help, both in financial support as well as in sending recruits; however, the American-based foundations were expected to be self-supporting and to attract vocations to religious life. All congregations, however, had problems in recruiting members, especially during the early years of a foundation.

A cultural divergence separated the French-born sisters and the girls who came to them for an education. Language was one major part of that divergence. The French-speaking sisters often lacked sufficient fluency in English to teach it as a subject. These sisters experienced trouble finding and retaining English teachers, which was one cogent reason for their need to attract native vocations. A second major cultural difference discouraging vocations was that a high proportion of the students were non-Catholic. At St. Cecilia's in Nashville, for example, three-fourths of the students taught by the Dominicans at the time of the Civil War were not Catholic.[18]

The young women who came to be educated in boarding schools, moreover, usually came from comparatively well-to-do families that were not likely to foster religious vocations in their daughters. Mother

---

[15]Sister Mary Xavier Holwarothy, I.W.B.S., *Diamonds for the King: A History of the Congregation to 1945* (privately printed, 1945), p. 18.

[16]Callan, *Philippine Duchesne*, pp. 310, 319.

[17]McCants, ed., *They Came to Louisiana*, p. 87. In many orders the sisters collected donations from their own families as well.

[18]Sister Aloysius Mackin, ed., "Wartime Scenes from Convent Windows: St. Cecilia, 1860 through 1865," *Tennessee Historical Quarterly* 39 (1980): 411.

Duchesne wrote about the situation prevailing in Grand Coteau, saying that several students showed signs of a vocation. But she cautioned the sisters to be "very prudent in this matter because of their [the students'] wealth and the opposition of their families." Mother Duchesne also observed that it was very difficult to explain religious life to people who spoke a different language and knew only different kinds of food and clothing.[19]

Young women unaccustomed to hardships were not deemed likely to persevere in religious life. When the Madames of the Sacred Heart learned that they had promise of an English-speaking Irish novice, Mother Duchesne believed that the candidate should get a true picture of the conditions, which she portrayed in the following words: "Inconvenience in everything, especially our lodging, having no place even to put a sewing basket or writing pad, not a table for one's own use, food that is often disgusting, and very little variety in it, severe cold, prostrating heat, and practically no spring weather. God alone and the desire of His glory: nothing else matters."[20]

The American-based foundations did not have to contend with culture shock, and those sisters who entered religious life from Kentucky were not unacquainted with pioneer conditions. However, the severity of the life took its toll even among these frontier women. When a decision was made to establish an American congregation of Dominican Sisters to assist the Dominican priests by training children in their faith, the priests took into account the fact that "the young women of the parish were accustomed to the hardships of wilderness life" along Cartwright Creek in Kentucky. However, four of the original nine applicants could not endure the rigors and hardships of the life, and did not persevere.[21]

Temperamentally, as well as spiritually, the women who became sisters had to resolve the difficulties they faced when they had a firm conviction that they had a call from God and that they were meeting real needs of people, but were nonetheless ordered by legitimate ecclesiastical authorities to disband. They had to discern when to acquiesce and when to confront. They had to make decisions about when to complement the work of the priests and when to strike out on their own and meet other needs.

---

[19]Callan, *Philippine Duchesne*, pp. 314, 330.

[20]Ibid., p. 332.

[21]*Commemorative Booklet*, pp. 10-11.

Response to grass-roots needs is, perhaps, best exemplified by the two congregations of Negro women who "saw a need, rolled up their sleeves, and put their hands to the plow, in spite of obstacles and in the midst of an inimical milieu." They did not "wait for some directive from their ecclesiastical leaders, nor did they fail to act, complaining because of some perceived lack of leadership on the part of 'higher-ups.' " They had "no precedent to fall back on, only creative courage and persistent faith. They did not wait for perfect conditions in which to act, nor for the best of all possible worlds."[22]

The role of the sisters in the deep South was affected by the role of women in general. Southern society was a patriarchal one, and women were trained to be submissive to the patriarchs. For example, in a letter to his newly married daughter, the president of a Virginia college admonished the young woman never to oppose her husband, and never to show displeasure, because a man had a right to expect his wife to place perfect confidence in his judgment. One of the more articulate spokesmen for both slavery and for the subordinate role of women wrote that as long as a woman was "diffident and dependent," men will worship her. Like children, women had but one right, he said, "the right to protection."[23]

Women's expressions of unhappiness centered on two areas, namely, their relationship to slaves and their limited opportunities for learning. Slaves were troublesome property; they made many psychological as well as time-consuming demands. Women were to learn "only so much as would not unfit them for their appropriate role in the patriarchy." Men who had prohibited the education of slaves, remarks Anne Firor Scott, "should have understood that it was risky to educate anyone whom they wished to keep in a degree of subjection," including women.[24]

Sarah Grimké, the daughter of a distinguished Charleston judge, spoke out on her perceptions of women's role in an 1837 publication entitled *Letters on the Equality of the Sexes.* The heart of the problem, she believed, was that women were "taught to regard marriage as the one thing needful, the only avenue of distinction," and from this basic prem-

---

[22]Michael J. McNally, "A Minority of a Minority: The Witness of Black Religious Women in the Antebellum South," *Review for Religious* 40 (1981): 267.

[23]Anne Firor Scott, *The Southern Lady: From Pedastal to Politics, 1830-1930* (Chicago, 1970), pp. 6, 17.

[24]Ibid., pp. 46, 52, 72.

ise many other evils followed. Women did not wish to appear intellectual lest men shun them; therefore, the education of women was neglected and children were shortchanged in their education, which in the early years came from their mothers.[25]

Religious women could be viewed as being in the vanguard of the women's movement, without conscious intent. They were better educated than most of the women in the South, because they had training for such "professional" work outside the home as teaching and nursing. Moreover, they did not have the strictures imposed by marriage upon women in the Southern patriarchal family structure. For the most part, their strictures came from working with clergymen in a relatively patriarchal church system.

A standard organizational feature of diocesan religious congregations of women at this time was the priest-director who had considerable influence over the internal affairs of the congregation. If he was a man of prudence, wisdom, and organizational skill, he could be a tremendous help and a strong advocate in ecclesiastical circles; however, if he exercised excessive control he could have a stifling effect on the congregation he directed, and create instability and insecurity. Therefore, many congregations that encountered difficulties sought to become pontifical, or independent of the local ecclesiastical authorities.[26]

When a new school was to be constructed, or any debt contracted, the sisters generally had to have some man vouch for them and agree to repay the debt in the event of default. Usually, their priest-director undertook this responsibility; however, when the director died, moved to another locality, or became bishop, the sisters ran the risk of being without a director for a time, or of having a director appointed who lacked understanding and sympathy.

The Dominican Sisters at St. Catharine, Kentucky, for example, were under the direction of the local Dominican Prior, Richard Miles, when they incurred a debt of $2,000, in 1825, for the construction of a new school. Before the debt was repaid, Miles was assigned to another diocese, and a Spanish Dominican named Raphael Munos was appointed their director. Father Munos did not understand what the Sisters were attempting to do, and disapproving of active congregations of religious

---

[25]Ibid., p. 62.

[26]Cf. McNally, "A Minority of a Minority," p. 268.

teachers, he repeatedly urged the Sisters to disband. Unacquainted with frontier life, he gave the excuse that "he deplored seeing women endure hardships in this new country with such little results." When Father Munos learned about the debt of $2,000 that the Sisters had incurred, and that Father Miles had signed the note, he became determined to put to an end "the foolish experiment" of a group of active women who had dared "to establish a school of seculars"—and girls at that![27] Without consulting the Sisters, he decided that they must sell the land given them by the parents of one of them, their home, and the new school, take off their religious garb, and return to their homes. In consternation, the Sisters read the mandate, and unanimously decided, by secret ballot, not to disband, but to confront Father Munos. They informed Father Munos of their decision, and pleaded with him for time to repay the debt. He became indignant at what he regarded as "feminine insubordination" and wrote to the Dominican Master General in Europe and to the bishop about the Sisters' opposition. To punish them, he refused them services in their chapel and removed the Blessed Sacrament. This meant that the Sisters had to walk a mile, over a muddy and rocky path to the nearest church, if they wished to receive the sacraments.

Alarmed at this turn of events, the Sisters' creditors demanded payment. The bishop finally wrote to the Dominican Master General in Rome and presented the case, asking for the sale of the property. He remarked: "So great and pressing are the wants of the sisters, and so urgent the necessity of liquidating this debt that I think they will consent to it rather willingly." In a postscript, the bishop added that it might be advisable for the Sisters "to disperse their community for awhile and devote themselves to various duties" in the diocese. If the Master General agreed to this, then the bishop wanted the Sisters to "assume a habit of black color" rather than the white habit of the Dominicans.[28]

The Sisters reacted by writing their own letter to the Master General, saying: "We will not agree to such a tragedy for we know it was God who called us to the religious life. Father Wilson secured the approval of the Holy See for us, and as long as the community is faithful to the purpose for which it was organized it cannot be disbanded without the consent of

---

[27] *Commemorative Booklet*, p. 28.

[28] Ibid., pp. 31-32.

the same community. Best of all, the Sisters are happy in their religious vocation and joyous in the service of their God."[29]

The master general resolved the problem by replacing Father Munos in 1830. Although the priest who replaced Munos was credited with taking care of the difficulty with the debt, the Sisters did their share of cooperating. They "disposed of every piece of furniture and salable article not absolutely necessary" and began the year 1830 "in the bleakest poverty they had ever experienced."[30]

The Oblate Sisters of Providence had a similar experience. When the health of their first priest-director, Sulpician Father James Joubert, began to decline, their material and spiritual fortunes also faded. No Sulpician came to replace Joubert, for these priests were under orders from their higher superiors to give up all work except that of working with seminarians. After Joubert's death, in 1843, the Oblate Sisters suffered such financial straits that they turned away postulants who had no clothes or money, they watched the enrollment at the Academy dwindle, and they fed themselves and the orphans on their meagre earnings from washing, ironing, and mending. By 1847, only twelve sisters were left, including two who had regular employment at the seminary and who had "disassociated" themselves from the others.

Since they had no priest to administer to their spiritual needs, the Oblate Sisters went to the nearest church, staffed by the Redemptorist Order. Their plight became known to John Neumann, the Superior of the Redemptorists in the United States, who asked a fellow Redemptorist, Thaddeus Anwander, to care for these sisters. But in the meantime, the archbishop of Baltimore, Samuel Eccleston, decided to disband the Oblates. Neumann told Anwander to promise the archbishop that he, Neumann, as head of the Redemptorists, would guarantee the support of the Oblates. The archbishop reportedly asked, "For what purpose?" Nonetheless, after some emotional pleading, the archbishop relented. Anwander went from house to house in Baltimore, begging for money and asking parents to send their children to the Oblate Academy. By 1849, the Oblates were again financially solvent.[31]

When the Sisters of Mount Carmel went from New Orleans to set up

---

[29]Ibid., p. 33.

[30]Ibid.

[31]McNally, "A Minority of a Minority," pp. 265-66.

their second establishment in Lafayette, then called Vermilionville, they had to contend with a very forceful pastor, Antoine Megret. Megret voiced some of his reservations about religious women to Father Etienne Rousselon, the director of the New Orleans group; he regarded religious women as "usually difficult to direct, especially in regard to obedience." He added that "their fancy takes over," especially if the rules were insufficient, and concluded with the observation: "Who can understand all the eccentricities of the feminine fancy?"[32]

Father Megret often acted on the supposition that his was the only worthwhile viewpoint. For example, he decided to introduce music and drawing in the curriculum. The Sisters resisted, noting that the Sacred Heart school in the vicinity had these offerings and that their school was intended to "try to form good mothers of families and teach them to love God." Megret actually sent a piano to the convent in an effort to force the Sisters to comply. At another time he surprised the Sisters by an unexpected announcement that the convent was at the top of his list of pledges for the church—pledged for $50; however, the Sisters actually gave him only $20.[33]

Having a priest-director could, then, be a matter of concern to the sisters. Some congregations had trouble securing any director; others had directors who were lacking in understanding and empathy assigned to them by higher authorities; and still others had self-appointed directors with which to contend.

Another problem facing the sisters in the South was the issue of slavery and the care of the Negroes. Sisters did not escape direct involvement with slavery. The contract that the Company of the Indies made with the first Ursulines provided them with slaves as part of their inventory.[34] A by-product of the barter system was the custom of parents giving slaves as a dowry for a daughter entering a religious congregation.[35] When a congregation was getting started, and had no labor other than their own, they sometimes considered renting a slave. Classes were organized to teach religion to the Negroes, and the hospital set up by the

---

[32]Charles E. Nolan, *Bayou Carmel: The Sisters of Mount Carmel of Louisiana, 1833-1903* (Kenner, 1977), p. 29.

[33]Ibid., pp. 31, 36.

[34]Kiefer, *Dominican Sisters*, p. 17.

[35]McCants, ed., *They Came to Louisiana*, p. 71.

Daughters of Charity in New Orleans, Hotel Dieu, had a slave department with "superior advantages for this class of patients" and special rates for them.[36]

Slavery was a matter about which the European-born sisters had no previous experience. The letters written by Mother Hyacinth of the Daughters of the Cross to relatives and fellow sisters in France reveal how some of these sisters eventually absorbed the attitudes prevalent at the time.

In 1855, Mother Hyacinth wrote: "The white people do not work. . . . Bishop proposed that we buy one slave. I showed my repugnance, and he did not insist." The following year she wrote that they had tried to hire help but were unsuccessful. Moreover, the priest had not been able "to find a good negress for cash." Then, Mother added: "We must have one on account of the boarders." When the priest later decided to buy a slave, she wrote that "this might prove a good acquisition."[37]

On 24 March 1856, she wrote that the Daughters of the Cross had bought a slave, Simon, who was forty-five years old, and the father of eight children. Simon was sold at the death of his master, who left some debts. Later she described Simon: "Our slave is a good man, too, a good Christian, and a good worker. We also teach him. He is esteemed by his people, who consult him as they would an oracle."[38]

Two years after the Daughters had purchased Simon, Mother Hyacinth wrote that in Isle Brevelle they were considering renting a "negro of responsibility for a month or two (his master has three daughters in school)" and she would later "return with Simon to Avoyelles where he has so much work to do."[39]

In May of 1864, a battle between the Union and the Confederate forces took place near the Holy Cross convent, and Simon disappeared. Concerning him, Mother Hyacinth again wrote: "Our ugly Simon, tired of being happy, seems to have followed them [the Union forces]. We do not know what became of him. Some other slaves have come back to their masters, but as for Simon, not a word has been heard of or from him since

---

[36]Baudier, *Catholic Church in Louisiana*, pp. 105, 396.

[37]McCants, ed., *They Came to Louisiana*, p. 36.

[38]Ibid., pp. 39, 57.

[39]Ibid., pp. 71-72.

May 21, when he left, taking with him one of our horses. That's what a slave is!!!!"[40]

The Madames of the Sacred Heart apparently had several slaves to help them in Grand Coteau. When Mary Ann Hardey finished school there, her biographer recounts that "a number of negro slaves also found that it [Grand Coteau] was home. Old Martin, Phyllis with her three wee children, Frank and the wife whom Mother Murphy redeemed for him from another owner, these were not only made as happy as possible in their snug little cabins, but were gradually won to the light of faith and to the love of the Sacred Heart that was the reason for Grand Coteau's existence."[41] This biographer strongly suggests that these slaves were content with their lot and implies that their conversion was justification for their condition. No accounts from the slaves survive to confirm her impressions.

When the first recruits for the Dominican sisterhood were being trained for religious life in Bethany, Kentucky, some of them brought slaves as a part of their dowry. Parents of some of the novices gave only the work of the "hands" to the sisters, but retained ownership. These slaves relieved the young women of much of the hard labor in which they previously had to engage. This permitted the women to spend more time in study, to prepare themselves for teaching.[42]

According to the chronicles of the Kentucky Dominicans, "the relationship of 'master and slave' had never existed" between the sisters and the slaves they had brought with them as part of their dowry. "Mutual respect and love" prevailed, and the "trials suffered by all tended to bring them closer together" according to this account.[43] Thus, when the sisters were considering a larger chapel, the "hands," as the slaves were called, offered to do without the yearly supply of clothing that the sisters furnished them so that the chapel could be enlarged. They requested, however, that the chapel be made large enough to accommodate them so that they would not have to take a long walk in inclement weather to the church they had been attending.[44] "Even after the abolition of slavery,"

---

[40]Ibid., p. 168.

[41]Williams, *Second Sowing*, p. 103.

[42]*Commemorative Booklet*, p. 17.

[43]Kiefer, *Dominican Sisters*, p. 7.

[44]*Commemorative Booklet*, p. 26.

according to the chronicles, "the people and the Sisters remained close" and the descendant of one of the slaves was cared for by the sisters in her final illness.

Two congregations of women of African ancestry were founded to take special care of their own people: the Sisters of the Holy Family in New Orleans and the Oblates of Providence in Baltimore. Both congregations began their work in the 1820s, even though the official recognition of the Louisiana congregation did not come until 1842.

The Oblates were founded by French-speaking women of Negro ancestry who were refugees from their home in the Caribbean. Elizabeth Lange and three companions formed a community in Baltimore, under the direction of Father James Joubert, a Frenchman whose family had fled to Santo Domingo and then to Cuba. Their difficulties in securing a director and in surviving financially have already been recounted.[45]

The Sisters of the Holy Family were founded by Henriette Delille and Juliette Gaudin, both of whom were free people of color, that is, not slaves but either freed slaves or descendants of these freed people. Henriette's grandmothers were free quadroons,[46] and she was trained to follow the traditions of her mother and grandmothers—to be mistress to some aristocratic member of the white gentry. In addition to being educated to converse about French literature, to have a refined taste in music, and to dance with grace, Henriette was also instructed in the art of nursing.[47]

When Henriette was ten years old, Sister St. Marthe, a French member of the Dames Hospitalier, opened a school for young girls who were free people of color. This school became the nucleus for missionary activities among Negroes, bond and free. By the time Henriette was fourteen, she had entered wholeheartedly into the work of teaching religion to the slaves. While other young women of her class concentrated on dancing, Henriette and her companions visited the sick and the aged, fed the indigent, and taught religion.[48]

After two futile efforts to form an interracial group, Henriette Delille

---

[45]Sister M. Petra Boston, *Blossoms Gathered from the Lower Branches* (St. Louis, 1914), pp. 3-8.

[46]Quadroons were persons who were of one-fourth Negro ancestry.

[47]Sister Audrey Marie Detiege, *Henriette Delille, Free Woman of Color: Foundress of the Sisters of the Holy Family* (New Orleans, 1976), pp. 15-16.

[48]Ibid., pp. 18-19.

became the leader of a new religious congregation, with no white members.[49] The first work of the Sisters was teaching religion to the slaves. Later, they included free people of color and whites in their classes. Since free colored women were trained in their families to care for the sick, the early Sisters also engaged in this ministry, and in 1842 opened a home for the aged, the first of its kind, called the Hospice of the Holy Family. It was a refuge for the poor, the sick, and the needy. In 1852, they established St. Augustine School, and two years later an asylum for orphans in New Orleans. Only after the Civil War did they expand their work from this area.[50]

Both of these congregations of Negro religious encountered opposition, especially from the Know-Nothing movement, which attacked Catholicism. For example, adherents of this movement allegedly broke into St. Joseph's School operated by the Oblates in Baltimore. After the second break-in, in 1856, teaching had to be suspended until the lawlessness had abated.[51] This opposition could have been expected, but opposition from Catholics was more difficult to endure. The women who founded these congregations were reluctant to wear a distinctive garb, or habit, because of anticipated opposition—in the two most Catholic cities in the South, New Orleans and Baltimore. After their directors counseled them to wear a habit, they had to endure many insults; for instance, they were sometimes forced from the sidewalks into the streets.[52] However, both congregations survived, assisted and supported by churchmen and by their sisters in other congregations.[53]

All of the social services rendered by the sisters—care of the sick, the orphaned, and the enslaved—involved instruction in religion explicitly or by way of example. Teaching religion, as well as secular subjects, was the chief focus of most of the congregations.[54] In fact, all of the native

---

[49]Ibid., pp. 20, 28-29.

[50]"Did You Know?" Brochure on Sisters of the Holy Family (n.p.).

[51]Boston, *Blossoms*, p. 17.

[52]Ibid., pp. 8, 22.

[53]The Ursulines sometimes sent a sister to help teach in Sister Marthe's school, where Henriette Delille's vocation was fostered, and the Madames of the Sacred Heart graciously received the first sisters when Bishop Blanc was looking for a place for them to make their novitiate. Detiege, *Henriette Delille*, pp. 20, 43.

[54]With the exception of the Good Shepherd Sisters whose goal is to render service to women with personal, family, and social difficulties, all of the congregations list teaching as an apostolate.

congregations founded in Kentucky had teaching as their initial and primary apostolate.

District schools in Kentucky operated only a few months of the year, and in states bordering Kentucky on the north, elementary education was in the hands of itinerant teachers.[55] In Louisiana, the early settlers engaged private tutors, or, if they could afford to do so, they sent their children to France to school. Although some effort was made by the state to educate its citizens, it was not until 1874 that Louisiana finally organized its educational system and established a number of free schools.[56]

In Louisiana, plantation owners, who were land-rich and money-poor, often resorted to unusual means to finance the education of their children. Mary Ann Hardey, whose parents lived in Opelousas, sent some slaves over to Grand Coteau—about eight miles—to get the laundry of the students and later return the clean clothing as a form of payment for part of her expenses in boarding school.[57] Along Kentucky's Cartwright Creek where the Dominican Sisters converted an old still house into a school, students were allowed to bring provisions for a year, a barter system that was far from satisfactory. Some years the potatoes and apples rotted in their bins and the barrels of sorghum molasses could not be consumed.[58]

During the periodic outbreaks of cholera and yellow fever the sisters gave witness and dispelled prejudice by ministering to the sick. The 1832 epidemic in New Orleans, which was especially virulent, was described as follows: Asiatic cholera has "combined with yellow fever, small-pox and so forth" and "has brought to the grave daily nearly 200 persons." When the "terror is at its height, the dead are buried clothed as they are and pellmell; it is hard to find negroes who are willing to do this work."[59] In Baltimore, the Daughters of Charity went into hospitals and almshouses

---

[55]Sister Agnes Geraldine McGann, *Sisters of Charity of Nazareth in the Apostolate 1812-1976* (St. Meinrad, 1976), p. 102.

[56]Sister M. Mercedes Kennedy, "The Struggle for Education in the Parish (Civil) of Natchitoches, Louisiana, 1847-1951" (master's thesis, Our Lady of the Lake University, 1952), p. 8.

[57]Williams, *Second Sowing*, p. 49.

[58]Kiefer, *Dominican Sisters*, pp. 17-18.

[59]John Tracy Ellis, ed., *Documents of American Catholic History* (Milwaukee, 1956), p. 237.

to care for the sick, and in Kentucky, the Dominican teaching sisters entered the homes of Protestants and slaves to take care of the victims.[60] During the cholera plague of 1852, as well as the yellow fever epidemic of 1853, the Marianites of the Holy Cross in New Orleans not only cared for the victims but also relieved their poverty by becoming their almoners. Sometimes they were also instrumental in getting the dead buried. According to one account, a Marianite who found three dead men in an attic walked into a nearby cafe and persuaded three men who were drinking there to take the bodies down to the city cart which was carrying corpses away.[61]

The policy of the sisters of rendering assistance whenever and wherever there was need won them public and official commendation and reduced some of the animosity against them and the Church—an institution John Tracy Ellis described as the "most disliked and suspect of all the American churches" of the mid-nineteenth century.[62] In Baltimore, for example, the city council gave a cemetery plot and erected a monument to the two Daughters of Charity who died of the contagion they contracted in the epidemic of 1832.[63] On behalf of the citizens of that city, the officials expressed their "warmest gratitude and deepest sense of obligation for those services which were given without compensation."[64] When sisters were observed ministering to the sick, those who had questioned the meaningfulness of religious life found the answer to such perplexing questions as "What kind of 'ladies' labored in the fields like men at the side of their slaves?"[65]

In addition to the care of the sick, the care of orphans was one of the most pressing needs in the Old South. As early as 1729, when the Natchez Indians killed most of the inhabitants of the Natchez post, the Ursulines agreed to receive the children orphaned by the death of their parents. In fact, settlers came from distant places to select a wife from among the orphaned girls whom the Ursulines had trained to be good housewives.[66]

---

[60]*Commemorative Booklet*, pp. 7-8.

[61]*Marianite Centennial in Louisiana, 1848-1948* (New Orleans, n.d.), p. 34.

[62]John Tracy Ellis, *American Catholicism*, 2nd ed. (Chicago, 1969), p. 83.

[63]*Daughters of Charity, 1809-1959* (Emmitsburg, 1959), p. 20.

[64]Ellis, *American Catholicism*, p. 58.

[65]*Commemorative Booklet*, p. 8.

[66]Baudier, *Catholic Church in Louisiana*, pp. 106, 137.

The waves of epidemics of cholera and yellow fever left orphans in need of care. In 1837, the New Orleans Ursulines decided that the government-supported orphanages they had been operating would be maintained at their own expense.[67] The Daughters of Charity also had their own orphanage, St. Patrick's of New Orleans, and by 1839 they were caring for ninety children there. After the epidemic of 1853, these Sisters had to rent a house in nearby Carrollton to provide a home for some fifty additional orphans.[68] In 1849, Bishop Antoine Blanc of New Orleans requested the Marianites of the Holy Cross to assist the Brothers of the Holy Cross in conducting St. Mary's Male Orphanage, which was devoid of the barest necessities. The children had no beds, and food was obtained by begging from restaurants.[69]

To the north, the first orphanage in Maryland, St. Joseph's at Emmitsburg, was opened by the Charity Sisters in October 1814.[70] On the Kentucky frontier, the Sisters of Charity of Nazareth set up an orphanage shortly after Mother Catherine Spalding learned, in 1831, that two orphan children whose parents had died on the way from New Orleans to Louisville were friendless and destitute. The following year, during the cholera epidemic, these sisters gave up their own beds for the children. Subsequently they built St. Vincent's Orphan Asylum.[71]

The sisters were far ahead of their times in the methods they used in the care of orphans. In 1854, the Daughters of Charity of New Orleans established St. Elizabeth's House of Industry to train older girls to earn a living, and by 1858, children under seven years of age received special attention in St. Vincent's Infant Asylum.[72] The care of orphans remained a pressing need throughout the nineteenth century. The Civil War left many children orphaned, and new homes for children continued to be established, despite the postwar difficulties.[73]

---

[67]Sister M. Theresa Woulfe, *The Ursulines in New Orleans 1727-1925* (New York, 1925), p. 94.

[68]Baudier, *Catholic Church in Louisiana*, pp. 395, 397.

[69]*Marianite Centennial*, pp. 30-32.

[70]Ellis, *American Catholicism*, pp. 56-57.

[71]Joseph B. Code, *Great American Foundresses* (New York, 1929), pp. 166-67.

[72]Baudier, *Catholic Church in Louisiana*, p. 396.

[73]The Sisters of St. Joseph set up an orphanage in Baton Rouge after the war. See Veglia, "The Sisters of St. Joseph," pp. 69-70.

The carnage of the Civil War provided the sisters with further opportunities to give witness to gospel values. At the outbreak of the war, the Daughters of Charity were probably the best prepared of all the congregations to nurse the sick. They had done specialized nursing in the mental department at Maryland Hospital in Baltimore, and in New Orleans had worked at Charity Hospital since 1834, where they treated the mentally ill and leprosy patients.[74] The Sisters of Charity of Nazareth had also established hospitals in Kentucky,[75] and the Sisters of Our Lady of Mercy in Charleston had some thirty years' experience in the care of the sick in the hospitals of that city at the outbreak of the war.[76]

Sisters in the path of conflict undertook the care of the wounded rather than looking for a place of refuge. In Kentucky, which was in the line of march for contending armies, St. Catharine's Dominican Convent was transformed into a military hospital, and during the Battle of Perryville injured men were brought there in every conceivable kind of farm vehicle. Some of the Dominicans remained on duty at the hospital, while others went to the battlefield, helping to lift the wounded upon the wagons.[77]

When Galveston Island in Texas was under blockade in September, 1861, and the city had no trained nurses, the Ursulines offered their academy for hospital purposes and volunteered their services.[78] The morning of the siege of Galveston, 1 January 1863, General John B. Magruder offered to conduct the sisters in the army ambulance to a place of safety, but they refused to leave the city. During the continuous shelling of the city, the sisters were in the midst of danger on the field of battle. Using an old-fashioned lantern, they helped to find the wounded on the battlefield and took them to their convent, which they had converted into a hospital. An eyewitness reported that the wounded were laid out in rows on blankets—the boys in blue and the boys in gray—and they were

---

[74]Baudier, *Catholic Church in Louisiana*, p. 396.

[75]Anna Blanche McGill, *The Sisters of Charity of Nazareth, Kentucky* (New York, 1917), p. 148.

[76]Except for the sisters, there were no trained nurses among the Southern women. See Francis B. Simkins and James W. Patton, "The Work of Southern Women Among the Sick and Wounded of the Confederate Armies," *Journal of Southern History* 1 (1935): 479, 491.

[77]Jolly, *Nuns of the Battlefield*, p. 89.

[78]Woulfe, *The Ursulines*, p. 78.

all treated alike.[79] During this battle, the sisters gave up their own beds and even tore up clothing to serve as bandages.[80]

In Charleston, South Carolina, where Union soldiers were incarcerated and under fire from their own troops, the Sisters of Our Lady of Mercy begged fresh vegetables from the people of the city, and they distributed them to the prisoners who were suffering from scurvy. In some instances, they arranged for an exchange of prisoners, and borrowed money for them. In the summer of 1864, when yellow fever was rampant, and some of the doctors fled from it, the Sisters continued to nurse the sick.[81]

One of the effects of the gospel witnessing given by the sisters during the Civil War was the dispelling of suspicion and bigotry among soldiers who had never encountered a sister and who were acquainted with few, if any, Catholics. The soldiers of both armies, for example, were moved by the heroism of Dominican Sister Alberta Rumph, who was in the emergency ward of Memphis City Hospital when her younger brother was brought in, needing immediate surgical care. She was ordered to care for another soldier nearby, her brother's foe at Shiloh, a task which she did unhesitatingly.[82] A Union officer who was imprisoned in Charleston gave testimony to the impact of the sisters on his life in the following words:"I am not of your church, and have always been taught to believe it to be nothing but evil; however, actions speak louder than words, and I am free to admit that if Christianity does exist on earth, it has some of its closest followers among the Ladies of your Order."[83] Eventually, a memorial was dedicated to the sisters who served during the Civil War.[84]

---

[79]Jolly, *Nuns of the Battlefield*, p. 324.

[80]Woulfe, *The Ursulines*, p. 79.

[81]*The Petition of the Members of the Legislature of South Carolina to the Congress of the U. S. States in Favor of the Sisters of Our Lady of Mercy, Charleston, S.C. for the Rebuilding of their Orphan Asylum Partially Destroyed During the Bombardment of the City* (Charleston, 1870), pp. 14-15.

[82]Jolly, *Nuns of the Battlefield*, p. 95.

[83]*Petition of the Legislature of South Carolina*, p. 16.

[84]See "Memorial to 'The Nuns of the Battlefield,' " a speech of Ambrose Kennedy of Rhode Island in the House of Representatives, 18 March 1918, in the *Congressional Record* of that date. This speech gives detailed information about the congregations that served in the war and the names of individuals who rendered service.

At a time when Catholicism was a minority religion, viewed by adherents of the nativist movement as a religion of "foreigners," loyal to Rome, who engaged in "idolatry" and an elaborate ritual, the sisters openly identified themselves as devout and committed Catholics. They wore a distinctive religious dress or habit, sought ecclesiastical approval, and worked under the direction of Catholic clergymen.

The sisters were not stifled by the restrictions that Southern society placed upon women. They challenged the laws prohibiting the education of slaves and taught the blacks in spite of threats of punishment. White sisters formed meaningful and lasting relationships with blacks, and the black sisters not only worked within the limits of their environment but also transcended that environment. They recognized the prevailing "cultural and historical myopia," yet formed relationships with persons in the white community to support common projects for the common good.[85] These black sisters served the unmet needs of their own people—the orphaned, uneducated, and aged—and by their witness challenged the larger society to follow their example.

Through their vows, the religious women of the nineteenth century were liberated to express their love of God and neighbor and to give witness to gospel values. They had no fear of losing material goods, for what they had was at the service of their neighbor. They lived like the poor, with few comforts and many deprivations. They engaged in hard manual labor, contracted debts, and experienced abject poverty—to the extent that they were sometimes told to disband and to abandon their work of serving the needy.

Through their vow of celibacy, the sisters were free to defy the norms that marriage was the proper state of life for women, and that women should be dependent upon their husbands. At a time when women's place was in the home, the sisters were free to seek a formal education and to become teachers, not only of religion, but also of secular subjects. The sisters were free also to become surrogate mothers of orphans and to try new methods of caring for these children and preparing them to become self-supporting. They were likewise free to risk their lives in caring for the victims of cholera and yellow fever and to go on the battlefields and battleships to care for the victims of war. For the black sisters, celibacy

[85]McNally, "A Minority of a Minority," p. 267.

was especially a sign of contradiction. Negro culture "celebrated the human body, the begetting of children, and kin relationships," yet these religious "were celibate, covered from head-to-toe with a black bonnet (or veil) and a long black dress, having neither husband, lover or children, and living apart from their relations."[86]

Through their consecrated obedience, the European-born sisters came to live in an alien land, among alien people, with an alien culture and language. Although many of the native-born sisters, especially in Kentucky, were hardy pioneers, they had to endure extraordinary physical labors that their mothers and sisters would have relegated to the men or to the "hands." The responsibilities associated with building a school, operating a hospital, or caring for the orphaned or aged were responsibilities that few other women in Southern society had. The sisters had trust, that in answer to the call to give a particular kind of service, they would have the necessary spiritual support to carry on their witness.

Obedience also required the sisters to work with priests who were often lacking in empathy and understanding. At times, they were given a mandate to self-destruct; however, these women had the courage to resist orders to disband, because they were convinced that they had a special call to serve God's people, and that what they were doing and how they were doing it made a difference. A generalization about the Negro sisterhoods was, to some extent, applicable to all of them, namely, that "in the face of adversity, poverty, privation, prejudice, segregation, lack of support, insecurity, and ambiguity," the sisters "continued doggedly to witness to what they believed, carrying on their love affair with their God by serving his people."[87]

---

[86]Ibid., p. 269.
[87]Ibid.

"SPLENDID POVERTY": JESUIT SLAVEHOLDING IN MARYLAND, 1805-1838

by R. Emmett Curran, S. J.

In 1788 Patrick Smyth, an Irish Roman Catholic clergyman who had recently returned from a brief ministry in Maryland, published a pamphlet on *The Present State of the Catholic Mission, Conducted by the Ex-Jesuits in North America*. Smyth's conclusion was that any impartial observer could readily see why the mission was languishing. The ex-Jesuits, Smyth reported, were

> superbly lodged on the banks of the Potomack, or basking in the luxuriant climes of the Eastern Shore. . . .They have a prodigious number of negroes and these sooty rogues will not work, unless they be goaded, and whipped, and almost flayed alive.

"Oh God of Heaven!" he melodramatically exclaimed,

> and is it thus your widely extended vineyard is neglected? . . . Are your very ministers become taskmasters? they, who should cherish the hapless African in their bosoms, and share the sad burden of his afflictions?[1]

---

[1](Dublin, 1788), pp. 17-18.

John Carroll, one of the ex-Jesuits and the superior of the Church's missions in America, responded to Smyth in a pamphlet of his own, exposing the falsehoods and distortions that Smyth was spreading.[2] But the accusations and insinuations of the Jesuits as "Lords of the Land" persisted. They reached a climax with the mass sale of their slaves in 1838.[3]

Jesuit landholdings in Maryland by the nineteenth century were extensive, though small when compared to the former estates of their brethren in Latin America. In 1824 they amounted to something more than 12,000 acres, most of which consisted of four large estates in the southern counties of Prince Georges, Charles, and St. Mary's, and two smaller plantations on the Eastern Shore. In addition, the order possessed two farms totalling more than 1,700 acres at Conewago and Goshenhoppen in eastern Pennsylvania.[4] It had acquired these properties by grants from Lord Baltimore according to the Conditions of Plantation issued by the proprietor in 1636, by acquisitions, and by bequests from individual Catholics. From the beginning, the Jesuits depended upon their estates to support their ministries to settlers and Indians.

To work these lands, the Jesuits first relied upon indentured servants, a practice they never completely abandoned. As this form of labor became increasingly difficult to secure and retain in Maryland, the Jesuit missionaries, like their secular fellow planters, turned to slave labor. Although there is explicit evidence of Jesuit slaves only from 1711 on, it is highly probable that they were working the plantations for at least a generation by that time.[5] By 1765 there were 192 such slaves.[6]

---

[2]"Response to Patrick Smith," in Thomas O'Brien Hanley, ed., *The John Carroll Papers*, 3 vols. (Notre Dame, 1976),1:337-46.

[3]In May 1839, for instance, an official of the Society for the Propagation of the Faith, which had been supporting the Maryland Jesuits for years, confided to the procurator of the mission that the Society kept getting reports of the great wealth in land and slaves that the Maryland Jesuits possessed. The Jesuits went to great lengths to show how indebted they were (*Archivum Romanum Societatis Jesu* [hereafter *ARSI*], Maryland 7 I 13, Francis Vespre to Roothan, New York, 30 May 1839).

[4]Thomas Hughes, S.J. *The History of the Society of Jesus in North America: Colonial and Federal: Documents*, 2 vols. (London, 1908), 1, part 1:379-80.

[5]Hughes, *History*, 1, part 1:222. Andrew White, the first Jesuit in Maryland, brought two mulattoes to Maryland, in 1633 and 1635, but there is no evidence they were slaves (See Peter Finn, "The Slaves of the Jesuits in Maryland," [master's thesis, Georgetown University, 1974], p. 6); Whittington B. Johnson, "The Origin and Nature of African Slavery in Seventeenth-Century Maryland," *Maryland Historical Magazine* 73 (1978): 236-45. Joseph Zwinge, S.J. speculated from ex-slave reminiscences that two

In 1773 the Society of Jesus was suppressed by Pope Clement XIV. Every bishop in the world was instructed to take possession of the order's property within his jurisdiction. Since no bishop in British America was closer than Quebec, the order was never carried out in Maryland.[7] The lands there remained in the control of the ex-Jesuits. To protect the property, they organized, in 1783, the Select Body of the Clergy, and nine years later received legal recognition from the state of Maryland as the Corporation of the Roman Catholic Clergymen. The charter empowered three to five trustees, elected by the members of the Select Body, to administer the property. With this authority the trustees appointed the managers of the several plantations, distributed the revenue accruing from them, approved expenditures, and oversaw the general business of the estates.

In 1805 five of the former Jesuits in Maryland received permission to affiliate with the Russian Province of the Society of Jesus, which Catherine the Great had protected from suppression. John Carroll, now bishop of Baltimore and head of the Corporation, signed an agreement with Robert Molyneux, the Jesuit superior, allowing the Society to reenter into possession of its old estates. The Corporation, however, continued to be the legal owner and to control the operation of the land. Membership in the Select Body was limited to Jesuits after 1816, but the Jesuit superior had no direct authority over the Corporation.[8] Inherent in the rationale of the Select Body of the Clergy, out of which the Corporation grew, was the affirmation of a clear-cut separation between the spiritual and temporal realms. Such a separation should have ended with the reestablishment of the Society, but it did not.

In the years before its establishment as a province of the Society in 1833, the majority of Jesuits in the Maryland mission were foreigners.[9]

---

servants working on the plantation at St. Inigoes in 1644 were slaves ("The Jesuit Farms in Maryland," *Woodstock Letters* 41 [April 1912]: 204).

[6]Zwinge, "Jesuit Farms," p. 204.

[7]Richard Challoner, the vicar apostolic of the London District, to whom fell the task of carrying out the details of the Suppression, ruled out any American confiscation as being impractical (Hughes, *History: Text* III [unpublished redaction of 1933], p. 209).

[8]Maryland Province Archives of the Society of Jesus (hereafter MPA), Minutes of the Corporation, 19 June 1816.

[9]The catalogue of the mission in 1819 listed four Germans, 16 Irish, three French, eight Belgians, one Russian, one Italian, one Englishman, and 19 Americans.

All of the mission superiors during that period— with two exceptions—
were foreign-born. Since only citizens could be members of the Select
Body, the foreign superiors had no legal authority over the property.[10]
Persistent tensions continued between the native Jesuits and their foreign brethren. The American Jesuits tended to regard the immigrants—
particularly those from White Russia, Italy, and Belgium—as "ignorant
monarchists" who appreciated neither the republican traditions of this
country nor the peculiar position of the Society in Maryland as a large
landowner. Superiors like John Grassi and Anthony Kohlmann were
criticized for incurring large debts to promote unrealistic educational
schemes at Georgetown College, at the short-lived New York Literary
Institute, and at the Washington Seminary. Francis Dzierozynski, the
superior from 1823 to 1830, struck many as a good religious who was
more fit to "be governed than to govern."[11] The trustees of the Corporation particularly resented the financial burdens placed upon the mission
by the superiors' admission of novices from Ireland, Belgium, and elsewhere in Europe.

Many of the Jesuits from continental Europe, if not openly antidemo-
cratic, were critical of American institutions and values. Dzierozynski
wrote a young Maryland Jesuit in Rome that he hoped that the Marylanders studying there would shed their republican spirit.[12] Men like Dzierozynski, a native of Russia, and Stephen Dubuisson, who had left Santo
Domingo with his parents during the revolution there, found the American Jesuits too independent, too materialistic, and too little observant of
the rules of religious life. To Dzierozynski, Dubuisson, Fidele de Grivel,

---

[10]The Corporation's trustees, for instance, acknowledged in 1817 that with the death
of Archbishop Leonard Neale, an ex-Jesuit, spiritual jurisdiction of the estates had now
passed to the superior of the mission. It was understood that the trustees retained
temporal jurisdiction (MPA, Corporation Minutes, 11 October 1817).

[11]*ARSI*, MD 3 I 31, George Ironside to Aloysius Fortis, Washington, 10 October 1825.

[12]MPA, Peter Kenney to John McElroy, Tullahey, 28 June 1822. Kenney reported in
1833 that a story was making the rounds in Ireland that during the War of 1812 one of the
foreign Jesuits in Maryland "sallied out of the house & abused a number of American
soldiers who were drawing cannon through our grounds, Calling them rebels to their
King, & wishing that the fate of rebels might attend them." Bishop John England was the
bearer of such tales and his source, according to Kenney, was Benedict Fenwick, the
former Maryland Jesuit and then Bishop of Boston (MPA, Kenney to Dubuisson, Dublin,
28 October 1833).

and others, the American Jesuits were too much the children of their culture.

These factions and the poor financial condition of the mission caused the general of the Society, Thaddeus Brzozowski, to send an Irish Jesuit, Peter Kenney, as his special visitor in 1819. One of Kenney's assignments was to examine the state of the farms. He found "splendid poverty"—"so much apparent wealth & real poverty." "Complaints of bad managment, unprofitable contracts, useless & expensive experiments & speculations" greeted him on every plantation with the exception of the one at Newtown.[13]

Adam Marshall, the Jesuit charged with overseeing the plantations for the corporation, described them as "immense tracts of land resembling rather an Indian hunting ground than lands inhabited by men acquainted with the arts of civilized life."[14] Marshall reported to the general that St. Inigoes, St. Thomas, White Marsh, Bohemia, and St. Joseph's were all "in wretched condition." The dwellings for the slaves were "almost universally unfit for human beings to live in." Even the best farm within the mission, Conewago in Pennsylvania, was in debt. Accounts were incorrectly kept, if at all. In only two places could he reckon with any reasonable certainty the annual revenues and expenses. None of the estates had contributed anything to the general fund of the mission. The tobacco the Potomac plantations grew was of an inferior quality.[15] White Marsh, potentially the most valuable property they possessed, had a debt in excess of $6,000, despite the large revenues it had brought in for the past several years.[16] The general debt of the mission was nearly $32,000.[17]

Nor did Marshall think improvement a possibility. "We have no men capable of managing a farm."[18] During the colonial period brothers had been assigned this responsibility wherever possible, but their numbers were few so that priests, with the occasional assistance of lay overseers,

---

[13]MPA, X T 1, "Temporalities," 1820.

[14]MPA, 205 G 6, Marshall to Enoch Fenwick, 14 August 1820.

[15]*ARSI*, MD 2 II 5, Marshall to Fortis, Georgetown, 6 February 1821; same to same, 5 March 1821.

[16]*ARSI*, MD 2, same to same, White Marsh, 5 February 1822.

[17]*ARSI*, MD 6 II 1, Charles Neale to Fortis, Portobacco, 27 November 1822.

[18]*ARSI*, Marshall to Fortis, 5 February 1822.

most often served as managers. With the restoration of the Society in 1805, lay brothers slowly were given charge of the farms by the corporation. By 1820 brothers managed five of the six plantations in Maryland, with the exception of St. Joseph's at Tuckahoe in Talbot County. Two years later four of them had either been removed or demoted to the status of assistant manager under a priest, the apparent victims of Kenney's and Marshall's devastating reports.[19]

One aspect of the brothers' management that disturbed Kenney was their arbitrary treatment of the slaves. He had found general disaffection among the blacks. In some places the weekly ration of meat was only a pound and a quarter ("often this has not been sound"); pregnant women were being whipped; the behavior of the slaves was scandalous; and their practice of religion virtually nonexistent. At the conclusion of his visit in 1820, Kenney instructed the mission consultors to issue regulations concerning the treatment of slaves with which the local procurators would have to comply strictly. "Great zeal, piety, prudence & charity with a regular system," he concluded, "are requisite to check the evils attendant on the possession of slaves."[20]

As Peter Finn has shown in his thesis on "The Slaves of the Jesuits in Maryland," the Maryland Jesuits conscientiously attempted through word and example to influence their fellow Catholic slaveholders.[21] As early as the 1760s a Maryland Jesuit chastised his congregation for regarding their slaves as an "inferior species."[22] John Lewis, the last superior of the mission before the Jesuits' suppression, reminded his hearers of Saint Paul's warning that "he who takes no care of his domesticks is worse than an infidel and has denyed his faith." He urged them to regard their slaves as "Brothers in Jesus Christ."[23] The slaves, in the Jesuits' eyes, had certain basic rights: adequate food, clothing, shelter; proper care when they were

---

[19]Joseph Heard remained in charge of Bohemia, which Marshall had found recovering under Heard's careful management (*ARSI*, Marshall to Fortis, 5 March 1821).

[20]MPA, X T 1, Kenney, "Temporalities," 1820.

[21]Finn, "The Slaves of the Jesuits," ch. 2, pp. 45-74.

[22]Georgetown University Archives (hereafter GUA), Sermon Collection. The hand seems to be that of John Boone; the date 1765-1770.

[23]GUA, Sermon Collection, John Lewis, before 1761.

old or sick; a Christian marriage in which the spouses were not separated.[24]

By the 1820s the living conditions for the slaves on most of the plantations were less than adequate. The hard times of the early years of that decade were partly responsible. By 1823 the novice Jesuits at White Marsh subsisted on a diet of little more than bread and water before the Corporation closed the novitiate. Two years later the superior had to sell a portion of the estate to buy winter clothing for the blacks.[25] The high percentage of slaves either too young or too old to work also compounded the pressures upon the estates to provide for all those dependent upon them. Thus, in 1820, only fourteen of the sixty-one slaves at St. Inigoes were working the land; twenty-three were under fourteen years of age.[26] At White Marsh a higher proportion was working, thirty-two out of sixty-eight. Twenty-six were under fourteen, and fourteen were over forty-five.[27] These exceptionally high percentages of underaged or super-annuated slaves may be due to the general good care the blacks had received. At any rate, by the early 1830s the material condition of the slaves seems to have improved significantly as conscientious priests like Joseph Carberry, Ignatius Combs, and Peter Havermans were assigned to St. Inigoes, St. Thomas, and Newtown respectively.

Fidele de Grivel reported in 1831 that St. Thomas remained some-what in a "delapidated state" but improvements were taking place, and all, including the slaves, had plenty to eat.[28] Indeed, in their enjoyment of the rudiments of life, de Grivel thought that the blacks were "Lords" in comparison to the peasants of his native France. White Marsh was still struggling to meet its basic needs, although by 1832 Father Samuel Mudd had paid off all its debts.[29] The most thriving plantation was St. Inigoes, where Carberry had instituted a system of dividing the estate into several

---

[24]Finn, "The Slaves of the Jesuits," pp. 50-51; GUA, Brother Mobberly's Diary, 1820, pp. 142-43.

[25]*ARSI*, Dzierozynski to Fortis, Georgetown, 29 January 1825.

[26]National Archives, Census of 1820, St. Mary's County, Maryland.

[27]National Archives, Census of 1820, Prince Georges County, Maryland.

[28]*ARSI*, MD 4 II 9, de Grivel to John Roothan, Georgetown, 26 January 1831. According to de Grivel, forty of the sixty slaves were female. Kenney echoed de Grivel's conviction about the relative position of the slaves in comparing them with many of the peasants in Ireland (MPA, 206 Z 10a, McElroy Papers, Kenney to McElroy, 30 March 1822).

[29]MPA, 4-5-6, de Grivel to Nicholas Sewall, White Marsh, 30 May 1832.

farms. One farm he rented out to a white farmer. Another he worked himself with approximately half of the active slaves. The other five tracts of land he assigned to slave families at the annual charge of $1.25 an acre. These last families were responsible for providing for all their needs. By the mid-1830s, Carberry was claiming the success of this free enterprise project. The debt was paid off, the blacks had an incentive to produce for themselves, and their economic improvement led them to better moral and spiritual lives as well.[30]

The Jesuits' slaves on most of the estates were routinely able to earn money, either by doing extra work for their owners or by selling products they had made or produce they had raised in their own gardens or seafood they had gotten from the river. Joseph Mobberly, a Jesuit brother manager, estimated that the average family at St. Inigoes was able to earn from eighty to 100 dollars a year.[31] Carberry's experiment was the first attempt to increase productivity by giving at least some of the blacks the incentive of working their own fields exclusively.

The moral and spiritual condition of the slaves also was a concern in these years. Despite catechesis and required attendance at Mass, Kenney found their lives a moral wasteland and a scandalous reproach to the Society. At Bohemia he encountered illegitimacy: a *méage à trois* involving a slave, a free black, and an abandoned married woman; another slave living with a prostitute; still another's house serving as a "tavern for selling whiskey &c to ours & our neighbour's servants."[32] Except for an old woman, none had been to the sacraments for twelve years.[33] All this among a slave population of seven. Bohemia's slaves were particularly notorious, but Kenney received similar complaints at all the plantations in Maryland.[34]

Some Jesuits attributed this moral anarchy to the Society's own failure to discipline the slaves. To John Beschter in Baltimore the proverb, "he is as bad as a priest's slave," was all too warranted. "Our slaves corrupt . . .

[30]*ARSI*, MD 5 I 31, de Grivel, "Memoire Sur la Congregation Prov. du Maryland commences le 3 Mai le 8 Juillet 1835" [1835]; Carberry to Stephen Dubuisson, St. Inigoes, 25 April 1838.

[31]GUA, Mobberly Diary, 1:132-33.

[32]MPA, X T 1, "Temporalities," 1820; MPA, X P 5, "Observations made by R. F. Visitor at the Residence of St. Francis Xavier Bohemia Cecil Co., Mar., June 1831."

[34]MPA, X S 1, "Memorial Left with the Superior of the Mission, S.J. in Missouri by the Rev. F. Peter Kenney, Visitor of the Society in the United States, N. Amer. 1832."

with impunity," he wrote. Neither their moral offense nor their laziness was punished. It was no surprise to Beschter that the farms languished, given this moral climate.[35]

Brother Mobberly, who managed St. Inigoes from 1806 to 1820, shared Beschter's conviction that a lack of discipline lay at the root of the growing corruption and discontent among the slaves. "The better a Negro is treated," Mobberly wrote in his diary, "the worse he becomes."[36] Mobberly's own attempts to discipline his slaves had just the opposite effect. By the time Kenney visited the plantation in 1820, the blacks compiled a litany of complaints to cite against the brother. Kenney listened (as he had elsewhere), and the Corporation removed Mobberly within a month.[37]

Mobberly, a Maryland native, had given much thought to the place of "the peculiar institution" within the mission. He wrote a long tract in 1823 justifying slavery as a necessary good that provided for the forty percent of the human family that was "deficient in point of intellect ... & know not how to take care of themselves."[38] His long experience on the Jesuit plantations had convinced him that the present slave economy based on the raising of tobacco and corn was unprofitable and destroying the soil. Furthermore, abolitionist activity in Maryland among the Quakers and Methodists was causing the slaves to grow more restive. Fears of insurrection were growing. In 1814 an abortive uprising had occurred within sight of St. Inigoes. As early as 1815 Mobberly was urging that the mission rid itself of its slaves and entrust the land to tenant farmers and the production of wheat.[39]

The Corporation was actually ahead of Mobberly. In the fall of 1814, the trustees raised the issue of not only changing from slave to free labor but also of freeing the slaves themselves. The following June they resolved "to dispose for a limited time of the greatest part of the blacks on

[35]*ARSI*, MD. 3 IV 18, William Beschter to Parain, Georgetown, 27 March 1829.

[36]GUA, Mobberly Diary, 1:143.

[37]MPA, Corporation Minutes, 20 April 1820; MPA, X T 1, Kenney, "Temporalities," 1820. As Finn notes, the slave of the Jesuits had the unique opportunity of voicing his complaints and problems to a superior higher than his local master (Finn, "The Slaves of the Jesuits," p. 81).

[38]GUA, Mobberly Diary, 2:1-87.

[39]GUA, Mobberly Diary, 1:74-77; 139-41; MPA, 204 K 3, Mobberly to John Grassi, St. Inigoes, 15 February 1815.

the different plantations." They intended to set a term of service for each black acquired after which he or she would be free. As John Carroll, one of the trustees, explained,

> since the great stir raised in Engld. about Slavery, my Brethren being anxious to suppress censure, which some are always glad to affix to the priesthood, have begun some years ago, and gradually proceeding to emancipate the old population on their estates.[40]

Such deferred emancipation was a policy of the Corporation that predated the restoration of the mission in 1805.[41] Probably more common was the practice of allowing the slaves to purchase their freedom through their earnings. In 1801 the Corporation censured Peter Brosius of Conewago for manumitting a slave on that estate. Such a precedent, the trustees noted, would prove "not a little injurious to that subordination, which ought to be preserved among the other slaves belonging to the Corporation." They advised Brosius to have the slave purchase his freedom, at least on a *post factum* basis.[42]

During the 1790s, when the Abolition Society in Maryland was fostering many slave petitions for freedom in the courts, several blacks on the estates at White Marsh and St. Thomas adopted this strategy of suing for their freedom through the aid of sympathetic lawyers. None apparently was successful, although one of the cases remained in the courts until 1811.[43]

The resolution of the Corporation of 1814 was never carried out.[44] At a meeting six years later the trustees repealed it with the explanation that "mature reflection" had convinced them that such a plan was "prejudicial."[45] By 1820 two things had happened: Kenney had been appointed

---

[40]MPA, Corporation Minutes, 14 June 1814; John Carroll to John Troy [1815], in *Carroll Papers*, 3:313.

[41]MPA, 203 T 8, John Carroll to Francis Neale, Baltimore, 3 October 1805.

[42]MPA, Corporation Minutes, Newtown, 1801.

[43]MPA, Proceedings of Representatives, St. Thomas, 3 June 1795. See Jeffrey Brackett, *The Negro in Maryland: A Study of the Institution of Slavery* (Baltimore, 1889), pp. 54-155.

[44]The only sale in accordance with the resolution was apparently that of a nineteen-year-old male slave for twelve years, after which he would be free (MPA, 99a R 3, Draft [1816]).

[45]MPA, Minutes of Corporation, St. Thomas, 22 August 1820.

visitor, and Carroll's successor as archbishop of Baltimore, Ambrose Maréchal, had initiated his claims against the Jesuit estates on the grounds that they were meant to support the Church in Maryland, not merely the Jesuits. Kenney agreed to support the Jesuits' desire to "part with the slaves" on the two conditions that the change be well planned and that they were certain that it would be for the better.[46] The archbishop's threats to go to court with his claim may also have caused the trustees to delay any mass sale of slaves.

As the debts of the mission grew in 1822, the trustees mortgaged White Marsh and its blacks.[47] A month later, they authorized the agent, Adam Marshall, to sell as many as thirty slaves from that plantation, if he judged it could survive without their labor.[48] Again, the sales did not take place.

Maréchal had taken his cause not to the civil court but to Rome. In July 1823 Pope Pius VII ordered the Maryland Jesuits to surrender White Marsh with all its slaves and equipment to the archbishop. They refused, claiming that they could not in conscience hand over their property to the archbishop because its incorporation gave it a civil nature that a bishop could not touch. If Rome forced them to give up White Marsh, it would constitute foreign interference with the civil rights of American citizens.[49]

In that same summer the general, Aloysius Fortis, had appointed another foreign superior, Francis Dzierozynski of White Russia, to resolve the controversy and to break the power of the Corporation as an independent authority. To Fortis the real cause of their impoverished state was that they loved property too much and obedience not enough. "Let them renounce the property," he exhorted Dzierozynski, and God would bless their work.[50] Within two years the trustees reluctantly

---

[46]MPA, 205 H 3, Kenney to Louis De Barth, 24 April 1820.

[47]MPA, Corporation Minutes, St. Thomas Manor, 16 October 1822.

[48]MPA, Corporation Minutes, 20 November 1822.

[49]The chief clerk of the Department of State, George Brent, a relative of the Neales, warned the archbishop that "the government of the United States . . . can never view with indifference any future appeals to such foreign states, touching the administration of temporal concerns under its jurisdiction. . . ." (24 October 1824, quoted in Hughes, *History*, 2:1072). Shortly afterwards Maréchal expressed his willingness to settle for a pension.

[50]MPA, 500 39b, Aloysius Fortis to Dzierozynski, Rome, 25 March 1824.

renounced any right to administer the property without the consent of the general. Thereafter the Corporation steadily came under the control of the superior or provincial.[51]

In the fall of 1830 Peter Kenney returned to America as visitor. The General Congregation of 1820 had cut short his first visit. Now a new general, John Roothan, had instructed him to make a thorough investigation of the question of whether or not to sell the plantations. Kenney found them in much better condition than they had been a decade before. Almost all were debt-free. Only St. Joseph's seemed a bad investment for the future.[52] But the estates were still not supplying revenue to the general fund of the mission to support the training of Jesuits or Georgetown College. Indeed, regarding education, a traditional major apostolic activity for the Jesuits, Kenney concluded that the mission was "as perfectly destitute of means as if it had not one acre of landed property."[53]

Before the visitor could complete his investigation of the estates, Father General Roothan ordered that the Maryland Jesuits not sell but continue their efforts to improve them.[54] The premature decision apparently was the result of the intervention of the former superior, Dzierozynski, who had informed the general in January 1831, that, contrary to reports, the farms were producing and the mission debts were practically gone.[55]

The general had said nothing about the slaves. A year later, in August 1832, the consultors of the mission directed Kenney to make clear to the general "the State of public feeling on the subject of slavery & the other disadvantages attending the system." They wanted Roothan's permission to liberate in a gradual manner the mission from its slaves and to substitute free laborers in their place. Three of the five consultors, Fidele

[51]By 1825 most of the Maryland Jesuits who shared Carroll's vision of the strict separation of the temporal and spiritual orders were dead or advanced in age. Charles Neale, the superior who had defied the archbishop, general, and pope in 1822, died in April 1823. Adam Marshall died in 1825. At the same time, more foreign-born Jesuits were qualifying for membership in the Select Body. Thus, in 1825, John McElroy, Anthony Kohlmann, Matthew Lekeu, and Stephen Dubuisson all gained admission.

[52]MPA, Kenney to McElroy, St. Joseph's, 2 July 1832.

[53]MPA, X M 2, "Instructions given by Revd. F. Kenney to Revd. F. McSherry Procurator" [1833].

[54]MPA, 210 T 4, Kenney to Dubuisson, 20 July 1831; MPA, 210 T 8, Kenney to McElroy, 4 August 1831.

[55]ARSI, Dzierozynski to Roothan, 1 January 1831.

de Grivel, Thomas Mulledy, and William McSherry, strongly supported the proposal. Dzierozynski was just as opposed to it; Stephen Dubuisson favored it with great reservations.[56]

In 1820 Kenney had already been of the mind that ridding the estates of the slaves would remove "an immense burden" from the mission and "the odium" which the survival of slavery on the Jesuit estates in Maryland cast upon the whole Society.[57] The thrust for change, however, now came from a new breed of American Jesuit with no particular loyalty to the Maryland tradition. Mulledy and McSherry were among six young Jesuits that Kenney had sent to Rome in 1820 for their philosophical and theological training. By 1830 Mulledy was already rector of Georgetown and McSherry the assistant to the superior. To some of the older Jesuits in Maryland they seemed all too ambitious. One had the impression that they were trying to take over the mission with "grand plans of selling the farms ... putting the money in a bank ... and manumitting the slaves, at least after some years of service."[58]

Mulledy and McSherry both came from western Virginia, an area in which slaveholding was not so deeply implanted. McSherry himself had been raised on a large estate near Martinsburg, but both he and Mulledy were convinced that the problems that plagued the Society in Maryland—pressing debts, lack of funds, struggling colleges, corrupt slaves—all stemmed from the attempt of the Maryland Jesuits to be both priests and planters.[59] Of the two, Mulledy proved the more aggressive in urging the Society to abandon the "Maryland Way" that had prevailed since the 1630s. Shortly after he had returned from Rome in 1829 he petitioned Roothan to reopen the question. By 1833 he was telling the general that it was impossible to maintain both the estates and the colleges at Georgetown and Frederick.[60]

In that year the Maryland mission was raised to the level of a province and McSherry named the first provincial. He made his headquarters at St.

---

[56]ARSI, MD 4 I 23, 28 August 1832.

[57]MPA, X T 1, "Temporalities," 1820.

[58]*ARSI*, MD 3 IV 23, Beschter to Roothan, 15 February 1830.

[59]*ARSI*, 3 IV 20, Mulledy to Roothan, Georgetown, 7 January 1830. This concept of the hyphenated priest first appears in a letter from Richard McSherry to his Jesuit brother. It was a theme that both William McSherry and Mulledy repeated often in the next several years.

[60]*ARSI*, MD 5 III 4, Mulledy to Roothan, Georgetown, 28 October 1833.

Thomas Manor, where he had the opportunity to study closely the workings of that plantation, as well as those at St. Inigoes and New-town.[61] He "is verifying what I foresaw many years ago," Mulledy reported to Roothan in March 1835, "that these farms were a curse on the Society in this region. The negroes behave abominantly on many of them & the priests allow them to destroy soul and body. They are neither farmers nor priests, nor religious—but some bad combination of all."[62]

In 1830 Mulledy had suggested to the general that the slaves be sold on the basis of deferred emancipation in order that they might be prepared for their eventual freedom during their stipulated years of future service. The longer the Society kept the slaves, he went on, the more it would run the risk of being forced to sell some as they grew in numbers or became more restless under the influence of abolitionists. "Wouldn't it be necessary to separate families?" he conjectured. "And isn't this a hideous thing in America?"[63]

The Maryland Jesuits had long been sensitive to the changing climate concerning slavery.[64] By the 1830s Jesuits like Mulledy and McSherry were becoming increasingly uncomfortable about their status as slave-owners. At the same time, new legislation, triggered by the rampant fears among whites concerning the growing free black population, made it more difficult to pursue a policy of deferred emancipation.[65] Thus, the declining status of the free black in Maryland was making emancipation less acceptable as a goal while persistent financial pressures were making a mass sale more thinkable.

In May 1835 the Maryland Province held its first congregation. Out of the deliberations of the ten delegates came requests to the general to allow them to reduce the number of country missions, to sell the slaves

---

[61]Finn, "The Slaves of the Jesuits," pp. 119-21.

[62]*ARSI*, MD 5 III 6.

[63]*ARSI*, MD 3 IV 20. Mulledy to Roothan, 7 January 1830.

[64]One example of this occurred in 1817. The Corporation sold five blacks from its Bohemia estate to a neighbor who subsequently attempted to transport them to Louisiana. The blacks were intercepted and a Jesuit charged with kidnapping. When the charge was dropped, the Corporation bought back the blacks to avoid scandal (GUA, Mobberly Diary, 1:111-17).

[65]Ira Berlin, *Slaves Without Masters: The Free Negro in the Antebellum South* (New York, 1974), observes that "nowhere was the sense of crisis greater than in Maryland" (pp. 210ff.).

and some of the lands, and to work the remainder with tenant labor. This would enable the province, so the delegates reasoned, to focus its limited resources on establishing colleges and a mission band in cities like Baltimore, Philadelphia, and Richmond.[66] Mulledy, McSherry, James Ryder, and George Fenwick (all Roman-trained) were persuaded that the future of the Society in America lay in rapidly growing urban centers rather than the stagnant rural areas of southern Maryland and the Eastern Shore.[67] These four were joined by Stephen Gabaria (who had been in the country less than two years) and Francis Vespre to form the majority that supported the *postulatum* to sell the slaves.

Aloysius Young, the provincial's assistant, wanted the general to know that Mulledy, the dominant force in the congregation, and his supporters were biased against the rural tradition. Young claimed that Vespre, the province procurator, had succumbed to Mulledy's pressure but personally opposed the plan. He urged the general not to abandon the lands and institutions in Maryland, where Catholicism and the Society had flourished for over 200 years, simply to appease the empty fears about an imminent division of the Union and a possible civil war (two reasons that had been given in the congregation).[68]

Young, from an old Maryland family and now at St. Thomas, spoke for other native Marylanders who remained committed to the estates. Most of the local superiors opposed the sale. They pointed to the profits they were beginning to realize at Newtown and St. Inigoes, and contended that the blacks on their plantations, far from being corrupt, were leading truly edifying lives in the practice of religion and in their general behavior. They were skeptical about the superior opportunities to be found in the city. At least one local superior of an estate, Ignatius Combs at White Marsh, opposed slavery in principle.

One delegate to the congregation pleaded that the general consult the opinion of some of the older men in the province who knew it better than most of those who were supporting the sale.[69] To Roothan's query about

---

[66]MPA, *Acta Primae Congregationis, Provinciae Marylandiae Societatis Jesu*, 1835.

[67]Even Augustine Bally, a Jesuit missioner in rural Pennsylvania who was so successful during his long tenure at Goshenhoppen that the village was renamed for him, had to admit that Catholicism was advancing much more rapidly in the cities than in the country places (*ARSI*, MD, 7 VII 3, Bally to Roothan, Goshenhoppen, 31 January 1842).

[68]*ARSI*, MD 5 II 2, Young to Roothan, Georgetown, October 1835.

[69]*ARSI*, MD 5 II 4, Dubuisson Memorial, 1836.

seeking such wider advice, McSherry replied that he already knew what they thought and what weight to give to their opinion.[70]

It was the Europeans who were most vocal in opposing the sale. With the exception of Young, all those who had voted against the measure in the congregations were Europeans. Dzierozynski, the former superior, had wrestled as early as 1822 with the morality of selling the blacks in order to relieve the mission's financial pressures. By 1831 he was convinced that selling the lands and "our blacks" was "a dangerous...unjust" scheme.

> Lands are a patrimony from our Fathers . . . by what right can they be alienated? I consider the blacks under this respect only, that they are our sons, whose care and salvation has been entrusted to us by Divine Providence and are always happy under our Fathers.[71]

Peter Kolchin has pointed to the similarity in viewpoints that Russian noblemen and Southern planters exhibited toward serfs and slaves respectively.[72] What is striking about the arguments used by the European Jesuits in Maryland is the manner in which they tend to imagine the master-slave relationship as an idealized master-serf relationship. They tended to see the slaves as innocent and pious, gathering as families to recite their rosaries, working hard when treated properly, bringing consolation to the missionary by their staunch faith despite their lowly position. In the Europeans' view the lot of the country slaves was a blessed one compared to that of the corrupt, impoverished free blacks in the cities.[73]

The European Jesuits regarded the estates not only as a sacred trust but as a refuge from the cities and as a guaranty of their status in society.

---

[70]*ARSI*, McSherry to Roothan, Georgetown, 1836.

[71]*ARSI*, MD 2 I 51, Dzierozynski to Fortis, Georgetown, 12 April 1822.

[72]"In Defense of Servitude: American Proslavery and Russian Proserfdom Arguments, 1760-1860." *American Historical Review* 85 (October 1980): 809-27.

[73]*ARSI*, 5 IX 7, *Memoire du Pere Stephen Langaudelle Dubuisson de la Campagnie de Jesus, missionaire aux Etats unis d l'Amerique Septentrionale, Mai 1836*. Dubuisson told of blacks with Protestant masters who had stoically suffered whipping for converting to the Catholic faith. John Grassi, born in Parma and educated in Russia, had written in 1818 about "the very great consolation which the negroes bring to the missionary; for amongst them, although they are poor slaves and so abject in the eyes of the world, are found chosen souls filled with such beautiful sentiments of true piety, that they move one to tears. . . ." (*Notizie varie sullo stato presente della repubblica degli Stati Uniti dell'America settentrionale scritte al principio del 1818* [Milano, 1819]).

As Fidele de Grivel observed to Roothan in 1835,

> The Protestants have, up to now, appreciated us only because of our large
> estates; if we sell them, they will consider us no better than Methodist preachers
> who crisscross the country to accumulate money.[74]

To Jesuits like Dubuisson and de Grivel a bond existed between the
Society and its blacks that could be broken only for the most extreme
reasons, such as incorrigibility, but not need of money. They argued that
selling them would lead to the slaves' physical and moral ruin, and would
give great scandal to Protestants and Catholics alike. Dubuisson informed
Roothan while in Rome in 1836,

> There is in general a great repugnance among the blacks of Maryland to being
> sold south. Without doubt [our slaves] . . . would despair when they should be
> dragged from their ancient manors and churches. Isn't the very idea of being
> forced to go with new masters a cruel one?

What it meant, Dubuisson concluded, was that the Maryland Jesuits
would be collaborating with planters from the deep South to parlay the
labor of their blacks into immediate financial gain. The abolitionists, he
warned, would not miss the meaning.[75]

Selling slaves was not new to the Maryland Jesuits. But the sales had
usually taken place to keep families together or to punish refractory
slaves, such as at Newtown in 1774 or at Bohemia in 1832. In 1835,
however, McSherry began to sell blacks to meet financial needs. Fourteen
were sold from St. Thomas, then eleven from St. Inigoes.[76] The latter
were sold to Henry Johnson, the ex-governor of Louisiana, and Thomas
Jameson, a planter from the same state. McSherry claimed, against the
objections of Dubuisson and others, that it was not possible to sell them
to neighbors, and that Johnson had promised to provide for their reli-

---

[74]*ARSI*, MD 5 I 21, de Grivel, *Memoire Sur La Congregation* [1835].

[75]*ARSI*, MD 5 II 4, Dubuisson Memorial. The one European to support the sale,
Gabaria, was merely concerned about the persons to whom they would be sold. He judged
the sale itself would cause little stir. (*ARSI*, Gabaria to Roothan, Georgetown, 20 January
1837).

[76]de Grivel claimed that one of the slaves sold at St. Thomas was actually exchanged
for a horse, and that the trade had given great offense to the Catholics in the area. "They
were saying," he reported to the general's assistant, "even priests engage in the business
of human flesh." "After a month," he added, "the horse died and the Catholics rejoiced."
(*ARSI*) MD 5 II 1, de Grivel to Aloysius Landes, 24 October 1835).

gious needs in the same manner the Jesuits themselves had cared for them.[77]

In October 1836 Roothan finally approved the general sale of the slaves, provided that their religious needs be met, that families not be separated, especially spouses, and that the money be invested for the support of Jesuits in training.[78] The Panic of 1837 delayed the sale. "We could not at the present time," McSherry wrote Roothan in May 1837, "obtain one tenth part of what we could have obtained last year for them."[79] Poor health and the burdens of office forced McSherry to ask to be replaced as provincial. In October 1837 the general appointed Mulledy to succeed him.

Mulledy wasted little time making the final sale. In June he agreed to sell 272 slaves from the four estates in southern Maryland to Johnson and a partner, Jesse Batey, for $115,000. The pair paid $25,000 and were given ten years to complete the transaction. Eight thousand dollars went to the settlement of the archbishop's claims against the estates, and $17,000 was applied to the $30,000 debt Georgetown had incurred through Mulledy's ambitious building campaign when he had been rector. The remaining $90,000 was to be invested for the support of the Jesuits in formation. "All the Catholics who live near our estates, with no exceptions," Mulledy wrote Roothan, "approve the sale. They say it should have been done 20 years ago." He admitted that the Jesuit superiors on the plantations were quite upset "because they no longer will be great lords." He hoped, however, that this would make them better Jesuits.[80]

Rumors of a mass sale had been circulating among the slaves since at least 1832. To give the local procurators no chance to encourage their blacks to escape, Mulledy arrived without notice, accompanied by Johnson and a local sheriff. Thomas Lilly, stationed at St. Thomas Manor, was outraged. "They were dragged off by force to the ship and led off to Louisiana. The danger to their souls is certain," he wrote to Roothan. "The buyers have promised they will be treated in a Christian fashion. But given the laws and customs of that region it will be very difficult to keep

---

[77]*ARSI*, 5 II 3, McSherry to Roothan, Georgetown, 30 August 1838.

[78]MPA, F 3 A[2] - F 5 E, Roothan to McSherry, 27 October 1836.

[79]*ARSI*, MD 5 I 39, McSherry to Roothan, Georgetown, 13 May 1837.

[80]*ARSI*, MD 7 I 5, Mulledy to Roothan, Fredericktown, 9 August 1838.

them." Lilly, a native of Pennsylvania, did not believe the general could have permitted such a scandal, had he been properly informed, or had he consulted more of the members of the province. The majority, he reported, were appalled.[81]

One is tempted to wonder whether the sale would have happened had the Corporation still been a semiautonomous body. Carberry, Combs, Dubuisson, Dzierozynski, and de Grivel all had the seniority that had normally meant membership on the Corporation before it became subservient to the provincial.

The main body of the slaves was sent in a second ship in November 1838. This time there were runaways at White Marsh and St. Inigoes. Joseph Carberry and (apparently) Ignatius Combs warned their blacks to hide in the woods. At least nine did so at White Marsh and two at St. Inigoes. There is reason to believe that some escaped at St. Thomas as well.[82]

By late November the only blacks who remained, except the elderly and runaways, were those who were married to spouses on other plantations or to free blacks. Mulledy wrote John McElroy, on 11 November 1838, that Johnson had left behind these slaves in order to attempt to purchase their spouses as well.[83] It would seem at this point that Mulledy was already resigned to shipping them with or without their spouses. Four days later he was again at Newtown rounding up the remaining slaves. Peter Havermans from Holland, who was as disturbed as Lilly about the sale, recorded a particularly pathetic scene in which the slaves submitted to their fate with "heroic courage and Christian resignation."[84] At the end of November a third ship carried the last of the slaves south. The available evidence suggests that, despite the elaborate instructions of Father General Roothan, families were separated.[85]

---

[81]*ARSI*, MD 7 II 7, Lilly to Roothan, St. Thomas, 2 July 1838.

[82]Zwinge, "Jesuit Farms," p. 195; in the census of 1840, fourteen slaves were listed for St. Inigoes, six at White Marsh, and seventeen at St. Thomas.

[83]MPA, 212 M 16, Mulledy to McElroy, Georgetown, 11 November 1838.

[84]According to Havermans, one old woman sought his blessing on her knees and begged to know what she had done to deserve this. "All the others came to me seeking rosaries. . . . If ever any one had reason to despair, it was I," he told Roothan (*ARSI*, MD 7, Newtown, 15 November 1838).

[85]According to Fidele de Grivel, all the blacks married to spouses not belonging to the Society were sold to their spouses' masters or to those nearby. Some children, however,

The scale of the sale created something of a sensation within the Catholic community. Benedict Fenwick, the bishop of Boston and one of the Fenwicks of Maryland, thought it "extraordinary news. Poor Negroes! I pity them," he wrote his brother in September 1838. The bishop supposed that the antislavery party was ultimately responsible for forcing the Maryland Jesuits to resort to such an extreme measure.[86] Many others, however, did not share the bishop's judgment about where the blame lay. Stephen Dubuisson wrote the general from his parish in Alexandria that the sale had badly affected the Society's reputation both in Washington and Virginia.[87] Havermans told Roothan that Catholics and Protestants alike were scandalized. What Mulledy had done, Havermans charged, was "the stock of slave traders who value nothing except money," or the desperate recourse of those overwhelmed by debts.[88]

Dubuisson and Haverman's readings of the reaction were undoubtedly colored by their own convictions about the morality of the sale. Evidence exists, however, that other people were highly disturbed by what had happened; that some took their complaints to the archbishop of Baltimore, Samuel Eccleston; and that Eccleston carried their charges to Roothan.

Eccleston had proposed to McSherry, in 1837, that the Province sell both its land and slaves in order to concentrate on urban missions and colleges, which he promised to help them found.[89] At that time he already knew about the slaves McSherry had sold to Louisiana. Although the complete Eccleston-Roothan correspondence has apparently not survived, it would seem that the core of the charges he brought to the general was the separation of families.[90]

---

had been separated (MPA, 212 G 9, de Grivel to Charles C. Lancaster, Georgetown, 4 May 1839). de Grivel was living at Georgetown now. The sale records appear to indicate that at least some of the couples were separated (MPA, 112 W O, Newtown Account Book). Some complex situations could exist. One father at White Marsh reportedly escaped to Baltimore with his three children. The wife was nonetheless willing to leave without him because the husband was living with another woman (MPA, 212 M 5a, de Grivel to C. C. Lancaster, Georgetown, 11 November 1838).

[86]MPA, 212 N 2, Benedict Fenwick to George Fenwick, Boston, 1 September 1838.

[87]*ARSI*, MD 7 I 14, Alexandria, 24 June 1839.

[88]*ARSI*, MD 7 I 9, Havermans to Roothan, Newtown, 20 October 1838.

[89]*ARSI*, MD 5 II 5, McSherry to Roothan, Georgetown, 13 March 1837.

[90]Thomas Hughes, who knew intimately the Roman Archives, wrote in 1907 that "it was Eccleston . . . who . . . when people threw up their hands highly scandalized, . . . ran

In the late fall Roothan began a correspondence with the former provincial, McSherry, about the "scandal" Mulledy had created. Roothan evidently was ready to remove Mulledy as provincial, but McSherry counseled delay.[91] By August, however, Roothan became convinced that there no longer could be any doubt about what had happened and that greater scandal would be given if nothing were done. The general ordered McSherry to inform Mulledy to resign as provincial, at least until he could clear himself of the charges, which the general doubted he could. If he refused, he was to be dismissed. Roothan concluded:

> In some way it must be understood even in America, that men of the Society, unless they are motivated by the spirit of the Society . . . and the observance of the Rules, not only will not be a great help, but will make for great ruin![92]

By this time, however, Mulledy was already on his way to Rome. In late June Eccleston and McSherry had persuaded him that, for his own sake, he had to step down as provincial and take his case to Roothan himself. Apparently Mulledy had cause to leave hastily since he left Georgetown for Rome within a week.[93]

Peter Havermans congratulated the general for taking such decisive action. What Mulledy had done, Havermans pointed out, was "a sad example that many can follow" but decent men had now seen in Mulledy's

---

forward and denounced Mulledy to the General" (GUA, Hughes to E. I. Devitt, Rome, 29 January 1907).

[91]MPA, 500 84b, Roothan to McSherry, Rome, 14 February 1839.

[92]MPA, 500 84c, same to same, 3 August 1839. It is clear from Roothan's letter that Eccleston's testimony had been crucial. In December 1839 Pope Gregory XVI issued an apostolic letter in which he denounced the slave trade in which blacks "as if they were not men, but mere animals, howsoever reduced into slavery, are . . . contrary to the laws of justice and humanity bought [and] sold. . . ." He condemned any eccleciastic or lay person who "shall presume to defend that very trade in negroes as lawful under any pretext or studied excuse." (*In Supremo Apostolatus fastigio* in *Acta Gregorii Papae XVI* [Austria, 1971], 2:387-88; English translation in John England, *Letters to the Honorable John Forsyth on the Subject of Domestic Slavery*). Benedict Fenwick later thought that the Maryland Jesuits might have had advanced notice of this papal letter and thus accelerated their efforts to sell their slaves before it was promulgated (Archives of the Archdiocese of Baltimore, Eccleston Papers, 24-U-1, Fenwick to Eccleston, Boston, 11 March 1840). There is no evidence that Mulledy or any of the Maryland Jesuits knew that such a letter was coming. But it is quite likely that Roothan was aware of it.

[93]*ARSI*, MD 7 I, Eccleston to Roothan, Georgetown, 27 June 1839. Eccleston urged Roothan not to dismiss Mulledy from the Society. The latter was in shock. He wrote in his mass book: "No Mass (unwell). *Ave Crux. Spes unica*" (GUA, Mulledy Diary, 27 June 1839).

removal that the Society did not approve of such things. They would see it even more clearly, Havermans suggested, should Mulledy not return from Europe.[94]

Mulledy remained in Europe for three years. When he finally was allowed to return to America, he came back to Georgetown. In an address to the debating society he contrasted the peaceful liberty that Americans enjoyed with the conscription that was becoming the curse of Europe. The worst feature of conscription, he told them, was the cruel way in which it separated parents from children, wives from husbands. Prize liberty, he instructed them, and work to make right what is wrong in America. But be cautious, he warned, for "if special care be not taken in eradicating the vice you will root out the virtue too."[95] Mulledy would seem to have had more than conscription in mind.

Thus ended the Society's history in Maryland as a large slaveholder. The change to exclusive tenant farming eventually proved a profitable one by the late forties, as sharecropping was gradually introduced. Ironically, the Society abandoned its slave labor at the very time the estates were beginning to produce. In Carberry, Combs, Havermans, and Lilly, the Society finally had a set of effective managers. Had the alliance between the European Jesuits and the local procurators had its way, there might well have been increasing efforts to make the Jesuits' estates models of Christian slavery, such as Christian evangelists were attempting to create elsewhere in the South. Most Maryland Jesuits, including those on the farms, seemed to have perceived by the 1830s that slavery's days in Maryland were numbered. They might then have begun consciously to prepare the slaves for freedom, as Carberry was in effect doing at St. Inigoes. But few seemed prepared to go against the prevailing climate. For much of their history Maryland Jesuits had been outcasts, if not outlaws, but still very much the children of their culture who wanted to prove that they belonged. This tradition, economic expediency, and the urban vision of a younger American generation of Jesuits prevailed. The sale of 1838 with all its consequences was part of the price of progress and a morality play worthy of Harriet Beecher Stowe.

---

[94]*ARSI*, MD 7 VI 7, Havermans to Roothan, Frederick, 14 February 1840.

[95]GUA, Mulledy Papers, Address to the Philodemic Society (1843).

PART TWO

Society and Church

THE FAILED MISSION:
THE CATHOLIC CHURCH
AND BLACK CATHOLICS
IN THE OLD SOUTH*

by Randall M. Miller

The story of black Catholics in the Old South is largely unwritten. It is easy to see why. The population was small and elusive. Except for the Gulf region and pockets in Maryland, South Carolina, Florida, and Kentucky, Catholicism rarely touched black slaves, or whites too for that matter. Catholicism among black slaves in America left no legacy of resistance; it built no solid foundation for future black social and political activity; and it declined steadily among blacks throughout the nineteenth century. The black church in America grew out of the slaves' secret gatherings in groves and hollows—out of the Afro-American community's striving for cultural and spiritual autonomy. Catholicism was no part

*Reprinted, with minor revisions, with the author's permission from Edward Magdol and Jon L. Wakelyn, eds., *The Southern Common People: Studies in Nineteenth-Century Social History* (Westport CT, 1980), pp. 37-54. Research for this essay was completed under a faculty research grant from Saint Joseph's College, Philadelphia, and a grant from the American Philosophical Society.

of this process. The few Catholic slaves in the Old South lived as a people apart. As such, they slipped into historical obscurity.[1]

This is understandable, if unfortunate. The records on Catholicism among enslaved Afro-Americans are fragmentary and misleading. Few Catholic slaves left autobiographical or personal accounts of what their religion meant to them in their daily lives. Few remnants of their beliefs are preserved in Afro-American folklore. Catholic masters and the Church either cared so little about the slaves' religious lives or were so ignorant of the slaves' private world that they did not observe or record religious activity in the quarters. Much of the story of Catholicism among slaves of the Old South must be stitched together in a patchwork design from scattered, randomly created, and sometimes doubtful and conflicting evidence. There are many tantalizing clues, but the researcher should proceed with extreme caution.

Still, the records suggest patterns of slave values and behavior that provide revealing, if brief, glimpses into the interior world of slaves. They also adumbrate the nature of master-slave relations on the sensitive subject of religion. The history of Catholicism among slaves in the Old South reiterates the central theme of much of Afro-American life—the quest for a distinct identity. The Catholic slaves, like their Protestant counterparts, adapted the master's religion to fit their own community needs. They were not passive recipients of the slaveholder's culture. They defined and preserved their own religious values capable of surviving the rigors of bondage. In so doing, they put distance between themselves and their masters. But they also put distance among themselves.

The Afro-American experience has been one of division as well as common struggle. Real differences in occupational status, proximity to the master, social status, and sometimes age divided the slaves.[2] Real differences in religious values and style also separated the black slaves in the Old South. These divisions grew in the variegated social and cultural climates in which the slaves lived. Slaves in the upper South, for example, responded to different religious cues than those in the Gulf region. Urban

---

[1]For a general survey of the literature on the subject, see Randall M. Miller, "Black Catholics in the Slave South: Some Needs and Opportunities for Study," *Records of the American Catholic Historical Society* 86 (1975): 93-106.

[2]On ranking within the slave community, see John W. Blassingame, "Status and Social Structure in the Slave Community: Evidence from New Sources," in Harry P. Owens, ed., *Perspectives and Irony in American Slavery* (Jackson MS, 1976), pp. 137-51.

slaves had a wider range of denominational choices than did rural slaves. African-born slaves had less to do with Christianity than did American-born bondsmen. Catholic slaves lived in greater social isolation than did Protestant slaves.

The best estimates put the number of black Catholics in the South at 100,000 persons in 1860. But these people did not compose a distinct ethnic group. They were divided by culture, geography, and circumstance. Even though Catholics lived throughout the South, they tended to congregate in particular neighborhoods. There were five regional divisions among Catholics and within these several caste divisions. An older white and black Catholic population existed in Maryland and spilled over into Virginia. A small colony of French and German Catholic settlers in western Kentucky kept some slaves who professed Catholicism. Low country South Carolina, especially Charleston, harbored a Catholic population, many of whom were émigrés from the West Indies. Florida also had a tiny Catholic enclave. The largest concentration of Catholics was in the Gulf region, particularly in and around New Orleans. The American acquisition of Florida and Louisiana significantly altered the character of the American Catholic population, as did the migration of several thousand black and white Catholic refugees from the Caribbean between 1790 and 1810. Increasingly, the Catholic population derived from non-British origins, and in the case of the refugees, it became an urban population. But most Catholics continued to reside on farms, and with the westward movement in the early nineteenth century, Catholics in the Gulf region became a minority population.

Within the regional concentrations of black Catholics, caste barriers sometimes separated slaves, free blacks, and Creole free persons of color. The latter group was peculiar to Louisiana and established a unique ethnic identity that has survived into this century. They constituted a recognized and self-perpetuating third caste in antebellum Louisiana. They occupied a precarious middle ground between white and black, and they jealously guarded their autonomy. They celebrated their French and Spanish heritage, sloughed off their African cultural ties, and staked off clear racial and cultural boundaries between themselves and their own black slaves, indeed all blacks.[3] Likewise, free blacks did not always identify with the

---

[3]On this point, see Gary B. Mills, *The Forgotten People: Cane River's Creoles of Color* (Baton Rouge, 1977); and Sister Frances Jerome Woods, C.D.P., *Marginality and Identity: A Colored Creole Family Through Ten Generations* (Baton Rouge, 1972), ch. 3.

aspirations and interests of their enslaved Afro-American brethren. Much depended on their economic status and place of residence, of course—free black urban entrepreneurs being the most isolated in culture and attitude from the slaves and poorer free blacks—but real tensions sometimes marked relations between free and enslaved black people.[4] Although many black Catholic slaves lived or worked in New Orleans, they largely remained a rural people in residence and attitude. In time, many in the city succumbed to "Americanizing" pressures and gave up their faith. On the farms, however, many Catholic slaves retained a Catholic identity of sorts, although the insidious American influence steadily corroded their Catholic attachment. The haughty manner of colored Creole and white Catholic masters took its toll; so too did the prejudices and hostility of poor farmers and Irish immigrants toward the slaves. The process of religious survival and accommodation among the slaves on the farms forms the substance of this essay.

Except perhaps in lower Louisiana, the Catholic Church in the Old South was not equipped to be the guardian of the slaves' moral and physical health. It was not the arbiter of the planters' or poor whites' social and moral lives. The Church recognized slave marriages, but it lacked the power to enforce planter compliance in allowing, or honoring, the sacrament of marriage among slaves. Unlike the Church in Spanish America, the Church in the Old South largely abdicated its evangelical role among the slaves. Local parish records indicate a high rate of baptisms among slaves throughout the antebellum period, particularly in lower Louisiana. But there is little evidence of high rates of slave identification with Catholicism in terms of attendance at Mass, marriage in the Church, or other signs of Catholic activity and devotion.[5]

During the nineteenth century, the Church was besieged with financial and staffing problems that interrupted or prevented it from reaching out to the rural folk of the South. Perhaps the most fundamental cause of the Church's meager achievements in evangelizing was the Church's dependence on immigrant clergymen. As Jay Dolan has shown, the Church recognized the need to evangelize among its scattered and declin-

---

[4]Ira Berlin, *Slaves Without Masters: The Free Negro in the Antebellum South* (New York, 1974), pp. 271-83.

[5]My observation is based on samples of church records in Louisiana, Mississippi, Alabama, and Maryland.

ing population. In the voluntaristic world of America, the Church had to compete for converts. Parish missions staged revivals and rekindled Catholic commitment in the nineteenth century, but the Church's revivalistic efforts in the antebellum period were sporadic and largely confined to the cities. New Orleans was well served by revival preachers. Central and northern Louisiana hardly saw them. Too many of the priests who did come to the South were foreign-born. Many came from provincial farming backgrounds in Europe, and so at least had an affinity to the rural folk. But even the best of them missed the nuances of Southern religious and social culture. The worst alienated Protestant and Catholic alike and set back Catholic efforts to win converts and social acceptance—the necessary preconditions to establishing permanent missions in the countryside.[6]

Foreign-born priests frequently had trouble with the language. As late as the Civil War, the Church continued to rely on priests with a poor command of English. In 1862, for example, a white Catholic girl in Louisiana observed that her family avoided Mass because they did not want to suffer Father Larneudie's preaching. As always in such things, the priest's reputation preceded him. The previous Sunday he had "preached one hour and a half," but nobody understood anything he had said. The word was passed. Avoid the good father thereafter. John Nevitt, an Adams County, Mississippi, planter who was a member of the board of trustees of the local Catholic church, briefly drifted away from attendance at Mass because he found local Protestant preachers more comprehensible than the local priest. His church was later without a priest and turned to itinerant Protestant preachers for Sunday services. Unlike the immigrant priests before them, these preachers evoked a positive response from the otherwise taciturn Nevitt. The evidence of general inadequacy of preaching among foreign-born priests was ubiquitous in the Old South, and it hurt.[7]

The faithful chafed under the burden of poor preaching and alien ministers. The less devout stayed away. As the Catholic population shifted and hordes of non-Catholics invaded the Gulf region, Catholic

[6]On Catholic revivalism, see Jay P. Dolan, *Catholic Revivalism: The American Experience, 1830-1900* (Notre Dame IN, 1978), pp. 3-12, 15-24, 33-49, 65-66, and passim.

[7][Tennessee Robertson] to Mary Jane Robertson, April 1862, Mary Jane Robertson Papers (Louisiana State University); John C. Nevitt Journal, 31 May 1829, 11 March 1832 (Southern Historical Collection, University of North Carolina at Chapel Hill).

attendance declined and Catholic power evaporated. And the Church was slow to respond in the South. It was not until 1850 that Archbishop Antoine Blanc provided organized religious and educational life for Catholics in Louisiana, the stronghold of Catholicism in the South. And the establishment of dioceses and parish missions rarely extended real Catholic influence into the backcountry. The rich Catholics could travel to towns to participate in organized religious life, and they could send their children to Catholic schools. The poor, black and white, waited for the priests' annual visits to remind them of their Catholic sacramental life. Churches fell into disuse for want of clergy and lay interest. Indignities occurred. The church at St. Stephens, Alabama, for example, was sold and converted to a brothel. In St. Mary's Parish, Louisiana, which had four Catholic churches in 1860 capable of seating fourteen hundred persons, church attendance was so low that one observer wryly remarked that the situation would not improve unless the grogshops were closed on Sunday. Catholic planters put plantation duties before religious ones: Church was not sufficiently appealing or necessary to them to warrant a trip to town. One Catholic woman confessed that she chose not to attend Mass during the summer and fall simply because it was "too hot." The church at Houma, Louisiana, tried to make it easier for parishioners to attend services by paving a walk from the main street of the town to the church, but its efforts were not rewarded. Poor roads were not the problem. It was indifference on the part of the Catholic parishioners, whatever their income or social status. This religious indifference would not go unnoticed by the slaves of Catholic masters. A faith that was not worth observing when it was hot or inconvenient was no faith at all.[8]

---

[8]A.B. Moore, *History of Alabama and Her People* (Chicago, 1927), p. 182; Franklin (LA) *Planter's Banner*, 2 August 1849; Tennessee Robertson to Mary Jane Robertson, 29 June 1861, Robertson Papers; Raleigh A. Suarez, "Religion in Rural Louisiana," *Louisiana Historical Quarterly* 38 (January 1955): 62. It is worth noting that in rural, lower Louisiana the number of churches grew steadily from 1850 to 1860, but attendance did not keep pace with the growth. On religious indifference among Catholics, see Mother Mary Hyacinch Le Conniat to her parents, 6 December 1856, 19 August 1857, in Sister Dorothea Olga McCants, ed., *They Came to Louisiana: Letters of a Catholic Mission, 1854-1882* (Baton Rouge, 1970), pp. 56, 66-67. As Dickson D. Bruce, Jr., argues in *And They All Sang Hallelujah: Plain-Folk Camp Meeting Religion, 1800-1845* (Knoxville TN, 1974), p. 45, Southerners "generally displayed a good deal of apathy and even hostility toward organized religion" in general, and even revivals did not change that. Indifference to and ignorance of formal religion was not peculiar to Catholics, and even after a wave of Protestant revivals only about 20 percent of the whites in the Old South were churched by 1860.

Catholicism had an image problem in the nineteenth century. It was a religion of "foreigners" who professed loyalty to a foreign power. It was a religion that exercised few social restraints on its followers—witness the drunkenness and poverty of the immigrant Irish, who were despised equally in the North and the South by Protestant whites and blacks. It was a religion that lacked the directness and simplicity of message of "American" religion. Catholics engaged in too much chanting, too much "idolatry," too much elaborate ritual, and too much hierarchical organizing for American egalitarian tastes. And American Protestants would have none of it. During the Civil War, even when the Church labored mightily for the Confederate war effort, one Louisiana woman reacted strongly to the nature of the Catholic service. Given her location, she should have been less sensitive about such things. But when a Catholic companion commented on her refusal to participate in a Catholic Mass that she had attended, the woman replied sharply that she did not care what the priest thought of her actions and would not worship when she did not know what was going on. It is significant that even in lower Louisiana, the seat of Catholicism, non-Catholics remained suspicious and ignorant of Catholic services and intentions.[9]

Worse, many non-Catholics believed that Catholics were ungodly. Southerners regarded Catholics as inveterate gamblers and drunkards, and they deemed the foreign-born priests to be the worst of the lot. Such attitudes led to ugly doings. In Louisiana, in 1857, for example, an Italian-born priest was murdered at a grocery across from his church. Twenty persons had witnessed the crime, but nobody helped the priest. Indeed, his body lay in the street all night. A local Protestant blamed the priest's alleged lust for women and craving for money as the cause of the murder. This response neatly fit prevailing interpretations of the "low life" of Catholic immigrants. Nativism ran strong in the 1850s. Anti-Catholic feelings discouraged conversions to Catholicism. During the Civil War, when religious intensity swelled in the South, one brave lady came out for Catholicism. She had wanted to convert "for a long time but had not the courage, to resist so much opposition as she knew she would be sure to encounter." But not everyone was brave. The Catholic Church in the South did not grow significantly during the great wave of religiosity

---

[9]Priscilla "Mittie" Munnikhuysen Bond Diary, 24 January 1864 (Louisiana State University).

in the 1850s and 1860s. It remained on the defensive—too weak to be a bastion for the slaves and the poor, or an attraction to them.[10]

The Catholic Church in America traditionally has followed a course of political caution. In the nineteenth century, particularly in the South, the Church lacked the numbers, wealth, and internal strength to stride with confidence into political and social controversy. Whenever possible, the Church avoided conflicts with local powers. In the Old South to be different was often to be damned. Catholic leaders were sensitive to the Church's minority status in the Protestant South and so tried not to be different on the basics. It was having enough trouble establishing control over church finances and policy. The laity held the purse strings in most parishes, and wealthy laymen exercised a decisive influence in church affairs. They ensured that their churches would serve their needs alone. This often meant ignoring the social needs of poor parishioners, black and white, and it even led to the exclusion of black parishioners from services.[11] If a priest challenged lay power, he often suffered humiliation and defeat. The wardens of one church settled a dispute with their parish priest by locking him out of the church during Holy Week. At another church the white parishioners resisted the priest's efforts to allow blacks to worship there, and although the priest had enough prestige to prevent the whites from harming the blacks, his own ministry never fully recovered after the incident. In this instance, the planters knew what they were doing, for however much slaves and lower-class whites distrusted one another, they could make common cause against planters. For that reason planters encouraged rivalries between slaves and poor whites—letting the whites bully the blacks and allowing the slaves to denigrate the poor whites as "trash." Hostilities between Irish Catholic immigrants and

---

[10]Effingham Lawrence comments in Magnolia Plantation Journal, 4 October 1857, Henry Clay Warmoth Papers (Southern Historical Collection, University of North Carolina at Chapel Hill); Kate Sully to Mary Jane Robertson, 28 June 1864, Robertson Papers.

[11]On the Church's position, see John T. Gillard, *Colored Catholics in the United States* (Baltimore, 1941), pp. 42-43; Madeleine H. Rice, *American Catholic Opinion in the Slavery Controversy* (New York, 1944); and James J. Pillar, *The Catholic Church in Mississippi, 1837-1865* (New Orleans, 1964). On lay control of the churches, see James J. Pillar, "Catholicism in the Lower South," in Lucius F. Ellsworth, ed., *The Americanization of the Gulf Coast, 1803-1850* (Pensacola, 1972), pp. 38ff.

slaves only intensified this rift separating lower-class black and white Catholics.[12]

Church leaders got the message. Only the most devout Catholics heeded Church teachings that ran against their material interest in slavery. The Southern bishops comforted them that compliance was not always necessary. Indeed, by their public support for Southern "rights" and planter hegemony, the bishops pointed the way to Catholic acceptance in the South. With declining numbers of white Catholics, rising Protestant opposition to Catholic missions, and the return of agricultural "flush times" in the 1850s, the Church was in no mood to offend anyone on the issue of slavery. As Madeleine Rice has shown, Catholic leaders opposed antislavery reform as a New England Protestant movement closely aligned with nativism and anti-Catholic activity. In addition, many Catholic clergymen who came from Europe linked abolitionism in America with the rationalism and anticlericalism that threatened Catholic teaching in Europe. Like the dominant Protestant churches of the Old South, the Catholic Church mirrored the racial values of its followers and reinforced planter hegemony by supplying biblical justifications for slavery and a conservative social order. In neither teaching nor example did the Church create a moral climate conducive to manumissions or humane treatment of slaves. Individual clergymen interceded on the slaves' behalf and called for Christian charity, but their numbers were few and their power illusory. Catholic masters remained the sole arbiters of discipline and treatment on their plantations and in their communities. The slaves had to fend for themselves and to reach accommodations with their masters; the poor white farmers had to defer to the stronger economic and social power of the planters. The Church did not figure in the lower-class whites' and enslaved blacks' strategies for survival.[13]

Bishop William Henry Elder of Natchez summed up the problem in a letter to the Society for the Propagation of the Faith, written in 1858. He

---

[12]Minutes of the Meetings of the Fabrique (Archives of St. Paul's Church, Mansura LA); *American Catholic Quarterly Review* 14 (1889): 483. On the relations between the Irish immigrants and slaves see, for example, Earl F. Niehaus, *The Irish in New Orleans, 1800-1860* (Baton Rouge, 1965), pp. 49-54; Frances Anne Kemble, *Journal of Residence on a Georgia Plantation* (New York, 1863), pp. 79-80.

[13]Rice, *American Catholic Opinion*, pp. 90-103; Maria G. Caravaglios, *The American Catholic Church and the Negro Problem in the XVIII-XIX Centuries* (Rome, 1974), pp. 182-84; Michael V. Gannon, *Rebel Bishop: The Life and Era of Augustin Verot* (Milwaukee, 1964), pp. 33-39; Niehaus, *Irish in New Orleans*, pp. 47-55, 160-62.

noted that few slaves of Catholic masters and few poor white farmers received regular spiritual instruction. Several planters hired preachers to attend to their plantations and to deliver sermons on Sundays, but the preachers were generally Protestants. Many masters refused to let their Catholic slaves attend services off their plantations because the masters feared that the slaves might run away. Planters sometimes encouraged black slaves to preach, but this naturally excluded the Catholic priest from control or direction of the slaves' religious concerns. As teachers of catechism, the masters performed poorly, if at all. The masters failed to do their part in bringing up their slaves as Catholics. With widely scattered churches, few priests, and no money, Elder and the other bishops could not meet the needs of the slaves or the white Catholics. The priests who were available devoted their attention to winning and hold-ing white Catholics, and some priests evoked fear or, worse, ridicule among the slaves who did not understand them or perceived them to be arms of the masters' authority.[14]

No sermon notes survive to tell us what the priests said on those occasions when they ministered to the slaves. The few contemporary accounts suggest that priests did not avoid special pleading, which surely alienated the slaves. How could the slaves on Colonel Carroll's Maryland plantation respect the priest who insisted that they obey their master and who defended slavery as good for their upbringing and maintenance? The problems of style and language aside, the priests lacked credibility among the slaves. To be sure, some priests displayed kindness and concern for the slaves. They tried to provide health care and educational and spiritual guidance for Catholic slaves. Other priests, however, betrayed confi-dences, which had a devastating effect on the slaves' loyalty. The Church, after all, was the servant of the slaveholders, and the priests knew their masters. So did the slaves. One Catholic slave woman said it all when she quit Catholicism because her confessor was a proslavery apologist who

---

[14]Elder letter printed in John Tracy Ellis, ed., *Documents of American Catholic History* (Milwaukee, 1956), pp. 335-36. For a Catholic priest's account of planter resistance to his mission in Louisiana, see John M. Odin's letter of 2 August 1823, printed in "Letters Concerning Some Missions of the Mississippi Valley, 1818-1827," *Records of the American Catholic Historical Society* 14 (1903): 189. A vigorous priest could win converts and acceptance; for some examples, see Pillar, *Catholic Church in Mississippi*, pp. 37-42; and Joe Gray Taylor, *Negro Slavery in Louisiana* (Baton Rouge, 1963), p. 140. On scattered Catholic churches in the South, see Edwin S. Gaustad, *Historical Atlas of Religion in America*, rev. ed. (New York, 1976), p. 105.

informed on slaves expressing sentiments for freedom.[15] Slaves might suffer dull priests, but they were not about to countenance hypocritical ones.

In the end, the priests did not count for much in the Catholic slaves' religious world. The priests were transient figures who passed hurriedly and often unnoticed through the slaves' lives. Their visits to the plantations were too infrequent to establish rapport with the slaves, and their ministry, although often well intentioned, was too unrelated to the slaves' daily sufferings to have much meaning for them. Catholic slaves and slaves of Catholic masters rarely commented on the priests in their past. And that silence speaks volumes. Catholicism, then, would be a product of plantation circumstances. As in so many things, the master would put his imprint on the religion, and the slaves would accept and adapt those parts of it that met their peculiar needs.

In the absence of priests, Catholic masters held prayer meetings, taught catechism, and otherwise tried to conduct religious services for the slaves. If mixed with good treatment and if culturally isolated, the slaves responded favorably to such training. Each Sunday, for example, the Catholic mistress of one Kentucky plantation drilled the slave children in catechism and the Lord's Prayer. Although many of the children later became Baptists or Methodists, they gratefully acknowledged her teachings and thanked her for leading them to Christ.[16]

But countervailing forces often undermined the Catholic masters' efforts to bring up their slaves as good Catholics. Many slaves recoiled from the embarrassment of sitting in segregated pews or galleries in the rural Catholic churches.[17] The presence of black slave preachers, who were not Catholics, competed effectively for the slaves' attention, and the advance of Protestant culture among slaves overwhelmed the small number of Catholic slaves. More directly important was the relationship between the master's treatment of the slaves and their acceptance of his religion. The slave La Son Mire refused to attend Mass, partly because he

---

[15]William Howard Russell, *My Diary North and South* (New York, 1863), p. 184; Octavia V. Rogers Albert, *The House of Bondage, or Charlotte Brooks and Other Slaves* (New York, 1860), p. 69.

[16]George Rawick, comp., *The American Slave: A Composite Autobiography*, 19 vols. (Westport CT, 1972), volume on *Indiana*, 6:108. See also Rawick, comp., *Texas*, 4:2:60, 62; *Mississippi*, 7:120-21.

[17]Segregated seating was the norm outside of New Orleans.

found the segregated seating obnoxious and degrading, but largely because his Catholic master exhibited no evidence of Christian character in his regular dealings with the slaves. Catholic masters who broke the Sabbath, whipped their slaves excessively, denied food and adequate shelter to their slaves, and in other ways abused the slaves obviously earned the enmity of the slaves, but they also discredited Catholicism. The slaves noted that Catholic Mass failed to temper the wickedness of one Maryland slaveholder who repeatedly began "fighting amongst the colored people" after Mass. She was "never satisfied" and once beat a slave woman viciously with a walking stick. A Virginia slave showed no respect for his master or his master's faith because the master, "a good Catholic, though very disagreeable," drove the slaves hard and abused them with coarse language. Odel Jackson of Mississippi put it more succinctly in describing the character of her Catholic owner, whom she would never follow: "De ole Missus was mean."[18] Catholic masters were no better or no worse than Protestant masters in their treatment of the slaves. Neither in Louisiana nor outside of it did Catholicism restrain the excesses of barbaric masters or otherwise serve to ameliorate the conditions of bondage for the slaves. For that reason, Catholicism deserved no special attention from the slaves.

Masters generally allowed their slaves to follow the religion of their choice. Masters won respect for setting up chapels for slaves and not interfering in the slaves' religious practices. In the Gulf states wise Catholic masters who purchased slaves from the Protestant upper South acquiesced in the inevitable by allowing the non-Catholic slaves to go to their own churches or listen to black preachers.[19]

There was not much masters could do to impose their own religious values on the slaves because the slaves resisted the slaveholders' often clumsy attempts to rule their private lives. In this regard, the case of John Thompson is instructive. Thompson, a Methodist slave, once was hired to a Catholic tobacco farmer in Maryland. All the slaves on the tobacco farm were Catholics, save for Thompson, who lived in isolation due to the circumstances of his religion and his status as a hired slave. The master

---

[18]Rawick, comp., *Texas*, 5:3:107-109; William Still, *The Underground Railroad: A Record of Facts, Authentic Narratives, Letters, &c.* (Philadelphia, 1872), pp. 71, 461, 524; Odel Jackson narrative, Louisiana, W.P.A. Slave Narratives (Louisiana Department, Louisiana State Library, Baton Rouge).

[19]Rawick, comp., *Texas*, 4:2:62; *North Carolina*, 15:2:336-37.

prayed three to four times daily, and on Sunday he called the slaves to prayer. Thompson refused to participate, and he further enraged the Catholic slaveholder by singing Methodist hymns while working. Eventually, Thompson could no longer stand the pressures to conform or the abusive master, and he fled the plantation. For Thompson, as for many slaves, religion was too important to be left to a white man's direction and misuse.[20]

Slaves used religion to insulate themselves from their masters and to preserve their own heritage. In so doing, they showed that they did not love their masters so much that they sought to accept the masters' religion. And the slaves suffered much to nurture their own religious culture free from the slaveholders' interference.[21] Elizabeth Ross Hite, a former slave of a French Catholic master in antebellum Louisiana, described the slaves' struggle to define their own religious identity. She recalled that at Pierre Landro's "Trinity Plantation" the slaves were christened as Catholics and were "supposed to be Catholics." But "lots didn't like that 'ligion." Some slaves were from Virginia, where they had been practicing Protestants, and their children sought to follow the religion of their parents. The slaves also had a deeper commitment to religion than the master. For them, religion was no casual affair; rather, it was the central feature of their Afro-American community's identity. Landro tried to raise the slaves in the Catholic faith. He brought a black man from France to teach the slaves "how to pray, read and write." The slaves, particularly the women who were more religiously vocal than the men, disliked French-trained preachers because they would not let the slaves "shout an' pray lak ya wanted to." But, "Prayin and be free to shout" was the essence of the slaves' religion. "Gawd says dat ya must shout if ya want to be saved. Dats in de Bible." The slaves preferred to risk Landro's

---

[20]John Thompson, *The Life of John Thompson, Fugitive Slave* (Worcester MA, 1856), pp. 52ff.

[21]On the place of religion in the emerging Afro-American community of the quarters, see John W. Blassingame, *The Slave Community: Plantation Life in the Antebellum South* (New York, 1972), especially pp. 60-75; Vincent Harding, "Religion and Resistance Among Antebellum Negroes, 1800-1860," in August Meier and Elliott Rudwick, eds., *The Making of Black America*, 2 vols. (New York, 1969), 1:179-97; Donald Mathews, *Religion in the Old South* (Chicago, 1977), pp. 185-236; Eugene Genovese, *Roll, Jordan, Roll: The World the Slaves Made* (New York, 1974), especially pp. 159-284; and, especially, Albert Raboteau, *Slave Religion: "The Invisible Institution" in the Antebellum South* (New York, 1978).

wrath rather than God's, so they turned to their own black exhorters, who let them shout and pray all night. Another reason for their preference for black exhorters was that the slave exhorters worked on the plantations "lak ev'rybody else." The exhorter at the Landro place was a trusted member of the slave community who knew the slaves' sufferings by his personal experience. The Catholic priests, however, espoused a stiff, foreign religion, and they were outsiders. In the closed world of the plantation all outsiders were suspect—the master's hirelings more so. This was a major obstacle confronting Catholic preachers, and they never broke down the barriers of suspicion.

The slaves at Landro's plantation attended their own church, which was hidden "in de brick yard way out in de field." Every night they gathered there to sing, pray, and hear Bible lessons from "Old man Mingo." Although he prided himself as a religious man, Landro opposed the slaves' nightly services. He feared that an excess of slave religiosity would "give him all religion an' no work." By staying up late each night the slaves were too tired to work or started late on the next day's tasks. Still, the slaves persisted in their nocturnal devotions despite frequent whippings from Landro. In that way they demonstrated their independence and their real devotion to religion. Needless to say, Landro won no converts by his actions.[22]

It worked both ways. Catholic slaves sold to Protestant masters might demand the right to attend Mass, even if this meant traveling to town, and some masters gave in rather than risk unnecessary and dangerous confrontations. When a Protestant master prevented his Catholic slaves from praying during the week, they sneaked off to do so. For them, religion was a means of expressing their autonomy. It was not so much what Catholicism or Protestantism taught theologically that counted among the slaves as it was who controlled the churches and how the religious affiliation affected the masters' collective behavior. Living away from any Catholic church, one slave refused to accept Protestantism and kept alive his Catholic identity by observing dietary and personal religious customs. In that way he retained a link to his personal past, and he set himself apart from his new master's total control.[23]

[22]Elizabeth Ross Hite narrative, Louisiana W.P.A. Slave Narratives (Louisiana Department, Louisiana State Library, Baton Rouge).

[23]James B. Sellers, *Slavery in Alabama* (University AL, 1950), pp. 322, 323; Rawick, comp., *Texas*, 5:4:132; Pillar, *Catholic Church in Mississippi*, pp. 120-21.

Catholicism had a material attraction for some slaves. The priest's visit meant a holiday on the plantation, and many slaves of Catholic masters took part in the Mass for that reason. Charity Parker, a former slave from Louisiana, remembered how "when dere was Communion on de place dere was a big celebration. De marse an' mistres would send down cake and ice cream and nobody worked dat day." Another slave was happy to see the master bring a priest to the farm to baptize the slave children because the master treated the slaves to "real beef meat" after each baptism. Matthew Hume of Kentucky confessed that despite assiduous efforts of the devout Catholic mistress to teach the slaves their catechism, he attended classes solely to get the sugar and candy that were dispensed afterward. Vanity also served God. Slave girls looked forward to christenings because they received pretty dresses for the occasions. At the Dermot Martine plantation in Louisiana the Catholic slave girls enjoyed primping in front of the mirror to see who was "pretty enough to go to church." Attending Mass promised a trip to town or a nearby plantation. Such events broke the monotony and loneliness of rural life, but the slaves' participation did not always lead to a greater Catholic devotion on their part.[24]

Catholicism was, of course, more than presents and holidays. The mysticism and high moral code of nineteenth-century Catholicism appealed to some slaves. Charity Parker of Louisiana is a case in point. As a girl, she was disappointed that the outbreak of the Civil War prevented her from making her first communion. She was "lookin forward to havin dat white dress, veil an' candle dat dey gave everyone of dem slaves" at their first communion. But, for her, Catholicism also meant spiritual cleansing. In old age, after converting to Protestantism, she sometimes wished that she had remained a Catholic. As she put it: "If you pure to de Lord, yer pure to everythin'. When you go to confession you gotta have in yo' mind dat you ain't gonna do anythin' ya tell da priest ya ain't gonna do, an' yo' gonna say 'Lord, when I go befo' de priest, don't let me do no more behind his back den I confess to his face.' "[25] Catholicism was a personal religion that demanded daily devotion and an honest self-assessment of one's moral life. It was also a sedate religion that had few of the public

---

[24]Charity Parker narrative, Louisiana W.P.A. Slave Narratives, Dillon MSS, Melrose Collection (State University of Louisiana), copy courtesy of Margaret Dalrymple; Rawick, comp., *Texas*, 4:1:308; *Indiana*, 6:108; *Texas*, 4:2:226.

[25]Charity Parker narrative.

displays of unbridled emotion that sometimes characterized Southern evangelical religion. Some slaves found in this a greater measure of truth in religion. They recoiled from the crude religious practices of their more vocal Protestant counterparts. Thus Donaville Broussard of Louisiana distinguished Catholic slaves as civilized because they "didn't have to half-drown when they got religion." And Carlyle Stewart of Louisiana identified himself as a Christian who "never got that 'ligion that makes you shout and carry on." Rather, he prayed in his home at night—a sure sign of genuine commitment.[26]

The syncretic process of Afro-Catholicism that developed in the Caribbean never flowered in the Old South, but enough elements of the slaves' African heritage must have transferred to Catholicism to give it some appeal among them. Direct evidence of this transfer, however, is not available. Catholic feast days, the use of candles, burial rites, and liturgy all provided disguises for African religious traditions. The syncretism that occurred, however, largely took place in and around New Orleans, which had a large concentration of black Catholics and fresh infusions of African culture. There are examples of slaves who elevated Catholic priests to the status of healers, thus comparing them with the healer/exhorter of West African religions. Even proximity to the Catholic clergy suggested divine powers. The slave Simon, who lived with the Daughters of the Cross mission in Louisiana, was "esteemed by his people who consult him like they would an oracle." Indeed, one day "a negro came to ask him to bless his marriage." But the syncretic process in the Old South is too elusive to document with confidence.[27]

Catholics in the rural South lacked the properties necessary for the emergence of a vigorous, syncretic Afro-Catholicism. Catholic feast days and religious ceremonies were observed too infrequently, and after the

[26]Rawick, comp., *Texas*, 4:1:151; Carlyle Stewart narrative, Louisiana W.P.A. Slave Narratives (Louisiana Department, Louisiana State Library, Baton Rouge).

[27]On the syncretic process, see Roger Bastide, *African Civilisations in the New World*, trans. by Peter Green (New York, 1971), ch. 7. On the priest as comforter and healer, see, for example, Rawick, comp., *Texas*, 4:2:226, for a planter-initiated call; and Adam Hall narrative, Louisiana W.P.A. Slave Narratives (Louisiana State University), for a black's turning to a priest for healing. On Simon, see Mother Mary Hyacinth Le Conniat to her parents, 6 December 1856, in McCants, ed., *They Came to Louisiana*, p. 56. The veneration of Catholic saints and observance of Catholic rites could blend with voodoo: See, for example, "External Love Christian Faith No. 1." in "Life Histories for *Gumbo-Ya-Ya*," folder 5, box 11, Lyle Saxon Collection (Tulane University).

American acquisition of Louisiana, the Gulf South was overrun by Afro-American slaves carrying an Afro-Protestantism that effectively challenged Catholic teaching among the slaves. An illiterate people must be shown religion. This can be accomplished through miracles and through the good example of religious leaders. Catholic masters and priests were not providing miracles. Indeed, their religion was hardly visible in large areas of the Gulf South, the most "Catholic" of regions. And white priests and masters could not win the slaves' confidence. Inexorably, the Afro-Protestantism of the newcomers took hold and captured the Catholic slaves' attention and affection.

The meeting of Catholic and Protestant slaves in the Old South revealed the different cultural reference points among the slaves. Black Protestants and black Catholics approached one another warily. Initially, at least, each group practiced endogamy, but in time the rising number of Protestant slaves and the declining number of Catholic slaves throughout the South made this impossible for Catholics. Some Catholic masters tried to preserve Catholicism among their slaves by selling Catholic slave families intact and only to Catholic masters. Others tried to retain a French cultural and language orientation on the plantations to combat the Americanizing influences.[28] But economic pressures and, more generally, planter ignorance or indifference to the slaves' religious preferences led to increased mingling of Protestant and Catholic slaves. Still, as late as 1863, Thomas Wentworth Higginson could wonder how his black regiment of ex-slaves from South Carolina would react to a contingent of new recruits: "We have recruits on their way from St. Augustine, where the negroes are chiefly Roman Catholics; and it will be interesting to see how their type of character combines with that elder creed."[29]

Higginson need not have worried. Catholic and Protestant slaves were combining everywhere in the South by 1860. The war only accelerated the process. The decline of Catholic influence among the slaves in the rural South occurred at different times in different places, of course;

---

[28]On Catholic masters' selling slaves to other Catholics, see, for example, Louisville (KY) *Catholic Advocate*, 26 January 1836, 14 September 1839. On the French culture among slaves, see, for example, Frances and Theresa Pulszky, *White, Red, Black: Sketches of Society in the United States*, 3 vols. (n.p., 1853), 2:271-72; and especially Henry Reed narrative, Louisiana W.P.A. Slave Narratives (Louisiana Department, Louisiana State Library, Baton Rouge).

[29]Higginson quoted in Miles Mark Fisher, *Negro Slave Songs in the United States* (Ithaca NY, 1953), p. 149.

but by 1860 the pattern of Afro-Protestant absorption of Catholic slaves was well established. Many Catholic slaves were familiar with the broad outlines of Southern Protestantism through the preaching of itinerant ministers employed by their masters or through the appearance of revival meetings in their neighborhoods. Others discovered Afro-Protestantism by listening to black preachers in the shadows of the quarters. Others still had relatives or close fellow bondsmen who were Protestants. Catholic slaves who left the Church did not wander aimlessly in a spiritual wasteland; rather, as "churched" slaves they sought a spiritual home in some kind of organized religion. The Afro-Protestantism of the slaves offered the most inviting opportunities for spiritual and psychological fulfillment.

The migration westward and southward of slavery introduced blends of Afro-Protestantism to the Gulf region. By sheer numbers the Protestant-oriented slaves simply overwhelmed the Catholics. For some Catholic slaves the "new" religion heralded a total transformation of values. They traded the dignity and solemnity of formal Catholicism for the emotional richness of Afro-Protestantism. Rather than worship alone, they joined the Afro-Protestant community to sing and dance together in the new religion. One slave woman nicely detailed her conversion to what she significantly termed the "American" religion. She had been raised a Catholic but "never knowed how good the 'Merican religion was till I married John. He was a member of the 'Merican church, and he got me to go with him on Sundays to his church; and the more I went the more I liked it." She had been a practicing Catholic for many years and had denigrated Protestantism until she met her husband. She reported that since she joined his church, "I been changed, I feel like I been new born." The American religion "makes any body feel happy all over; it runs through you, down from your head to the very soles of your feet!" As for Catholicism, it was "all doings and no feeling in the heart." Likewise, Henry Reed of Louisiana observed that he did not know "how to talk" until he met a "real American" who drew him away from Catholicism and French culture.[30] Like so many others, they were guided by family interests. Reed's mother was a Baptist, and Reed credited her example as the principal cause of his conversion. Charity Parker left a

---

[30] Albert, *House of Bondage*, pp. 68-69; Henry Reed narrative.

congenial Catholicism to follow the religion of her Baptist mother. Religion meant community and family solidarity.[31]

The only rural Catholic group of any size to survive the American acculturation onslaught was the colony of Creoles of color centered at Isle Brevêlle in Louisiana. In their self-imposed isolation they established Catholicism as the only religion. They ruthlessly stamped out African-isms among the slaves and insisted that all men, slave and free, practice their brand of Catholicism. Despite segregated worship and a denial of their African heritage, the slaves apparently followed Catholic teaching. Religion is both a public and a private event. To be successful, it must be visible, and in the chapels and religious festivals at Isle Brevêlle it was very much so. The Catholic calendar of feast days and special devotions and regular attendance at Mass fixed the timetable of life in the colony and reinforced Catholic identity for Creole and slave alike—something that also occurred in diluted form among Catholics in New Orleans. Cultural isolation, of course, was crucial to this process, but until the barriers fell during the Civil War, the colony existed as a historical anomaly out of time and place in the American and Protestant Old South.[32]

Emancipation allowed most Southern blacks to express their religious preferences openly. Most visibly, the freedmen retreated from white churches to form their own. Just as they sought economic and political independence, they refused to take religion from their former masters. For Catholics this was not so easy. The Church lacked the resources to establish separate black and white churches, and congregational auton-omy was not a recognized church practice. To remain of the faith meant having to suffer the humiliation of sitting in segregated galleries or pews in the old churches. In some cases it meant having to travel thirty miles or more to find a Catholic church. Not everyone wanted to or was able to make the journey.[33] Black Catholics pressed for changes in seating policy

---

[31]Henry Reed narrative; Charity Parker narrative.

[32]Mills, *Forgotten People*, ch. 6; Louis Joseph Piernas narrative, Mississippi W.P.A. Slave Narratives (Mississippi Department of Archives and History).

[33]On the tendency of freedmen to leave white churches, see, for example, Peter Kolchin, *First Freedom: The Response of Alabama's Blacks to Emancipation and Recon-struction* (Westport CT, 1972), ch. 5; and Edward Magdol, *A Right to the Land: Essays on the Freedmen's Community* (Westport CT, 1977), ch. 3. On traveling long distances to church, see, for example, Henri Necaise narrative, Mississippi W.P.A. Slave Narratives (Mississippi Department of Archives and History).

and for their own churches. Black Catholics in St. Martinville, Louisiana, for example, petitioned the state legislature to repeal an 1858 statute that allowed only whites to incorporate churches there.[34]

But many former slaves of Catholic masters were not interested in removing such legislative obstacles or facing white racism each Sunday. They left the Church. This move made the break with their former masters and slavery complete. It reflected the freedmen's desire to locate in a religious environment more compatible with their own peculiar spiritual, psychological, and social needs. The freedmen's movement out of the Catholic Church was also an attempt to reclaim their family roots. Recall Henry Reed: During slavery he had regularly attended Mass with his Catholic master. Catholicism, however, had kept him in cultural isolation in rural "French" Louisiana, and he found Catholicism to be an empty faith. He later blamed his "ignorance" of American ways on his sheltered religious life, and after emancipation he became a Baptist preacher. The reasons were complex, but one stood out: "I had a good maw," he said, and "she was the cause of me being converted." He became part of the larger Afro-American community growing in the seedbed of the black Protestant churches of the postwar South.[35]

French-speaking Catholic freedmen, however, did not generally join the exodus out of the Catholic Church. They were already a people apart from the larger Afro-American community, and many chose to remain so. They married in the Catholic Church, baptized their children there, and worshiped there. Each act of participation reconfirmed their faith. Even in the face of evangelizing by Northern Protestant missionary-teachers, who were often aghast at the Sabbath breaking of the French-speaking ex-slaves, they stood their ground.[36] Perhaps they liked a religion that allowed them to work on Sundays—no mean consideration for farmers scratching out a living. More likely, they were simply prisoners of their cultural and physical isolation from American blacks, or they

---

[34]Charles Vincent, *Black Legislators in Louisiana During Reconstruction* (Baton Rouge, 1976), p. 161.

[35]Henry Reed narrative. See also Charity Parker narrative; and Rawick, comp., *Texas*, 4:2:60.

[36]Rawick, comp., *Texas*, 4:1:92, 252-53; 4:2:227; 5:3:274-75. For a Northern missionary's description of a Creole settlement, see Edmonia G. Highgate to the American Missionary Association, 17 December 1866, American Missionary Association Archives (Amistad Research Center, Dillard University).

fondly remembered the good priests and paternalistic Catholic masters who had comforted them when they were sick and otherwise had treated them decently.[37]

On the whole, however, the Catholic record during Reconstruction was not good. Many Catholic ex-slaves left the Church, and others grew angry and frustrated with the Church's halting and fumbling ministry. The Church was slow to meet the needs of the freedmen. The Second Plenary Council of Baltimore (1866) promised a fresh approach to establishing missions among Southern blacks. The bishops addressed the problems of providing educational and material assistance to the freedmen, but little came of their deliberations. The bishops quarreled over the amount and the direction of such assistance. Only Bishop Augustin Verot of Savannah recognized the desperation of the freedmen in the dislocated postwar South. But special efforts to educate and to support the ex-slaves were not forthcoming. Waves of new immigrants from Europe after the war exhausted the Church's attention and resources nationally, and the general confusion of Southern and national political, social, and economic life after the war dissipated reform efforts. The Church's brief interest in Southern blacks lapsed. It would not revive until the Third Plenary Council of Baltimore in 1884.[38]

In the meantime, the Catholic ex-slaves were left to themselves. What aid the Church did provide was often disorganized. Individual priests attempted to establish schools for the ex-slaves, but outside the cities few prospered. In one case, however, a Catholic school brought together ex-slave children and the children of Creoles of color who had refused to mix with blacks before the war. The church school thus showed a potential for socializing black and Creole Catholics and forging a larger Catholic community among the colored lower classes of the South. Generally, the few freedmen who received instruction in the parish schools described it as poor. One Catholic ex-slave in Texas, for example, attended classes run by some nuns and a German priest, but he thought

---

[37]See, for example, Rawick, comp., *Texas*, 4:2:226-27.

[38]On the Plenary Council, see Edward J. Misch, "The American Bishops and the Negro from the Civil War to the Third Plenary Council of Baltimore (1865-1884)" (doctoral dissertation, Gregorian University, Rome, 1968), ch. 3. The priests were not idle. An energetic priest supported by an interested bishop could win converts to Catholicism and deliver much aid to people in need. For one case, see William Henry Elder to John B. Mouton, 14 September 1866, Elder Papers (Natchez-Jackson Diocesan Archives).

that the education they offered did not amount to anything.[39] Despite propitious conditions to win friends among blacks by imitating the Protestant missionary associations, the Church continued to lose influence among the blacks.

Catholicism was a captive religion that was unable to reach a captive people. The history of Catholicism in the South suggests that institutional religion adjusted to fit local norms and conditions. Representing a minority religion and population, the Church catered to those in power, and in so doing ignored the powerless. Catholicism in the Old South operated within the peculiar world that the slaveholders made, and its limited role as teacher and arbiter for the slaves, and for lower-class whites too, cannot be understood apart from that context. For the slaves, Catholicism often lacked immediate purpose. It did not provide a place for slave preachers and exhorters; it did not hold out the promise of temporal release from slavery's torments; it did not function independently from the formal, and for the slaves alien, institutional structure of the planter-dominated Church. The wonder is not that Catholicism declined among the slaves of the rural South but that it survived at all.

---

[39]Louis J. Piernas narrative; Rawick, comp., *Texas*, 5:3:93.

PIETY AND PREJUDICE: A COLORED CATHOLIC COMMUNITY IN THE ANTEBELLUM SOUTH

by Gary B. Mills

The free man of color in the antebellum South is an amorphous element of American Catholicism. His status was ambivalent and his subsequent historical treatment has been more patronizing than perceptive. In present studies he is scarcely distinguishable from the slave, and little or no distinction is normally made between significant racial categories within the nonwhite population. Yet the free colored Catholic who was under the domination of no master and was free to choose his own mode of worship represents a unique opportunity for the study of Catholic evangelization among nonwhite Americans.

Within the Roman Catholic Church, as in all North American society before the Civil War, the free man of color was the proverbial fish-out-of-water. Moreover, he refused to be thrown back, and even the Holy Mother Church in pre-Darwinian America had difficulty coping with the social invertebrate who insisted upon recognition as a fully evolutionized and divinely created *homo sapiens*. The reaction of ecclesiastical authority to the emergence of a free nonwhite society vacillated considerably. Many pastors persisted in segregating parishioners according to race, without regard for distinctions in classes or degrees of culture, aspirations, or religiosity. Others approved of the upward mobility of the social evolutionary process and readily admitted all free nonwhite Catholics to the privileges and amenities accorded all free and pious Christians. The work of Bishop Miles at Springfield is frequently noted in studies of American Catholicism, as is Father Charles Nerinckx's acceptance of five free black girls into the Society of the Friends of Mary at Lorette, Kentucky, and Bishop John England's schools for free nonwhites in Charleston. Scattered references may be found in secondary works to the Church's establishment of free Negro schools in Nashville, Tennessee; Pine Bluff, Arkansas; Alexandria, Virginia; Georgetown and Washington, D.C.[1]

Where the greatest clusters of free nonwhite Catholics existed— Louisiana, the Mobile district of Alabama, and Maryland—the work of the Church is most evident. The first religious order of Negro nuns in the United States, the Oblate Sisters of Providence, was established in Baltimore in 1829, and a second at New Orleans, the Sisters of the Holy Family, in 1842. At Mobile, the free people of color who descended primarily from French and Spanish Catholics suffered minimal handicaps fulfilling their spiritual and educational aspirations.[2]

Throughout most of these areas, however, one significant factor was present, and to some degree it impeded Catholic evangelization. Seldom did the clergy treat the free man of color (that is, the man of both African and Caucasian ancestry) as he most commonly envisioned himself—as a race apart. Such a distinction may or may not have been *spiritually* justified, but the bulk of the free nonwhite Catholics fell into this racial category, and most seem to have resisted any form of segregation, even spiritual, which categorized them as *black*. Even where clergymen succeeded in winning spiritual concessions for their nonwhite congregation,

[1]Mother M. Agatha, *Catholic Education and the Negro* (Washington, 1942), pp. 3-5; John T. Gillard, S.S.J., *Colored Catholics in the United States* (Baltimore, 1941), pp. 20, 24-27, 30; Camillus P. Maes, *The Life of Rev. Charles Nerinckx* (Cincinnati, 1880), p. 510; John England, "Early History of the Diocese of Charleston," in Sebastion C. Messmer, ed., *The Works of the Right Reverend John England First Bishop of Charleston*, 7 vols. (Cleveland, 1908), 4:298-337; John La Farge, "The Survival of the Catholic Faith in Southern Maryland," *The Catholic Historical Review* 21 (1935): 14.

[2]A Member of the Order of Mercy, *A Catholic History of Alabama and the Floridas* (New York, 1908), pp. 339-40; Ira Berlin, *Slaves Without Masters: The Free Negro in the Antebellum South* (New York, 1974), pp. 108-14; Agatha, *Catholic Education*, pp. 4-5; Gillard, *Colored Catholics*, pp. 30-31; Roger Baudier, *The Catholic Church in Louisiana* (New Orleans, 1939), p. 376.

the colored Catholic often declined to accept these if blacks were included, lest even a limited spiritual association with blacks should jeopardize the political and social advantage he had won through a self-imposed segregation.

Ecclesiastical inconsistencies in the segregation of free men of color from whites and blacks have also created special problems for the student of history. An excellent example is found in Louisiana, where the largest concentration of free colored Catholics existed. In 1795 Bishop Luis Penalver y Cardenas of the diocese of Louisiana and the Floridas decreed that two each of every type of register should be kept in each parish, one for whites and the other for Indians, Negroes, and mixed breeds,[3] but an analysis of the various parish registers reveals ambivalent compliance. Some pastors subsequently recorded the administration of sacraments to all free nonwhites in registers labelled *Negros y Indios* or *Esclavons*, while others entered sacramental records on their free colored parishioners in registers labelled *Blancs et des Indiens* or *Blancos, Pardos y Indios*. Even within a given community, successive pastors followed their own inclination rather than the practice of their predecessors. Similarly, some pastors distinguished their free nonwhite parishioners with the identification *gens de couleur libres* or *nègres libres* while others did not.

As a consequence, any effort by historians to segregate the free nonwhite Catholic for historical analysis necessitates extensive genealogical study of many Catholic families who had white, black, and colored members, as well as minute scrutiny of the registers themselves. While published, translated, abstracted, and indexed editions of many Catholic registers have been made available by genealogists in recent years, few are of value to the historian who studies nonwhites, since genealogical inquiry has been the traditional domain of whites in America.[4]

---

[3]Decree of Bishop Penalver y Cardenas, 25 November 1795, University of Notre Dame Microfilm Publications, *Records of the Diocese of Louisiana and the Floridas, 1576-1803*, roll 1.

[4]A few exceptions deserve note. Perhaps the most extensive collection of sacramental data published on black Catholics appears in Elizabeth Shown Mills's translated abstracts from the oldest permanent settlement in the Louisiana Purchase, *Natchitoches: 1729-1803; Abstracts of the Catholic Church Registers of the French and Spanish Post of St. Jean Baptiste des Natchitoches in Louisiana*, Cane River Creole Series, vol. 2 (New Orleans, 1977); and *Natchitoches: 1800-1826: Translated Abstracts of Register Number Five of the Catholic Church Parish of St. Francois des Natchitoches in Louisiana*, Cane River Creole Series, vol. 4 (New Orleans, 1980). Fully 50 percent of the 6,392 sacramental entries in these two volumes represent nonwhite Catholics. Margaret Kimball Brown and

There exists in Louisiana, however, one civil parish where many of the problems inherent in nonwhite Catholic research have been transcended. The state is also home to a two-hundred-year-old colony of Catholic *creoles de couleur* who afford a unique opportunity for the study of Southern nonwhite Catholic life. The civil parish is Natchitoches, once the western outpost of the Louisiana colony and now a fringe of Creole society superimposed upon the Anglo-Protestant culture that dominates north Louisiana. The colony lies in the heart of this parish, where a fertile stretch of land known as Isle Brevêlle lies between two rivers. The heart of the colony is the Church of St. Augustin, established in 1829 as a mission of the Catholic parish of St. François des Natchitoches. Its founder was the colony's patriarch, the venerated Nicolas Augustin Metoyer, f.m.c., who lived to see the fulfillment of two of his most cherished dreams: the establishment in 1856 of a separate Catholic parish to serve the needs of "his people," *Paroisse de St. Augustin de l'Isle Brevêlle*, and the founding of the Convent of St. Joseph for the proper training of the young ladies of his family.

The Metoyers of Isle Brevêlle have long been fabled in Louisiana lore. Numerous writers have romanticized the illicit, interracial alliance of Metoyer's parents, the black slave Coincoin and the young French merchant, Claude Thomas Pierre Metoyer; and their tales have usually exaggerated the already phenomenal success that the family achieved after manumission. In recent years, more serious scholars have analyzed the family and its accomplishments with far more objectivity;[5] still the

---

Lawrie Cena Dean's *The Village of Chartres in Colonial Illinois, 1720-1765* (New Orleans, 1977) also included black entries from the Church of Ste. Anne des Chartres, the Chapel of the Visitation at St. Philippe, and the chapel at Prairie du Rocher later known as St. Joseph's Church. The Reverend Donald J. Hebert has included some discussion of Catholic records and black genealogy in his monumental series, *Southwest Louisiana Records*, 22 vols. (Eunice LA, 1974-1980), and notes the extreme importance of these records to a full exploration of the history of Louisiana, though he expresses the opinion (not necessarily concurred with by this researcher) that "it is extremely difficult if not impossible, to be able to use these records in order to trace a family history" (2:xii).

[5]For example, see Gary B. Mills, *The Forgotten People: Cane River's Creoles of Color* (Baton Rouge, 1977); and Sister Frances Jerome Woods, *Marginality and Identity: A Colored Creole Family Through Ten Generations* (Baton Rouge, 1972); also the complementary analyses presented in Mills, "Coincoin: An Eighteenth-Century 'Liberated' Woman," *Journal of Southern History* 42 (1976): 205-22; Mills, "Patriotism Prostrated: The Native Guards of Confederate Natchitoches," *Louisiana History* 18 (1977): 437-51; and Mills, "A Portrait of Achievement: Augustin Metoyer," *Red River Valley Historical Review* 2 (1975): 333-48.

relationship between the colony and the Roman Catholic Church warrants far more exploration. This essay seeks to fill some voids, although an ultimate anaysis of the impact that Catholicism played upon their lives, and of the role that they in turn played in the course of Louisiana Catholicism, is not yet possible. To fully analyze the religiosity of one isolated segment of a society, there must exist comparative interpretation of the other components of that society, and north Louisiana culture has been an anomaly traditionally ignored by Southern historians.[6]

Undeniably, Catholicism was the backbone that metamorphosed the colony from the social status of slaves to the highly civilized society it developed on Isle Brevêlle. Directly and indirectly, Catholicism nutured them at every step of the evolutionary process. It was Catholic respect for the family that resulted in the *Code Noir* provision that slave families could not be separated by sale in colonial Louisiana,[7] and this clause had significant influence upon the development of the Metoyer colony. It was the active concern of a Catholic pastor for all segments of his frontier flock that prompted the family's initial manumission in 1778. Most significantly, it was the family's piety, its dedication to the Catholic Church, that earned it the community respect which even wealth could not bring and which sheltered it from the ever-increasing restrictions that Anglo-Americans introduced into antebellum Louisiana. When Civil War and Reconstruction destroyed the 18,000-acre, 500-slave plantation empire they created, and white reaction to masses of black freedmen stripped them of much of that community respect, their faith was their refuge. Today, in a very secular twentieth century, it remains their most treasured legacy. For two centuries the colony has traditionally rejected all stereotyped labels. They still refuse to stamp themselves as either black or

---

[6]A comprehensive study of social, religious, and family life in the north Louisiana parish of Natchitoches is currently being made by Elizabeth Shown Mills, a certified genealogist and University of Alabama student who specializes in the Latin heritage of the deep South. Although the study focuses upon only the first one hundred years of the settlement's existence (1717-1816) when it embraced all ten thousand square miles of northwest Louisiana, Ms. Mills has extended several aspects of her study in order to develop comparative analyses vital to the present essay. Credit must be given the Mills study for many of the statistics presented herein.

[7]*Code Noir ou Loi Municipal Servant de Reglement* (New Orleans, 1778); "Royal Regulations for the Education, Treatment and Occupation of Slaves in the Indies and Philippine Islands. Printed in Mexico by Antonio Bonilla in March 1790, and Published in Bexar on November 14, 1790," Microfilm Publications of the University of Texas Archives, *Bexar Archives, 1717-1803*, roll 1, frames 852-58.

white. But there is one label they wear proudly: Roman Catholic.[8]

The piety of the colony's founder is legendary, and well deserved. As a child of scarcely nine, Augustin Metoyer first stood as godparent to a slave-born cousin, and before he assumed the responsibilities of parenthood at the age of twenty-five, he had already accumulated a dozen godchildren.[9] That number multiplied many times over before his death in 1856. A study of the published Catholic registers in the parish of St. François des Natchitoches, which served the colony during its early years, reveals that Augustin appeared more often in the parish registers during the first quarter century of the 1800s than any parish contemporary of any race, and he stood as *parrain* to more infants, both slave and free, than did any other man.[10]

That first quarter of the nineteenth century was a period of religious neglect at Natchitoches. The sale of Louisiana to the United States resulted in a transfer of the Louisiana diocese to an understaffed American Church. Years elapsed during which northwest Louisiana had no resident priest at all; fires and legal difficulties robbed Catholics of both a house of worship and financial resources. When, in 1828, a younger brother of Louisiana's future Bishop Antoine Blanc was sent to serve as the full-time pastor of the newly rebuilt church of St. François, the pious Catholics of northwest Louisiana were heartened,[11] none more so than Augustin Metoyer.

Early in 1829, Metoyer set aside a portion of his plantation and built a chapel thereon, in order (according to tradition) "that having a house of the good God in our midst, our people will live a better life, will love one another, and will live in harmony."[12] On the thirteenth Sunday after Pentecost, 1829, Reverend Jean Baptiste Blanc rode out from Natchi-

[8]For a comprehensive discussion of the colony's development and decline, see Mills, *The Forgotten People.*

[9]Elizabeth Shown Mills, *Natchitoches, 1729-1803*, entries 1489, 2130, 2304, 2392, 2434, 2480, 2560, 2623, 2642, 2702, 2736, 2811.

[10]Elizabeth Shown Mills, *Natchitoches, 1800-1826.*

[11]Monsignor Henry Beckers, *A History of the Immaculate Conception Catholic Church, Natchitoches, Louisiana, 1717-1973* (privately printed, 1973), unnumbered pages. Immaculate Conception is the present name of the old church of St. François.

[12]Rev. J. J. Callahan, et al., *The History of St. Augustine's Parish: Isle Brevelle, Natchez, La.; 1803-1953; 1829-1954; 1856-1956* (Natchitoches, 1956), p. 36. It should be noted that the tradition related by Callahan erroneously dates the erection of the colony's church as 1803. For a detailed analysis of the conflicting evidence, see Mills, *The Forgotten People*, pp. 147-51.

toches to Augustin's plantation some fifteen miles down river, and
dedicated the little chapel that was not just the third Catholic church in all
northwest Louisiana, but was the first Catholic church built by nonwhites
in America.[13] Returning from his pastoral visit Father Blanc recorded:

> I, the undersigned, pastor of the Church of St. François of Natchitoches, have
> proceeded to the blessing of a chapel erected on Isle Brevêlle on the plantation
> of Sieur Augustin Metoyer through the care and generosity of the above-named
> Augustin Metoyer, aided by Louis Metoyer, his brother. The above-said chapel
> having been constructed to propagate the principles of our holy religion shall
> always be considered a mission of the church of St. François of Natchitoches.
> The said chapel erected on Isle Brevêlle having been dedicated to St. Augustine,
> shall be considered as under the protection of this great doctor.[14]

Twelve years later Augustin himself expressed the pious and Christian
spirit that created the chapel of St. Augustine.

> A portion of land of three-fourths *arpent* of frontage by one and a half
> *arpents* of depth, situated on the portion of land above given to my children
> Joseph and Gassion, at its upper part, does not belong to me. The Church of St.
> Augustin of Natchitoches was built there by me and my family, principally for
> our usage, except that I desire, and such is my wish that *étrangers* professing our
> holy, Catholic, apostolic and Roman religion will have the right to assist at the
> divine office in the said chapel and shall enjoy, moreover, all the rights and
> privileges which I and my family are able to have there. After my death I wish
> that this portion of land continue to be destined for the preservation of the same
> church and of a cemetery and that it should never be able to be used otherwise, in
> any manner or under any pretense that may be; with the privilege to my
> successors of making officers of the said church the Catholic priests who will
> suit them and not the others.[15]

The *étrangers*, the outsiders, whose religious needs concerned Augustin, included all free men of the Isle, regardless of race. Throughout the
nineteenth century, Spaniards, Frenchmen, Indians, and Anglos, poor
and prominent, heard Mass at St. Augustin's where the front pew was
always reserved for Augustin and his family and where the whites took a
back seat to these men of color with no sense of affront. Those whites
who worshiped at St. Augustin's clearly considered the colony to be a race
apart from either black or white. Even the strained relations that devel-

---

[13]Gillard, *Colored Catholics*, erroneously attributes the honor of the first nonwhite
congregation with its own church to Baltimore, 1859; see pp. 29-30.

[14]Book 6, p. 116, Parish of St. François des Natchitoches (Archives of Immaculate
Conception Church).

[15]Last Will and Testament of Nicolas Augustin Metoyer, Book 25, *Notarial Records*,
77-80, Article 5 (Natchitoches Parish Courthouse).

oped between the races in the wake of the Civil War were scarcely evident at St. Augustin's. At no point in that troubled era did whites withdraw from the church completely, in spite of improved transportation and an increased number of churches within the area; nor did they take control.

Yet Metoyer's own account of his church's founding graphically points to the ambivalent treatment that his family (and all *gens de couleur libre*) suffered within the Church. He specifically decreed that as long as the chapel remained in use, his people should choose those "Catholic priests who will suit them and not the others." Entries recorded in the minutes of the parish of St. François in Natchitoches during that era spotlight the problems that forced the pious Augustin to make this condition. In 1848, for example, the *marguilliers* decreed that henceforth all nonwhites must remain seated after Mass until whites had left the church and that a separate holy water basin must be established for use of the "colored." The following year, the provision was repealed; but taken together the two entries illustrate the ambivalent and uncertain status of the free nonwhite Catholic even within his own church.[16]

Undeniably, the piety displayed by the colony, reinforced by their provision of a house of worship for Isle whites who had none of their own, earned a great measure of the social acceptance and community respect that they enjoyed. Moreover, as north Louisiana became increasingly settled by Anglo-Protestants, the cultured and affluent Catholic *creoles de couleur* enjoyed a spiritual and cultural bond with white leaders of the *ancien regime* that never could have existed between white Latin Catholics and Anglo-Protestants. Race, for many decades, would be a far less important factor than faith, heritage, and culture, and that factor was of extreme significance to the welfare of the colony. The alien whites who soon dominated north Louisiana brought with them a foreign political, economic, and social philosophy that progressively restricted the community role and privileges of the free nonwhite Louisianian, and it also rankled men of the *ancien regime* who resented changes in their traditional customs. The Catholicity that they shared with the wealthy *homme de couleur libre* was a symbolic element that bound the two races together against the Anglo, the Protestant, and the often-poor white.

---

[16]*Registre des Baptêmes, Mariages, Sepultures des Blancs, Compris dans la Paroisse St. Augustin, Isle Brevèlle*, rectory files, St. Augustin's Church, Natchitoches LA. Interview with confidential source, Isle Brevèlle, 26 April 1974. See also unlabeled minute book beginning 1848, Parish of St. François.

Consequently, many members of the Latin aristocracy became staunch defenders of the rights of the *creole de couleur*—and the astute *homme de couleur libre* who controlled Isle Brevêlle was keenly aware that "his people" must maintain their reputation for piety and devotion to the Catholic faith if they were to survive in the new social climate.

The efficacy of Augustin's leadership cannot be questioned. The colored parishioners of St. Augustin's Church were far more than nominal Catholics. Attendance at Mass and similar outward signs of devotion are not quantitative elements, given the nature of the parish records, but other criteria that are considered indicative of Christian morality can well be measured, and every comparison drawn between the colony and the various other components of Natchitoches society supports the colony's general reputation for morality. They also suggest some interesting nuances of the spiritual and social growth of free nonwhite society in general.

Traditional discussions of free Negro morality in Louisiana dwell upon a host of sensational travelogues in which one general pattern is present. The free woman of color is almost routinely portrayed as a courtesan, fulfilling her life through a series of liaisons with whites who enable her to improve her financial lot and to lighten the color of her offspring in hopes they might one day pass into the privileged ranks of white society. Her male counterpart, however, is sexually handicapped, rejecting his own women for their immorality (or being rejected by them for his low caste), while he dare not aspire to the interracial alliances that his womenfolk enjoy. The *femmes de couleur libres* of Isle Brevêlle have not escaped this generalization in popular literature, even by writers who recognized the colony's uniqueness.[17]

An analysis of Catholic society in the civil parish of Natchitoches does lend some degree of support to the generalized portrayal of interracial morality, but it provides no justification for an indictment of the colony. Moreover, the spiritual growth that it maps parallels, in many respects, the moral development of any frontier society, and it suggests the directions in which other free nonwhite Catholics may have been moving.

For the purpose of this analysis, sacramental registers were used from

---

[17]For example, see Frederic Law Olmsted, *Journey in the Seaboard Slave States in the Years 1853-1854* (New York, 1856; reprinted New York, 1968), pp. 636-37.

all four of the antebellum Catholic churches in the civil parish.[18] Not only do Metoyer family entries appear in all, but a comprehensive analysis of extant Catholic registers in the region produces comparative standards on the various Catholic ethnic groups that settled there. Of particular interest is an analogous *creole de couleur* colony in the Campti region of north Natchitoches Parish, a colony perhaps largely descended from a sister of the Metoyers' slave-born ancestress Coincoin. Like the Metoyers', the Campti colony was an extended community of interlocking families. In general, they boasted a higher degree of French blood, including *haute nobiliare*, yet their social characteristics and their community role never became so clearly defined as those of the Isle Brevêlle cousins with whom they occasionally intermarried.

Unfortunately, parish registers do not present the perfect tool for historical analysis. They are not infallible sources of data. Minute scrutiny of the registers of any church reveals discrepancies, contradictions, and clearly obvious errors, including crucial statements on legitimacy or racial identification. For the purpose of this study, family groups have been reconstituted to ferret out such irregularities in the sacramental entries and to facilitate the weighing of contradictory evidence. In the process, two significant patterns emerged:

- Presumption was usually weighed in favor of legitimacy, although a significant number of the comparative white population were married in civil ceremonies that the Church did not recognize.
- Racial identification in the 1800s appears to have been based upon appearance rather than an examination of pedigrees in the earlier parish registers. Countless free nonwhites appear in "white" registers, long after such registers were clearly restricted to the white population. Similarly, a significant number of Latins of undisputed, totally white, ancestry (but apparently darker complex-

---

[18]The four parishes were: (1) St. François des Natchitoches, where most of the Metoyer family sacramental entries were recorded between 1735 and the 1856 establishment of St. Augustin Parish. (2) St. John the Baptist at Cloutierville, just below the Isle, which was formed in 1817, became inactive in the late 1820s, and was reorganized in 1847. Metoyers and allied families who lived at the lower end of the Isle and along the river below it contributed heavily to the cost of restoring the parish church and became regular parishioners. (3) The parish of St. Augustin de l'Isle Brevêlle and its mission Ste. Anne, whose registers date only from the 1856 establishment of the parish rather than from the 1829 creation of the mission of St. Augustin. Curiously, the Chapel Ste. Anne was attended entirely by whites, a singular situation in which a white congregation constituted a mission of a nonwhite parish! (4) The Church of the Nativity at Campti, together with its Mission Ste. Rose, whose registers date from 1851.

ions) were recorded in the registers or folios labelled *gens de couleur libres* by
pastors new to the parish. Moreover, the Indian population was ambiguously
designated free colored, mulatto, and even white.

The statistics herein presented have been adjusted on both accounts, but
only after a thorough analysis of all existing records.

Between 1800 and 1860 the Metoyer colony showed an overall illegitimacy rate of three percent. Incidences of irregularity peaked at eighteen
percent in the first decade of that century, when the shortage of free
colored males in the parish and the family's yet undefined sense of
identity encouraged two females to form illicit alliances with whites—
and when the Metoyer males were equally susceptible to sexual alliances
with slave women. A low of less than one percent occurred in the last two
decades prior to the Civil War, when group identity and peer pressure
were at their peak.

The analogous colony at Campti displayed a similar pattern of
increasing conformity with Catholic norms, although their pattern
trailed that of the Metoyers by one generation and their overall illegitimacy rate was significantly higher. From a consistent 100 percent in the
first two decades of the nineteenth century, their illegitimacies declined
to twenty-one percent on the eve of the war—an overall rate of thirty-
four percent for the 1800-1860 period in comparison to the three percent
rate on Isle Brevêlle. Although no specific historical study has been
made of the comparative colony, evidence encountered by this researcher
in years of related study in the Natchitoches archives suggests that the
Campti community's development lagged a generation behind that of the
Isle colony in all respects—a fateful generation since the advent of the
Civil War precluded their continued development along the prewar
pattern they had established.

The remaining free nonwhite population of the parish may be
assigned to two broad ethnic groups: Negro (or part-Negroes who did
not segregate themselves) and Indian. Both exhibited strikingly similar
cultural situations and corresponding behavioral patterns. The free
Negroes at large, regardless of exact racial composition, were necessarily
of slave origin, had no stable family group with which they could identify,
and displayed little exclusivity in their social contacts. The Indian population also possessed some slave origins, and in general were isolated
individuals lacking group identification. The only pockets of group rein-
forcement were found in the neighboring parish of Rapides where the

small bands of Apalache and Biloxi Indians occasionally were served by Natchitoches ministers; and even these clusters were soon annihilated by disease, dispersed by encroaching whites, or assimilated into the population at large.[19] In both of these free nonwhite societies, illegitimacy was the norm (although they espoused Catholicism) with overall illegitimacy rates of eighty-two percent among the free Negroes and eighty-six percent among the Indians. Neither showed any indication of eventually conforming to the sixth commandment of the faith with which they were nominally identified.

By comparison, legitimate slave births throughout the antebellum period were relatively nonexistent. Baptismal entries routinely read "father unknown." Only one slave marriage was recorded at Natchitoches, one on Isle Brevêlle, none at Cloutierville, and only ten at Campti The slave baptisms recorded at Natchitoches by the Reverend H. Figary in the first months of his service there in the 1840s are tantalizingly nonconformist. While Father Figary frequently omitted names of owners (a practice no other priest followed), a large percentage of his entries identified fathers for baptized infants. The inference is that Figary recognized the stability of slave relationships even in the absence of a Church-sanctified marriage. Abruptly, then, Reverend Figary's entries revert to the format of his predecessors, possibly due to orders of Church authorities or pressure from his parishioners.[20]

Illegitimacy rates within the various segments of the white population were in some respects similar to that of the free nonwhite society. Natural births peaked early in the century, then steadily declined; however, the peak among white Catholics (fifteen percent) occurred in the 1810-1830 period when the parish was frequently without a pastor. At no point did it fall below three percent (the overall average for Metoyers) and the overall white rate 1800-1860 was a significantly higher twelve percent.

Group identity and/or peer pressure to conform does not appear to have played a significant role among white Catholics, although the different ethnic groups displayed notable variance. A study made of

---

[19]For a sketchy chronicle of the demise of these two tribes, see "Letters Received by the Office of Indian Affairs, 1824-1881," microcopy 234, roll 727, Red River Agency, 1824-1830, Bureau of Indian Affairs (National Archives, Washington DC).

[20]Register 10, Parish of St. François des Natchitoches.

ethnic origins for the last decade before the war indicates a negligible one-quarter percent illegitimacy rate among French Catholics (comparable to that within the Metoyer colony). The Anglo and German Catholic minority ranked three percent, while the many "Spanish" families (who were predominantly of Texas origins and often boasted a strong Indian heritage) led with an illegitimacy rate of nine percent.

A statistical analysis of these registers yields still further glimpses into the personal life-styles of the Metoyer colony and comparative Catholic groups, as well as into the community image that the various groups enjoyed. In only one case of illegitimate birth among the Metoyers did the church registers read "father unknown," and in later records that child named her father. In the smaller Campti colony there appeared forty-eight such baptisms (twenty percent of total illegitimate births). However, many infants of this community who were christened under this ecclesiastical epithet "father unknown" grew to adulthood using surnames of area white males to whom their mothers were not related. By comparison, fifty-five percent of the illegitimate free Negroes were labelled "father unknown," and an even larger majority used their mother's surname, while seventy-five percent of similar Indian births were classified "father unknown" and surnames were almost never used by either mother or child. By contrast, fifty-eight percent of white illegitimacies were labelled "father unknown."

Only two instances can be documented or assumed in the 1800s of a Metoyer male fathering children by a slave female, and no females within the colony appear to have become romantically involved with a slave. Similarly, neither males nor females among the Metoyers and their related families entered into a relationship with a black. Throughout this colony's development (as with the Campti colony and perhaps the majority of *creoles de couleur*) an important caste barrier existed between the part-Negro and the full-Negro.

Miscegenous relationships with whites, however, were common among nonwhites outside the Metoyer colony. Thirty-three percent of all illegitimate births among free Negroes at large represented recognized white fathers or children identified by a racial designation a degree lighter than their mothers. In the Campti colony an even higher overall percentage were apparently fathered by whites (thirty-seven percent), although these two nonwhite groups showed considerable variance in their pattern of relationships. Miscegenous unions remained statistically stable throughout the antebellum period for free Negroes at large, while in the

Campti colony it declined from a high of seventy-nine percent pre-1820 to a low of forty-six percent in the last decade before the war. Again, the Campti colony was clearly following the pattern begun by the Isle Brevêlle colony a generation earlier, in which the colony's founders, the children or grandchildren of miscegenous couples, began to view miscegenation as more of a threat to, than a tool for, racial advancement.

Society's more sensitive form of racial miscegenation, the white female-nonwhite male relationship, was not unknown, though rare, in the civil parish of Natchitoches. No similar incident is known to have existed within the Metoyer colony, and it is doubtful that peer pressure there would have permitted it, given the community ill will that this might have created and the threat that it could pose to the colony as a whole.

While a considerable segment of the Catholic free Negro population seems to have accepted miscegenation as a vehicle for social and economic mobility, the racially mixed Metoyers emphasized maintenance of the status quo. In this respect they came into direct conflict with one of the basic tenents of their faith. Along Isle Brevêlle group identity and racial privileges were maintained by in-group marriage. Young Metoyers could not legally marry whites, and, as shown, they did not condone illicit miscegenous unions. Neither would they marry blacks, and the number of free colored Catholics in the parish who were socially acceptable to them was limited. While a small number of *gens de couleur libres* were imported from New Orleans as spouses for the second and subsequent generations, most marital partners were chosen from the core group produced by the original children of Coincoin in their marriages to freed slaves of similar background. Throughout the history of the colony a small number of family names have dominated.

A study of the marital patterns exhibited by Islanders with the six predominant family names indicates that seventy percent of all prewar marriages were in-group marriages, and this obviously involved a great degree of intrafamily marriage within degrees of relationship forbidden by the Church. Studies of free Negro society in North America have almost universally pointed to the prevalence of intrafamily marriages, and at least one free Negro colony has been accused of inbreeding "to an appaling extent."[21] A cursory examination of parish marriage records

---

[21]James Blackwell Browning, "Free Negro in Antebellum North Carolina," *North Carolina Historical Review* 15 (1938): 33.

might create the same general impression of the Metoyer colony; but an in-depth study of all Catholic marriages recorded in St. François registers between 1810 and 1850 reveals that marriages within forbidden degrees of relationship were no more prevalent among the nonwhite Catholics of Isle Brevèlle than among the white Catholics of the parish. Only twenty-three percent of Metoyer family marriages were within the forbidden three degrees, while thirty-one percent of white marriages fell within this category. However, it appears that those Metoyers who did marry within forbidden degrees were prone to marry within closer degrees than did the white population in general, primarily because the limited size of the colony provided them with less choice of partners.

Intrafamily marriages within both the colony and the white Catholic population were often contracted without dispensations being obtained. Among the comparative white Catholics, twenty-two of the sixty-five intrafamily marriages (thirty-four percent) made no mention of the proscribed relationship. Among the colony, four of the seven intrafamily marriages (fifty-seven percent) within the studied years ignored the relationship. Family tradition holds that local Church authorities did not initially inform the Metoyers of the Church prohibition against intrafamily marriages and that once this proscription was called to the attention of Augustin he curtailed such marriages.[22] Perhaps tradition is correct in that the failure to seek dispensation was due to ignorance of Church law rather than to a desire to circumvent it, but parish records do not support the tradition that Augustin curtailed such marriages. On the contrary, the last generation to marry during his lifetime exhibited an even greater tendency toward intrafamily marriage than did the pre-1850 population.

Pastoral neglect of Natchitoches during the 1806 to 1828 period created further opportunity for deviancy from Church norms in marital patterns. In the absence of priests, both white and nonwhite Catholics contracted civil marriages that were later ratified when pastors were assigned to the parish. The Metoyers displayed a markedly smaller tendency to resort to civil unions. Among free Negroes and Indians at large, common-law marriages, rather than civil marriages, appear to have been the norm in the absence of Church pastors.

In yet another way, the Catholic registers of the civil parish reflect an important aspect of the colony's experience—its treatment of the human

---

[22]Interview with Mrs. Lee Coutii, Isle Brevèlle, 24 March 1974.

property it owned.[23] Descendants of the colony insist that their antebellum ancestors were exceptionally humane to their slaves, and extant records generally support the claim. However, evidence does not exist that, as devout Catholics, the Isle Brevêlle masters were exceptionally concerned with the *spiritual* welfare of their bondsmen. They certainly did not feel that all men were "brothers in Christ"; indeed, this aspect of their piety suffered drastically as a result of the more temporal necessity of maintaining the all-important caste barriers between themselves and the black/slave population.

The Metoyer colony dutifully presented slave infants for baptism, no more or less promptly than did white slaveowners. Evidence exists that they were somewhat more likely to keep records of slave birth dates and to provide these to the priest who administered baptism than were white planters, but it is debatable whether this indicates more concern for the individuality and humanity of slaves or more interest in careful record-keeping. At least it does not appear that the colony merited the type of criticism some Catholic masters earned, as evidenced by a pastoral complaint in south Louisiana that slaveowners were demanding baptism of adult Negroes without instruction and would send slaves "to be baptized without specifying the sex, the age, the name of the mother, whence result many blanks in the registers."[24] By contrast, the Metoyers and allied families were likely to appear as godparents to the slaves they presented for baptism.

The degree of instruction given to adult slaves of non-Catholic birth, prior to baptism, is a factor that is hard to quantify, or even to discuss with objectivity. Almost all evidence dealing with the subject depicts practices that are ecclesiastically deviant; it was this deviancy that usually created the record. Consequently, documentary evidence is strongly weighted in favor of neglect on the part of the masters.

To some extent it has been possible to find suggestive patterns among slaveowners in the colony. In June 1809, Augustin acquired a lot of African slaves from an Anglo trader; sex and age are given, but not names. Three of these were sold immediately to his brother, Louis. Twelve years later both Augustin and Louis presented several Guinea

[23]For a broader discussion of the colony's attitude toward slavery, see Mills, *The Forgotten People*.

[24]Report of Father Sebastien Flavian Besançon, O.M.C., St. Charles des Allemands, 29 December 1775, reel 1, *Records of the Diocese*.

Negro youths for baptism, all of an approximate age to be the same African youths purchased in 1809.[25] No other purchases of Africans were found in those intervening years to negate the possibility that the above slaves might be the same. The assumption might therefore be made that twelve years were allowed for the acculturation and Christianization of the imported Negroes.

Similarly, in March 1811, Augustin purchased a ten-year-old female from an Anglo trader, and this slave was also baptized in 1821. In the ten-year interval, she had borne three children (1815, 1819, and 1821) who were baptized at the ages of ten months, two and a half months, and three months, respectively.[26]

Again, on 26 August 1813, Augustin purchased from a south Louisiana man a slave family consisting of husband, wife, and *"her* three children," aged nine months, three years, and eight years. All three children were baptized within two years; and two subsequently born children were baptized in 1816 and 1820. However, the husband and wife were not themselves baptized until 1821.[27] The inference, once more, is that adult slaves were not so readily converted to Catholicism, although it can hardly be inferred whether this was due to a lack of proper instruction or to a feeling on the part of the master that the conversion must be thorough before the sacrament of baptism is administered. By way of comparison, it may be noted that the Royal Cédula issued by the Spanish Crown in 1788 expressed its opinion that slaves entering Spanish dominions could be sufficiently instructed and baptized within a year.[28]

Family tradition holds that the colony's slaves were regularly gathered in prayer and otherwise received spiritual guidance on a daily basis.[29] It is difficult to document this tradition. No records exist of legitimate Church marriages between Metoyer slaves. No record is found of any confirmations of their human chattel, nor is there found record of their deceased slaves being buried with a church ceremony or in any of the parish cemeteries. In this, the colony conforms to the general pattern set

---

[25]Elizabeth Shown Mills, *Natchitoches, 1800-1826*, entries 1455-1473, 1687-1690; Miscellaneous Book 1, pp. 28-29, Natchitoches Parish Courthouse.

[26]Mills, *Natchitoches, 1800-1826*, entries 1153, 1440, 1471, 2413.

[27]Ibid., entries 1463, 1473, 1816, 1820, 2522. Italics added.

[28]"Royal Regulations for the Education . . . of Slaves," ch. 1.

[29]Interview with Mrs. Coutii, 26 April 1974.

by white masters among whose slave households marriages, confirmations, and burials were extremely rare in the 1800s. Most assuredly, the Metoyers did not bury their slaves in the cemetery at St. Augustin's. Tradition holds that the slave cemetery lay across the road from their own, on the bank of the river.[30] Such a site, in front of the church itself, would seemingly indicate that the church played some role in slave burials, although the lack of burial records in any registers indicates that no priest was called from Natchitoches to officiate.

Similarly, tradition also holds that the colony's slaves, and those of the *étrangers* who attended St. Augustin's, were relegated to the galleries and the widely overhanging side eaves during Mass.[31] This segregation was necessitated to a great extent by the limited space inside the church, but other evidence indicates that the colony preferred such segregation for social reasons. This became most clearly evident in the postwar years when the sheer numbers of freedmen, many as light-skinned as their former masters, made it difficult for the Metoyers and allied families to maintain their racial uniqueness and superiority. In the wake of universal manumission, St. Augustin's parishioners appear to have effectively closed the church doors to their former slaves who were, admittedly, only nominal Catholics.[32] Most then drifted away to the numerous and probably more appealing black Baptist congregations. Clearly, the Catholicity of the St. Augustin congregation was as racially intolerant as that espoused by their white neighbors.

The Church's loss of black membership to Protestant faiths in the postwar years was an almost universal phenomenon in Catholic communities.[33] Yet despite the general conformity of St. Augustin Parish to this pattern, there did exist an exception which reflects the degree to which the colony had succeeded in establishing itself as the nonwhite elite of the region. The economic and social changes wrought by the Civil War and Reconstruction brought into the parish a number of light-skinned nonwhites who had also been free before the war but were of Anglo-Protestant origins. They, as well as the local light-skinned freedmen of

---

[30]Ibid.

[31]Woods, *Marginality and Identity*, p. 66.

[32]Ibid., p. 104.

[33]Randall M. Miller, "The Failed Mission: The Catholic Church and Black Catholics in the Old South," in Edward Magdol and Jon L. Wakelyn, eds., *The Southern Common People: Studies in Nineteenth-Century Social History* (Westport CT, 1980), pp. 49-50.

ambition, often saw in the Catholic Church a means by which they might climb the socioracial ladder. As one sociologist has pointed out in her study of the postwar Metoyer colony, "Being Catholic reinforced [their] claim to being old family."[34] Other ambitious nonwhites felt the same. Even though they were not "old family" in the sense that word is used, being Catholic might make them appear to be. The Catholic Church provided special contacts with the "old family" hierarchy of the parish and possibly would lead to intermarriage with those generally recognized as the nonwhite elite. The parish registers of St. Augustin and neighboring St. John the Baptist Church at Cloutierville, where most of the extended family of Metoyers attended Mass, reflect the introduction of these "new family" Catholics into the colony—all bearing such obviously Anglo names as Jones, Wilson, Taylor, Reuben, Hanson, and Hampton.

The Catholicity of these newcomers, however, is even yet questioned by certain of the "old family" descendants. Mrs. Smith,[35] it is said, moved with her husband and family to the Isle at the close of the war and then attempted to wed her daughters to the light-skinned Metoyer youths. The colony was slow in accepting them, despite the fact that the Smiths had survived the war in better financial health than any of the Metoyers whose acceptance they sought. Perceiving that St. Augustin's Church would be her family's most effective *entrée* into the nonwhite elite of the Isle, Mrs. Smith requested permission for her family to attend the "Metoyer family church." Permission was slow in coming. Ultimately, Mr. Smith offered to make a substantial contribution toward rebuilding the war-torn church in exchange for membership privileges, and the economically strapped colony accepted his offer. The Smith family took instruction and converted to Catholicism. Some time afterwards, it is related, Mrs. Smith rose during Mass to join the communion line, and her daughter conscientiously whispered, "But, Mama, you ate a biscuit right before we left home," whereupon the deep-voiced Mrs. Smith "whispered" back in tones her pewmates could easily hear, "Hush, child! Jesus don't know what I do in my own kitchen!"[36]

St. Augustin's Church remains the heart of the Isle Brevêlle colony,

---

[34]Woods, *Marginality and Identity*, p. 66.

[35]A pseudonym.

[36]Interview with confidential source, Natchitoches, Louisiana, 23 October 1973.

pulsating as strongly today as in the first fifty antebellum years. For those Metoyer descendants who have left the Isle it is the Catholic "mecca" to which they periodically make their pilgrimage. A sociological study of the postwar parishioners clearly reveals that Catholicity is still very much the way of life, although their degree of conformity to Catholic norms has diminished as in society as a whole. Illegitimacy and divorce rates have shown some small increase, but peer pressure to conform to Catholic standards of morality is still strong.[37] Moreover, the large number of vocations professed by descendants of the colony in the twentieth century reveals not only the family's faith but points to an extremely important adjustment in the attitudes that accompany that faith. Although religious orders for nonwhites existed prior to the Civil War, the pious *gens de couleur libres* of Isle Brevèlle had declined to join them because *blacks* were accepted also. Since 1900 a number of youths from St. Augustin's Parish and from their satellite colonies in various industrial cities have entered several of the Catholic orders, emerging as professed sisters, brothers, and priests to work within the black community.

In reviewing the spiritual development of this free nonwhite Catholic community, it is clearly obvious that racial prejudice was the factor that most seriously hamstrung its faith in the antebellum years—but it was a prejudice with a mirror image. The Isle Brevèlle colony suffered from pastoral neglect, but then most of their Louisiana contemporaries suffered in this respect. The ecclesiastical failure to see them as they saw themselves—as a special race of God's children—presented a serious test of their devotion, as successive priests followed personal inclination rather than a central policy and treated them on the one hand as they might treat any free Catholic and on the other hand relegated them to the ranks of the nominally Catholic slave. It was this ecclesiastical ambivalence that prompted Augustin Metoyer to found a church in which "his people" could choose "the Catholic priests who will suit them and not the *others.*"[38] But this racial prejudice was a two-sided coin and the otherwise devout Catholics of the Isle colony were as guilty of the sin of racial intolerance as were the priests who did not "suit them." In all other respects, both statistics and contemporary testimony agree that the

---

[37] Woods, *Marginality and Identity*, pp. 89, 98-99, 103, 116.

[38] Will of Augustin Metoyer, article 5; italics added.

colony's members were brilliant examples of Catholic morality, and their continued dedication to the faith clearly indicates that even though Catholic evangelization among nonwhites was limited in America, it produced permanent results.

TABLE 1

Racial Misidentification of Colored Catholics by Church Authorities*

	F.p.c. erroneously identified as white in "white" registers			White males erroneously identified as legitimate husbands of f.p.c. females in "colored" registers		
	Metoyer Colony	Comparative Colony	Other f.p.c.	Metoyer Colony	Comparative Colony	Other f.p.c.
1800-1809	-	-	-	-	-	-
1810-1819	-	-	-	-	-	-
1820-1829	5	1	1	-	-	-
1830-1839	8	4	1	1	1	-
1840-1849	23	6	7	-	2	-
1850-1859	-	2	2	-	6	1

*Based upon an analysis of 7,000 white and f.p.c. baptismal entries in the parishes of St. François des Natchitoches (1800-1860), St. Jean Baptiste des Clouterville (1821-1860), St. Augustin de l'Isle Brevelle (1856-1860), and Notre-Dame de la Nativite de Campti (1851-1860).

TABLE 2

Fluctuations in Illegitimacy Rate—
by Cultural Heritage and Time Frame

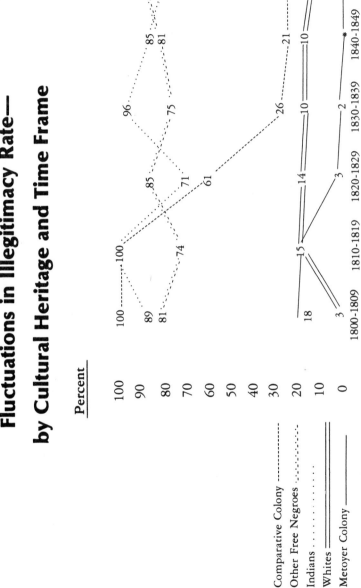

Percent

Comparative Colony ----------
Other Free Negroes ·············
Indians ················
Whites ══════
Metoyer Colony ─────────

*Less than 1 percent

TABLE 3

Church Recognition of Interracial Unions*

	White fathers identified in interracial liaisons			White mothers with free Negro children			White females married to Indians or slave-born metifs		
	Metoyer Colony	Comparative Colony	Other f.p.c.	Metoyer Colony	Comparative Colony	Community At Large	Metoyer Colony	Comparative Colony	Community At Large
1800-1809	2	-	-	-	-	-	-	-	2
1810-1819	2	4	3	-	-	-	-	-	2
1820-1829	-	-	-	-	-	-	-	-	-
1830-1839	-	2	5	-	1	1**	-	-	-
1840-1849	-	2	11	-	1	5**	-	-	-
1850-1859	-	3	10	-	4	1**	-	-	-

*Based upon an analysis of approximately 1,000 baptisms of free nonwhite children in the parishes of St. François des Natchitoches (1800-1860), St. Jean Baptiste des Cloutierville (1821-1860), St. Augustin de l'Isle Brevêlle (1856-1860), and Nôtre-Dame de la Nativite de Campti (1851-1860).

**These figures include one white female who bore children by a quadroon husband over a period of three decades. The marriage was termed legitimate in the church records, although the actual marriage record has not been found. It appears to have occurred in Texas. The quadroon in question was an in-law of the Isle Brevêlle colony who left the civil parish of Natchitoches to live as white, later returned, but severed ties with his sibling who had married into the colony.

THE SOUTH'S IRISH CATHOLICS: A CASE OF CULTURAL CONFINEMENT

by Dennis Clark

The social experience of the Irish Catholics in Southern states affords an opportunity to examine the regional differences that resulted in broad variations in the history of ethnic groups in American society. Most studies of ethnic groups have focused on local settings or have catalogued the panoramic presence of the group without attention to regional influences that distinctively shaped the traditions of major ethnic populations.[1] Hence the popular historical understanding of the diversity of the nation is largely innocent of the notable differences between Italians in California and those in New York, between Greeks in New England and those in Florida. The potency of regional cultures, the adaptability of ethnic minorities, and the capacity of ethnic consciousness to persist amid isolation and hostility all demand attention. An examina-

---

[1]See, for example, Carl Wittke, *The Irish in America* (Baton Rouge, 1956); and William V. Shannon, *The American Irish* (New York, 1963). Lawrence M. McCaffrey, *The Irish Diaspora in America* (Bloomington IN, 1976), tries to give a perspective on Irish-American dispersion, but does not examine the South.

tion of both Irish occupational and religious standing in the South should aid this process.

There is ample evidence of the presence of the Irish in the South during the earliest periods of exploration and settlement. Under both Spanish and English auspices, Irishmen found themselves in pioneer settings as adventurers and entrepreneurs. Often the adventurers were serving as military explorers or in garrisons in ill-defined colonial enterprises. As trappers, traders, scouts, or simply wandering renegades, the Irish crop up in the vast southeastern region. Irish priests in Florida's Spanish missions, Irish officials for the Spanish crown in Louisiana and Texas, Irish convicts in Georgia, Irish settlers in the Carolinas, and Irish traders among the Indians appear in the records of the seventeenth and eighteenth centuries.[2] These appearances in the landscape of a barely explored continent were part of the habit and legacy of exile that was one of the abiding misfortunes of Ireland's persecuted sons and daughters.

In Charleston and New Orleans active Irish communities existed from the time of the American Revolution. Strong merchant families with ties to Irish counterparts in Northern cities, the Caribbean, and England were their leaders, and through Hibernian societies they sustained a strong interest in Irish writing, politics, and culture.[3]

The Appalachian Mountains—that immense spine that imposed the principal geographic barrier to the physical unity of the South—were influenced by the Irish in an oblique but definite way. For generations, indentured servants formed a significant and regular component of the American laboring population. Indentured workers with terms ranging from seven to twenty-one years came to America as immigrants, and their importation was a common colonization procedure. The Irish comprised the most numerous group among this indentured class. In early America orphans, prisoners, runaways, delinquents, debtors, and vagrants were frequently seized by local authorities and indentured, with officials making tidy profits from the traffic, and with the labor for the

[2]See, for example, W. S. Murphy, "The Irish Brigade at the Capture of Pensacola, 1781," *Florida Historical Quarterly* 45 (January 1966): 215-25; John G. Coyle, "Cornelius Harnett of Wilmington, North Carolina," *Journal of the American-Irish Historical Society* 29 (1930-1931): 148-56; A. S. Salley, ed., *Warrants for Lands in South Carolina* (Columbia SC, 1973).

[3]Earl F. Niehaus, *The Irish in New Orleans* (Baton Rouge, 1965), pp. 4-5; John I. Cosgrave, "The Hibernian Society of Charleston, South Carolina," *Journal of the American-Irish Historical Society* 25 (1926): 150-58.

least desirable domestic and unskilled jobs benefitting tradesmen and householders while legal enforcement of the work contract was presided over by sympathetic courts. Slavery, of course, decreased the use of indentures in the South, but still they were not uncommon. From the eastern settlements in both North and South indentured servants escaped to the refuge of the mountain wilderness. Eighteenth-century provincial papers steadily carried advertisements with rewards for such runaways, and the Irish had the reputation for being the servants most likely to flee.[4]

Hence it was not only Ulster Irish Protestants such as those who moved South through the Appalachians as pioneers who peopled the deep mountains. Irish Catholic fugitives—whose attachment to what was basically an obligation under Anglo-Saxon law was bound to be slight considering their ancestral problems with that law—also made the mountains their own. This fugitive population gained security in the impenetrable mountains. They played a role in creating the mountaineer's distrust of strangers, authority, and inquisitive influences. As fugitives, such people were loath to tolerate governmental intrusions. Their hardy individualistic life-style, their racy Irish music, and their suspicious secretiveness were already a tradition in the Southern mountains from the Smokies of Virginia to the Ozarks before the Civil War.

The emergence of large concentrations of Irish in the South had to await the development of more major centers and the need for the kind of labor that characterized Irish employment in the period when Irish immigration swelled after 1820. As in other regions, the need for "internal improvements" from the time of Andrew Jackson onward created a strong market for menial construction labor. The canal and railroad construction that advanced across the terrain brought Irish digging crews into one territory after another, and afterward left them clustered along these lines of communication. As well, the need for longshore labor rose as the ports grew along the Atlantic and Gulf coasts. Riverboat and barge men were also part of the Irish diffusion along major lines of travel. This channeling of Irish labor was the chief medium for the settlement of the Irish in Southern ports, river and rail centers, and inland cities. Whether persistent communities of Irish Catholics resulted from these population clusters depended upon such factors as the size of the Irish enclaves, the existence of further economic opportunities, and the prospects for the

---

[4]Abbott Emerson Smith, *Colonists in Bondage: White Servitude and Convict Labor in America, 1607-1776* (New York, 1971), pp. 167, 212, 267.

maintenance of religious and social facilities. In New Orleans, Charleston, and a few other cities Irish communities had formed in the eighteenth century, as had been noted, but these were exceptions in the region.

During the 1850s, after the calamity of the potato famine had sent a vast tide of hungry refugees to American shores, the Irish were engaged in the urban labor that was part of the expansion of Southern cities in these years. They also continued their work as contract laborers for excavation, repair of levees, and lumber clearing, and were active in riverboat and railroad labor. In some respects they were more reliable and valued than slaves, especially if only recently arrived in the country. But in other respects they were expendable. Frederick Law Olmsted notes that in ports they were employed in dangerous loading because they had no monetary value as slaves did. They were, too, more intractable than black labor, and would strike for better wages and working conditions, as they did in New Orleans in 1853, tying up the entire steamboat traffic.[5]

The identification of the Irish with labor in opening the nation's transportation routes is no less significant for the South than for other areas of the nation. Their employment in canal building in the 1820s took them hundreds of miles from the Eastern cities, as Matthew Carey noted. The cholera, yellow fever, typhus, dysentery, malaria, and other epidemic diseases, in addition to the brutal nature of the excavation work, exacted a fearsome toll wherever the Irish work gangs labored. So grim was the toll that some planters expressed reluctance to use valuable slaves for it; also, most slaves were trained for agricultural work, not the body-breaking labor of the hard-driven digging crews. Strikes and violence marked canal construction in Virginia as routes to the tidewater were dug by the Chesapeake and Ohio Company and the 184-mile canal to Cumberland, fifty to eighty feet wide, progressed. Company bankruptcies, broken wage agreements, fury at the abusive gang bosses, and terrible working conditions caused repeated outbreaks. In one famous case, Simon Cameron shipped Irishmen from Philadelphia to work on the drainage and canal projects near New Orleans, and the result was a disaster of disease and exploitation. Whatever the human cost, much of the 500 miles of canal works built in the South prior to 1860 was the work of Irish labor.[6]

---

[5]Ella Lonn, *Foreigners in the Confederacy* (Chapel Hill NC, 1940), p. 28; David R. Goldfield, "Cities of the Old South," in Blaine Brownell and David R. Goldfield, eds., *The City in Southern History* (Port Washington NY, 1977), p. 64.

[6]Niehaus, *The Irish in New Orleans*, pp. 33, 44-45.

One episode reveals that colonization projects did on occasion accompany railroad development. In Georgia the building of the Ocmulgee and Flint Railroad was conceived as a combined commercial, colonization, and missionary venture. Abbott Brisbane, who had served with Irish-American soldiers against the Seminole Indians, became a Roman Catholic. He was an engineer and planned a wooden track railway from Mobley's Bluff to the Flint River near Albany, Georgia. With the aid of a Catholic priest, he recruited Irishmen from Charleston and New York in 1842 and began construction. Workers expected to receive settlement land near the railroad right-of-way to form a Catholic colony, the Mission of St. Ignatius, in the heart of Georgia. Immigrants were sought from Ireland. The scheme failed when the business structure for the road collapsed, the Irish workers stormed Abbott Brisbane's headquarters, and the priest involved died. Some of the Irish stayed in the area and settled land on an individual basis.[7]

Whether clearing right-of-way for the Natchez Trace, building wharves in the river cities and ocean ports, or heaving and hauling freight in the "J. Murphy" wagons of St. Louis (the competitors of the Conestoga wagons), the Irish threaded through the land on its travel routes. This usually meant that their presence was transitory and what residence they made was temporary at the beginning. For this reason, their first major treks through the South in significant numbers are largely without community record. The shelter for the male labor gangs simply consisted of shanties, lean-tos, and canvas stretched from wagons. Sanitation was primitive and food of the rudest kind. Poverty bound them to the work and moved them on to the next work site. The touring actor Tyrone Power encountered them repeatedly—clannish, strangers to the local population, sharing their own speech and secret morale. Their itinerant work on flatboats, railroads, and drainage gangs made them peripheral to the religious and social communities they touched.[8]

---

[7]Fussell Chalker, "Irish Catholics and the Building of the Ocmulgee and Flint Railroad," *Georgia Historical Quarterly* 54 (1970): 507-16.

[8]George Rogers Taylor, *The Transportation Revolution, 1815-1860* (New York, 1951), pp. 42, 75-84, 290. The unenviable position of Irish immigrants in relation to slaves posed a further cultural problem for them. In many work situations the two groups competed. Olmsted observed that some Virginia farmers preferred Irish field hands to blacks. The defensive reaction of the Irish workers to the manifest cruelties of slavery led them to insistently distinguish themselves from black slaves and workers. Although sharing many of the same social and economic disabilities with blacks, the Irish strove to

When priests did reach the transient Irish Catholics working on levees or building railroads, it was partly to beg money from them. "Working the Irish" for collections became a common practice on the Mississippi River in the 1850s, but it did not bring the workers into organized Catholic life. Nature and the lack of missionary priests made such visits brief and irregular. Work and contractual arrangements also interfered with religious observances. The sixty Irish Catholics repairing levees near Vicksburg, Mississippi, in 1853, for example, were denied fast-day food by labor contractors unwilling to purchase the more expensive fare.[9]

Gradually enough immigrant Irish workers clustered in cities to establish distinct community groups. Richard Wade has pointed out the decline of black population in Southern cities in the antebellum decade, even though commercial and manufacturing activity in most of these cities increased. The work force for their urban economic base was partially augmented by Irish increments.

Good examples of the Irish as urban workers existed in Savannah, Georgia, and Charleston, South Carolina. Conditions in Savannah were so chaotic and destructive of decency for the Irish that they gained reputations as "the grand movers in all disturbances." Larceny, malicious mischief, buying and receiving stolen goods, fraud, illegal voting, assault and battery, and murder were common offenses for which they were brought to court. Drunkenness and gambling were vices that, when spread among slaves by Irish grogshop owners, caused deep local concern. Also, on the Savannah waterfront shipping agents named Kelly,

---

confirm their own independence and identity, and this imparted a special individualism to Irish behavior in the South. See Eugene Genovese, *Roll, Jordan, Roll: The World the Slaves Made* (New York, 1974), p. 229; Frederick Law Olmsted, *The Cotton Kingdom*, 2 vols. (New York, 1861), 1:276. New England's Edward Everett Hale in 1852 wrote of the Irish immigrants: "They are fugitives from defeat, or, without a metaphor, from slavery.... Here in Masschusetts we writhe and struggle, really with one heart, lest we return one fugitive who can possibly be saved to Southern slavery; but when there come these fugitives from 'Irish bastilles' as they call them, we tax them first and neglect them afterwards." Hale, *Letters on Irish Immigration* (Boston, 1852), p. 8.

[9]On soliciting money from and serving the Irish workers, see, for example, Fr. F. R. Pont to Antoine Blanc, 25 November 1856; and Fr. Peter McLaughlin to Blanc, 29 January 1859, New Orleans Papers (University of Notre Dame). On the denial of fast-day food, see Fr. John Fierbras to Blanc, 3 February 1853, New Orleans Papers. I want to thank Randall M. Miller for these and other references.

Dunn, and Hussey became notorious for their victimization of sailors in the 1850s.[10]

In an excellent analysis of Irish workers in Charleston in the years 1840-1866, Christopher Silver has presented the best material on this immigrant group, outside of Earl Niehaus's study of New Orleans. Silver's investigation reveals the same pattern of Irish alteration of the population balance toward a predominantly white pattern that is noted by Wade and Niehaus. The pressure on black urban workers by Irish newcomers altered the occupational structure of the city. This was especially true in the heavy work of carting and drayage. Free blacks in trades such as blacksmith, carpenter, millwright, and tailor resisted the Irish penetration in a way slaves were unable to do, so the Irish intrusion did not sweep them from the occupational structure. Because of this accession to semiskilled and skilled work, many of the Irish were able to purchase property and move toward respectability. But the climate of Charleston, the diseases endemic to it, and the inability to displace blacks sufficiently led to a high rate of transiency for the Irish in the city. The Irish who came to Charleston were largely recruited from New York on a seasonal basis, and finding inferior conditions and a labor situation replete with black resistance, the immigrants soon concluded it was best to move on. Thus in the winter months packets arrived with immigrants, and in the summer months they departed with Irish passengers, sometimes causing a net annual loss for the port. Although Charleston's Irish maintained their religious institutions and identity, the city itself became increasingly "nativist" and reflective of rural Southern attitudes.[11]

By 1860 there were 84,000 Irish-born people in the Southern states, a total smaller than the numbers of Irish in individual cities in the North. Only Louisiana, Tennessee, Missouri, and Virginia had more than one percent of their population made up of Irish-born. Cities such as Richmond, Savannah, and Memphis had more than 3,000 Irish-born, but outside these centers there were few identifiable concentrations.[12] Whole states were thus barely acquainted with an ethnic group that was in the mid-

---

[10]Richard Haunton, "Law and Order in Savannah, 1850-1860," *Georgia Historical Quarterly* 56 (1972): 10-11.

[11]Christopher Silver, "A New Look at Old South Urbanization: The Irish Worker in Charleston, South Carolina, 1840-1860," in Samuel M. Hines and George W. Hopkins, eds., *South Atlantic Urban Studies*, vol. 3 (Columbia SC, 1979), pp. 141-71.

[12]Lonn, *Foreigners in the Confederacy*, p. 31.

nineteenth century having a far-reaching effect on politics, religion, and social development not only in the North but in the Old Northwest and Far West.

The religious organization of this widely scattered Irish population evolved slowly and unevenly. The primary problem was simply the difficulty of providing priests and even rudimentary ecclesiastical administration for a region of such great distances and varying conditions. In states such as Maryland, Virginia, and Missouri, the Irish were able to build church facilities, and because of geographic location and communications, maintain liaison with the major Catholic dioceses of the Northeast. In 1801 Irish, English, and French Catholics subscribed for their first church in the nation's capital, and in Louisiana the French-speaking Catholics made provisions for their Irish coreligionists. In Savannah, Mobile, and Natchez stable religious administration was possible, as it was in Charleston, but it was often a hard struggle. Priests declined to work in the South because of the poverty of the Catholics there, the circuit riding required to visit remote missions, and the heat and sickness that were part of the subtropical environment. Prior to 1850 there were never more than six priests in the Natchez diocese, and only twenty in the Mobile diocese, both of which lay close to the chief Catholic center of the South, the diocese of New Orleans, which by 1850 had a Catholic population of 170,000.[13]

It is clear from the sources used by John Gilmary Shea in his review of Southern dioceses that institutional development was very uneven. In 1850, in Savannah, two bishops died from fever, leaving the thin Catholic network of twelve chapels without episcopal leadership. The Charleston diocese reached into three states, and the bishop reported "poor and struggling congregations" in such places as Raleigh and Fayetteville. Bishop Ignatius Whelan of Charleston journeyed all the way to Paris to seek aid for his flock. Bishop Andrew Byrne reported that "Within the whole diocese of Little Rock there exists no means to erect a single altar." During this period of seminal labor even the largest concentrations of Catholics such as New Orleans, Charleston, Louisville, and Galveston

---

[13]N. T. Maguire, "Catholicity in Washington, Georgia," *American Catholic Historical Researches* 11 (January 1894): 17-28; Bishop John England, "Memoirs of the Roman Catholic Church in America: North Carolina," ibid., 11 (July 1894): 119; Donald A. Debats, "Elites and Masses: Political Structure, Communication and Behavior in Ante-Bellum Georgia" (doctoral dissertation, University of Wisconsin, 1970), p. 436.

remained heavily dependent upon the Society for the Propagation of the
Faith in Rome for annual subsidies. And although the Irish imparted
some militancy to Catholicism in the South in the 1840s and 1850s, such
militancy was a defensive response to the intimidation emanating from a
strident evangelical Protestantism rather than an expression of institutional assurance and power.[14]

Early Catholic prelates such as Bishop John Carroll and Bishop John
Hughes had acceded to a scheme of parish administration that vested
property control and adminstrative decisions in the hands of laymen. The
lay role was qualified and in missionary conditions entirely warranted. As
time passed, however, disputes inevitably arose among trustees and
clergy. The feeble Catholic dioceses of the South were weakened in the
1820s by such trustee disputes in St. Augustine, Florida, Charleston, and
St. Louis. Even New Orleans was not exempt, but in that city the disputes
initially emerged within the French-speaking community, and the Irish
strongly supported the bishop, who was French.[15]

From the outset of missionary activity in the region, Catholics had to
face the hostility of the overwhelmingly predominant Protestants in
most of the South. Even the long-established Irish in Charleston had to
refute charges that they were political foils of Rome. In 1824 such a refu-
tation was circulated from "A Catholic Clergyman, A Native of Ireland."
Nativist and Know-Nothing prejudice against the Irish flared repeatedly
in the 1840s, and Louisville, Savannah, St. Louis, and New Orleans all had
incidents of violence or fierce controversy.[16] Such hostility was not merely
part of the national effusion of Protestant militant sentiment in the
1840s and 1850s. In the South it was part of a regional tradition of
religious homogeneity of a Protestant character and an antagonism
against immigrants in a setting where vigilance with respect to maintenance of the existing social order was believed to be imperative because of
the potential for disruption inherent in a slaveholding society.

In addition to religious hostility, new Irish Catholics faced Southern
upper-class prejudice. The baronial life-style of England's upper class had

---

[14]John Gilmary Shea, *History of the Catholic Church in the United States*, 4 vols. (New York, 1892), 3:93, 285.

[15]James J. Pillar, "Catholicism in the Lower South," in Lucius F. Ellsworth, ed., *The Americanization of the Gulf Coast: 1803-1850* (Pensacola FL, 1972), pp. 34-43.

[16]Ray Allen Billington, *The Protestant Crusade* (Chicago, 1964), pp. 132, 168, 256; *American Catholic Historical Researches* 9 (January 1892): 43.

an attraction for the Southern plantation elite, particularly in Georgia, the Carolinas, and Virginia where both genealogy and education emphasized the cultural connection to England. From England the stereotypes, prejudices, and anti-Irish attitudes deriving from the ancient English-Irish conflict passed to much of the Southern leadership.[17] The presumption of Irish inferiority repeatedly led English travellers in the South to compare the Irish with the slave populations, often to the detriment of the former. Fanny Kemble's view of the Irish was not unusual among celebrated English visitors to the great plantation houses, for she saw them as "savage, brutish, filthy, idle and incorrigibly and hopelessly helpless."[18] The fact that there were wealthy merchant cliques, successful plantation magnates, philanthropists, and distinguished leaders among the Southern Irish-Americans was irrelevant to Anglophile ignorance.

Under such conditions the Irish communities of the South evolved in a slower and more deliberate way than the larger Irish concentrations in Northern and Western regions. It was 1833, a full century after prominent Irish leaders had emerged in New Orleans, before the Irish had a church of their own. The vitality of the Charleston community declined as that port's fortune receded. In 1860, only eight of the more than 1,800 churches in Georgia were Roman Catholic. Outside of Louisiana and larger urban areas, the religious organization of the scattered Catholics was tenuous at best. An occasional Catholic plantation owner would maintain a tiny religious enclave but the record was very uneven.[19]

Although social handicaps and lack of resources retarded religious development, Southern Catholics did have an episcopal leadership that was educated and committed to an orderly ecclesiastical growth. The folk Catholicism of Ireland was being transformed in both the old country and the United States by increasing regulation and administrative directives. At diocesan synods the bishops of Charleston and Galveston shared a concern for promoting the use of financial accounts, discipline in liturgy

---

[17]Robert Kelley, *The Cultural Pattern in American Politics* (New York, 1979), pp. 172-75.

[18]Francis Anne Kemble, *Journal of a Residence on a Georgia Plantation in 1838-39* (New York, 1961), p. 129.

[19]Niehaus, *The Irish in New Orleans*; Debats, "Elites and Masses," p. 429; John Tracy Ellis, *American Catholicism* (Chicago, 1956), pp. 75-89; Randall M. Miller, "The Failed Mission: The Catholic Church and Black Catholics in the Old South," in Edward Magdol and Jon L. Wakelyn, eds., *The Southern Common People: Studies in Nineteenth-Century Social History* (Westport CT, 1980), pp. 37-54.

and the contracting of marriages, stricter regulation of the clergy, and the encouragement of special devotions. The organizational elaboration of Catholic life was proceeding in spite of the handicaps, and this was a reassuring influence for the scattered Southern Catholics.

Probably the most outstanding Roman Catholic leader in the antebellum South was Bishop John England. Born in County Cork in 1786, he became bishop of Charleston in 1820. He was well-read in Irish history and deeply committed to the advancement of the Irish people. His addresses and writings on Irish subjects revealed not only a rich knowledge and acute judgment about Irish affairs, but a resolution to refute prejudicial opinions and submit the premises of his people's advancement to reasoned and democratic discussion. Bishop England's travels throughout the South made him widely known and respected. In cities like Savannah he even celebrated St. Patrick's Day with religious leaders from the major Protestant denominations. He wrote regularly for his own diocesan newspaper and contributed to others. Whether seeking support for Catholic emancipation in Ireland, seeking aid for his seminary from the seminary in Havana, begging charity for the families of fever victims, or recruiting nuns from France for his early schools, Bishop England worked arduously and intelligently. He was able to administer his diocese with great skill, astutely balancing the English and French priests with the growing number of Irish priests. His qualities of missionary zeal, administrative flexibility, and democratic outlook prefigured Irish-American clerical traits that were to become commonplace in American Catholicism.[20]

New Orleans offers another perspective on the impact of Irish Catholics in a Southern city. In New Orleans the Irish came into a Latin Catholic community already established. As the Irish had in France and Spain for generations before 1800, they adapted readily. A merchant class of Irishmen flourished in the polyglot Gulf metropolis. When the great Irish influx to America swelled in the 1830s, the newer, poorer Irish actually changed the demographic composition of the city. From being predominantly black, it became predominantly foreign-born with the Irish forming more than half the immigrant population. By the eve of the Civil War, out of a population of 168,000, which was eighty percent white, the Irish formed a component of at least one-fourth. Politically and

---

[20]Peter Guilday, *The Life and Times of John England, First Bishop of Charleston, 1786-1840*, 2 vols. (New York, 1927), 1:545; 2:8, 163.

economically this Irish augmentation was very important, but religiously it was decisive, since it challenged the Latin Catholicism that had set the historic social and communal character of the city. In both numbers and ecclesiastical ambitions, the Irish altered the city's Latin heritage and imparted a new kind of Catholicism to it.

The religious energy of the Irish immigrants was not immediately evident because of the poverty and affliction of the group. In their emergence from a rural folk Catholicism to an urban modernized church system, the Irish in New Orleans—and in other cities—were setting a pattern that would have broad effects on American Catholic life. This is one pattern for which documentation exists in numerous places. The more flexible Latin Catholicism, steeped in ties to aristocratic ideas and patronage, and rich with Latin cultural effusion, was displaced by a driving and rigorous religious movement that represented an Irish immigrant vision of free development after centuries of persecution. It was a novel Catholicism for the Irish and for those who beheld it, for it was popularly supported financially and popularly recruited in its leadership and ethnic vitality. It was, for all the European usages with which the Church was structured, distinctly un-European, for it simply lacked a European context. Its context was immigrant, Irish, and American. It was, because of Irish demographic weight and Irish religious and social affinity, a major force in American Catholic history. In New Orleans before the Civil War this process had been begun. Prior to 1860 the three Irish parishes' growing charitable and social groups, schools, and other institutions formed the matrix of the post-Latin Catholic establishment that would dominate the religious life of the city in the future.[21]

The result of this demographic and cultural minority position in an inhospitable region was that Irish Catholics came to be affected in a thoroughgoing way by the local mores. Although they succeeded, where sufficiently numerous, in establishing their own schools, orphanages, hospitals, and auxiliary groups for religious service, they were rarely in a position outside of Louisiana to exercise cultural leadership themselves.

---

[21]Niehaus, *The Irish in New Orleans*, pp. 98-111; Shea, *History of the Catholic Church*, 3:269, 291. For Irish religious development, see Emmet Larkin, "The Devotional Revolution in Ireland, 1850-1875," *American Historical Review* 77 (June 1972): 625-52; and Jay P. Dolan, *The Immigrant Church: New York's Irish and German Catholics, 1815-1865* (Baltimore, 1975), pp. 159-69.

In the border states this was not true, for in Maryland and Missouri there were vigorous Irish Catholic components.[22]

Texas also represented a special case. Texas shared only part of the cultural orientation of the South. Its frontier atmosphere, vast arid prairies, and connection with Hispanic culture made it a distinctive extension to the South proper. The Irish Texans forged several frontier colonies for themselves prior to the Lone Star revolt against Mexico. In the 1830s the San Patricio colony to the north of San Antonio drew Irish immigrants and petitioned for English-speaking priests. The Refugio colony near Corpus Christi, founded by James Power in the 1830s, sought immigrants from Ireland in famine times in the 1840s, but hundreds of those recruited in Ireland died in sea disasters and of disease on the journey to Texas. In these Irish-settled areas, and in the Beaumont-Liberty district, several Catholic chapels served the settlers. Some of these chapels were in ranch houses, and both Hispanic and Irish Catholics worshiped there. Religious practices brought from Ireland persisted in these colonies, such as the strict "Black fast" from all food in Lent, the family rosary at evening, and the presence of statues of Irish saints in the chapels. The Irish Catholics in Texas suffered greatly due to the turbulence of the territory, but they maintained a strong identity and active traditions of social service and charity, as exemplified especially by the career of Margaret Mary Healy-Murphy, foundress of the Holy Ghost Sisters. Irish Catholicism in Texas was more robust than that in many areas of the Old South.[23]

For most of the South, however, the Irish had to be content with a circumspect role. They maintained their identity where education and group ties were possible, but there was no parallel to the political, religious, and social impact they made in other regions.

In the factious politics of the antebellum South, the Irish figured only in a marginal way. Sectionalism and the eccentricities of local pressures effectively baffled Irish combination in the Democratic party, and Whig particularism had the same effect in the strongholds of the Whigs in

---

[22]Ellen Meara Dolan, *St. Louis Irish* (St. Louis, 1967); R. Emmett Curran, "From Mision to Province: 1805-1833,"in *The Maryland Jesuits: 1634-1833* (Baltimore, 1976), pp. 47-68; James Crotty, "Baltimore Immigration" (master's thesis, Catholic University of America, 1951), pp. 20-21.

[23]John B. Flannery, *The Irish Texans* (San Antonio, 1980), pp. 91-96, 103-108, 110-19, 129-32.

Kentucky, Tennessee, Georgia, and western Virginia. In urban areas the group did coalesce on occasion, but rarely sent its members to the level of state office. The minority position of the Irish in such cities as Memphis, for instance, generated resentment among them that proved significant for political activity in the post-Civil War years.[24] The keys to the weak Irish regional political profile were the lack of numerical strength almost everywhere outside of urban areas, and the inability of the group to advance its specific needs in the Southern regional context.

If the Irish were not capable of challenging the existing political alignments, they were on the whole less disposed to challenge slavery. While there were some antislavery Irish in the North, the dean of American Catholic historians says that "wherever they were the Irish adopted the local point of view regarding slavery."[25] Typical of Irish sentiment, Bishop John Quinlan of Mobile declared in 1861, "We must cut adrift from the North in many things of intimate social conditions— we of the South have been too long on leading strings."[26] This statement well illustrates the sectional mentality the Irish as a whole adopted.

Still, some Irish dissented from the proslavery outlook of their countrymen in the South. Much of what is known of Irish views in the South derived from travellers and commentators with little regard for the Irish or the contradictions of their local situations. Irish landholders in the South did not usually hold slaves themselves. Thus fifty families from Tipperary in Taliaferro County, Georgia, worked their own land successfully without slaves. While there were few such as Michael Healy, father of a Catholic bishop of mixed blood, who married blacks, there was a stubborn representation of Irish, Catholic and Protestant, who were at least pro-Union, and in a few cases sympathetic to moderate antislavery arguments. Their presence suggests that where the Irish had the benefits

---

[24]Ralph Wooster, *Politicians, Planters, and Plain Folks: Courthouse and Statehouse in the Upper South, 1850-1860* (Knoxville TN, 1975), p. 32; Kelley, *Cultural Patterns in American Politics*, p. 175; Debats, "Elites and Masses," p. 436; Joseph P. O'Grady, "Immigrants and the Politics of Reconstruction in Richmond, Virginia," *Records of the American Catholic Historical Society* 83 (1972): 87-101.

[25]Ellis, *American Catholicism*, p. 89. See also Robert A. Sigafoos, *Cotton Row to Beale Street: A Business History of Memphis* (Memphis, 1979), pp. 39-40.

[26]Quinlan to Bishop Patrick Lynch, 19 May 1861, Lynch Papers (Archives of the Diocese of Charleston).

of education, the hostility to blacks attributed to them was not at all automatic.[27]

Even as they blended into the regional consensus, however, the Irish retained their identity. By 1860, they had established their basic Catholic institutional network, thin though it was regionally. There were many examples of individual success, and group ties were nurtured. Southern Irish-Americans followed closely the activities of Daniel O'Connell's Repeal Associations, welcomed exiled nationalist leaders such as John Mitchel, and kept nationalistic aspirations alive in the years prior to the time when the Fenian Brotherhood would coordinate nationalist undertakings. The preexistence or swift creation of special Irish units for service with the Confederacy revealed the persistent group identity among the Irish, and the group's need to manifest its loyalty to the region. Not only did Mobile's bishop bless the banners of the Emerald Guards, but Irish units fought bravely in the Civil War.[28]

Thus, while the Irish were not numerous enough or distinctive enough to shape Southern institutions in the way they deeply affected labor, politics, religion, and urban growth in the North and West, they still defined an identity for themselves within the context of Southern life.

The antebellum presence of the Irish in the South also had long-range implications in two areas of further development. The communities and facilities built in this period formed the nuclei around which a much stronger network later was constructed with continuous aid from the large Irish Catholic centers in the North. The South's Irish also entered into collaboration with the Irish-American nationalist organizations that would steadily pursue Irish independence through agitation in the United States after the Civil War.

---

[27]Clement Eaton, *The Freedom-of-Thought Struggle in the Old South* (New York, 1964), pp. 249, 385-91.

[28]Lonn, *Foreigners in the Confederacy*, p. 31; Cosgrave, "The Hibernian Society of Charleston," pp. 150-58.

CATHOLIC ELITES IN
THE SLAVEHOLDING SOUTH

by Jon L. Wakelyn

$\mathbf{R}$ecent revisionist historical works have concluded that in order to protect their way of life the Southern elites had to secede from the Union. A particular world view based on their business interests, their class-based ideological commitment to such a way of life, and their cultural and religious values led them to support secession.[1] A few historians have demurred from this view. Some have claimed that the business elite had conflicting interests that may have divided them over secession, and others believe that some elites feared the revolutionary implications of secession enough to hesitate in their actions.[2] Few, however, deny that the elites require further study, especially as regards their increasing sense of being part of a minority section.

Right beside the dominant Protestant planter power structure lived

---

[1]Eugene Genovese, *The Political Economy of Slavery: Studies in the Economy & Society of the Slave South* (New York, 1965); *The World the Slaveholders Made* (New York, 1969), pp. 103-17.

[2]Carl Degler, *The Other South: Southern Dissenters in the Nineteenth Century* (New York, 1974); David Potter, *The South and the Sectional Conflict* (Baton Rouge, 1968), p. 257.

Catholic elites who knew what it meant to be a minority within their own minority section. Catholic elites had lived in the slaveholding states long before any self-conscious Southernism existed. Their roots went back into Maryland to the beginning of the American settlement. They had been part of a slaveholding elite from the earliest existence of domestic slavery and retained wealth and status to the Civil War. In the Old South—that Protestant, rural, often isolated, and increasingly minority-conscious section—some Catholics came into great wealth, owned plantations, had successful business and professional careers, and held political office. Many of them simultaneously identified with the region's values, ideals, and interests, and yet held fast to their own religious views. Fears of changing political structures, economic upheaval, and regional shifts also influenced the activities of that minority within a minority. Many factors went into developing identity and loyalty, and the Catholics had the added burden of just how they related to the dominant religious system, making them even more sensitive to their regional identification and cultural values. A look at Catholic elites in the various Southern subregions—in business, politics, and culture—at how they became Southern, and at their activities in the sectional struggle might tell us how they survived and thrived in that Old South cultural and political atmosphere that was becoming so narrow and hostile.

The first and perhaps most important aspect of Southern Catholic elite life is that it rose and fell in the slaveholding regions as those regions contracted and expanded as a result of internal migration, immigration, and changes in the economy. English Catholic elites first settled in colonial Maryland where they lived primarily in the southern counties and Annapolis. After the War of 1812, Maryland's Catholic population center shifted north to Baltimore because of the influx of southern Maryland Catholics and Irish and German Catholic migration from Europe. After the Revolutionary period, Maryland Catholics also moved west to the fertile lands of Kentucky and later Missouri. They tended to settle together, first in the farm lands around Bardstown, Kentucky, and later along the Mississippi and Missouri Rivers. With the westward migration of German and Irish Catholics, largely into the urban centers of Louisville and St. Louis, many of the original Catholic settlers became an ethnic minority among their coreligionists. The Catholic elites in the border slave states witnessed a clash between old and new settlers and a shift from a predominantly slaveowning agricultural society to urban commerce and manufacturing.

In the Southeast, English Catholics had early settled the Virginia, North Carolina, and South Carolina coastal towns and plantation regions. A few Virginia Catholics became great planters and had family and business ties to southern Maryland Catholics. Although the antebellum migration of German and Irish Catholics into southeastern towns also presented a dilemma for those older Catholic families, the commercial-agricultural system remained the same.

Along the Gulf Coast, especially in Louisiana, long before the Americans purchased the territory, French, Spanish, and a few Irish Catholic families had made up the financial wealth, the social elite, and the politically powerful. There Catholics vied with one another for power and prestige. By the antebellum period, many Protestants had moved into those Gulf Coast Catholic strongholds. Also during the antebellum days, Irish and German Catholics settled in the cities and created ethnic divisions among the Catholics. Although a significant landowning, slave-holding, merchant, and professional class, old Catholics had lost their majority.

In order to understand the magnitude of the changes to the elites in Southern Catholic regions, one must look at the regions separately and over the entire history of the Old South. No slaveholding region boasted an older Catholic elite than that of Maryland where they succeeded as planters and merchants. In the eighteenth century they had lost the right to participate in public life; so, families such as the Carrolls, Taneys, and Brents put their energies into business. Kept from religious practice and church education, those families became increasingly clannish. They intermarried, held private religious services secretly in their homes for themselves and poorer Catholics, and sent their children to secluded private schools and to the College of St. Omer in Flanders. At those schools the young elites reaffirmed their faith, gained a classical education suited to men who would hold important business and public positions, and made contacts with European and American counterparts who later traded goods and served with them in important offices.[3]

Those rich Maryland Catholics came to prominence during the American Revolution. Intensely loyal to the colonies, southern Maryland Catholic elites defended coastal towns and family plantations. Charles Carroll, the brilliant and wealthy leader of the southern Maryland

---

[3]John Tracy Ellis, *Catholics in Colonial America* (Baltimore, 1965), p. 319; John Thomas Scharf, *The Chronicles of Baltimore* (Baltimore, 1879), p. 27.

Catholic community, spoke for the right of independence and assisted in ending religious restrictions for holding office.[4] Because of his role in the Maryland non-importation proceedings, he was elected to the local committee of correspondence and to the Maryland constitutional convention. As a member of the Continental Congress, he was the only Catholic to sign the Declaration of Independence.[5]

When Daniel Carroll, Maryland's representative to the Constitutional Convention and a wealthy planter cousin of Charles Carroll, asked for advice on the proper form of government from his cousin, Charles's response revealed the influence of Catholic thought on his political opinions. Charles favored a religious toleration plank, supported a permanent chief executive, and rejected what he believed were democratic excesses in the new government. He also acted as a rich planter when he advocated restricting suffrage "to persons possessed of 150 acres of land in fee simple."[6] Well aware of previous majority prejudice, Maryland's Catholic elites desired specific protection for themselves, which was reflected in their conservative positions on the Constitution. In the new state government and in the federal Congress, the Carrolls, their relative Thomas Sim Lee, and John Eager Howard all were Federalists.[7]

The patriarch of Maryland Catholics, Charles Carroll of Carrollton, remained a wealthy planter, but spent more and more of his time with his business investments in Annapolis, Baltimore, and Washington. In old age, his circle of Catholic friends and family increasingly occupied his thoughts. He watched as his children married outside the Church, and when his son turned to drink, he sought solace in religious works. But he also managed his own plantation, gave religious and educational instruction to his slaves, and worried about slavery's future in his part of the South. One biographer called him a conservative abolitionist, yet slavery

[4]Mary Virginia Geiger, *Daniel Carroll. A Framer of the Constitution* (Washington, 1943), p. 26; Daniel Barber, *The History of My Own Times*, 3 vols. (Washington, 1827-1832); Scharf, *Chronicles*, p. 66.

[5]Thomas O'Brien Hanley, *Charles Carroll of Carrollton* (Washington, 1970); Thomas M. Field, ed., *Unpublished Letters of Charles Carroll of Carrollton* (New York, 1902), pp. 143-66.

[6]Celestine Joseph Nuesse, *The Social Thought of American Catholics, 1634-1829* (Washington, 1945), pp. 47, 59-62, 78; Philip A. Crowl, ed., "Charles Carroll's Plan of Government," *American Historical Review* 46 (1940-1941): 588-95.

[7]Nuesse, *Social Thought of American Catholics*, p. 55; *A Memoir of the Late John Eager Howard* (Baltimore, 1863).

was woven into the fabric of the life that he loved. And Carroll had always feared that he would set a poor example for other planters if he freed slaves who had no place to go. Perhaps that is why he joined other Southeastern planters in support of the American Colonization Society. Carroll had also grown to despise Jeffersonian Republicanism, and he bitterly opposed party politics. At the last, he described himself as a Southern planter, and he maintained the manners, courtliness, and clannish regard for family, and community loyalty that distinguished his class.[8]

Until the War of 1812, which Carroll actively supported, the Catholic elites continued to expand their commercial and agricultural holdings. But the war led to the destruction of many of those great estates by rendering the tobacco market destitute, which shifted commercial power to Baltimore. Leading Carroll lieutenants, such as the young Roger Brooke Taney, descendant of a Catholic family that had come to Maryland in 1660, left southern Maryland to practice law in Frederick and later in Baltimore. Taney realized that both the city and the state had changed in population and in economic interests; so, he joined the Jackson party and in 1828 became the Jacksonian Democratic leader in Maryland.[9] The world of Charles Carroll was rapidly coming to an end.

Taney's business and political patterns were reflective of what was happening to other southern Maryland Catholic elites. Many moved to Baltimore, Kentucky, Missouri, and parts of the Southwest. Basil Elder, Raphael Semmes and his cousins, and a Carroll left their ancestral homes to settle in the plantation lands of the Southwest. Basil Spalding Elder, the only member of his family who did not go to Kentucky, moved to Baltimore, succeeded in merchandising, and was a trustee of the cathedral.[10]

In Baltimore, Elder not only had business connections with Charles Carroll but he also dealt with new settlers to the city such as the Irish-born Luke Tiernan and the Charleston-born William George Read. Tiernan

---

[8]Kate Mason Rowland, *Life and Letters of Charles Carroll of Carrollton*, 2 vols. (New York, 1898), 2: 358; Daniel Brent to Charles Carroll, 22 November 1828; Charles Carroll to Charles Carroll of Homewood, 19 October 1826, (microfilm) Charles Carroll Papers (Library of Congress).

[9]Whitman H. Ridgeway, *Community Leadership in Maryland, 1790-1840* (Chapel Hill NC, 1979), pp. 17, 48-49; Carl Brent Swisher, *Roger Brooke Taney* (New York, 1935), pp. 3-51.

[10]Nuesse, *Social Thought of American Catholics*, pp. 163-69.

emigrated as a youth, worked his way through Mount St. Mary's College in Emmitsburg, and rose as a successful shipowner and importer of dry goods. This wealthy conservative Whig held minor political office. Tiernan also joined Charles Carroll in building the cathedral, served as trustee of the cathedral, and hired poor Irish laborers. Read, son of the Charleston Federalist Jacob Read, moved to Baltimore in 1822, where he studied law in the office of Robert Goodloe Harper, son-in-law of Charles Carroll. Along with his fellow Democrat William Jenkins, descendant of a southern Maryland Catholic family, Read published an *Address to the Catholic Voters of Baltimore*, in which he castigated John Quincy Adams's supporters for attempting to curry favor with Catholic voters. Fearful of Whig appeals to immigrant voters, Jenkins and Read wanted to organize those voters into a local Catholic party.[11]

Other issues soon occupied Maryland's Catholic elite. For along with the shift in location, business interests, and ethnic composition, they faced the rise of sectionalism that so divided the nation. Although few business reasons remained for Maryland Catholics to continue an attachment to the slaveholding South, the leaders of the 1850s were mixed in their support for Southern sectionalism. The career of Benjamin Chew Howard, whose father had been a Federalist and whose Chew ancestors were large slaveholders, is an example of both the business and social interests that made some of them unionists. Howard studied at Princeton, practiced law in Baltimore, invested in merchant trade, and with the support of immigrants, whom he at first disdained, had a distinguished career as a Democrat in the U. S. Congress. In 1839, he retired to private life, only to be called back to run for governor in 1861 against the Know-Nothing candidate. As a delegate to the Washington Peace Conference, Howard vigorously defended the Union.[12]

Other Maryland Catholics with historical ties to slave society were thoroughly Southern in their values and life-styles and supported the South in the sectional controversy. Roger Brooke Taney, perhaps because of excessive governmental powers and untoward Northern attacks on

---

[11]William Jenkins, et al., *An Address to the Catholic Voters of Maryland* (Baltimore, 1828); Edward F. X. McSweeney, *The Story of the Mountain*, 2 vols. (Emmitsburg MD, 1911), esp. vol. 1.

[12]Jean H. Baker, *The Politics of Continuity: Maryland Political Parties from 1858 to 1870* (Baltimore, 1973), pp. 50, 68-69; J. D. Warfield, *The Founders of Howard and Anne Arundel Counties* (Baltimore, 1905).

slavery, sympathized with the plight of the South. In the Dred Scott case and in countless other cases, Chief Justice Taney supported those who opposed oppressive central government. According to his biographer, Taney had once been a colonizer, but in later years he had come to believe "that a general and sudden emancipation would be absolute ruin to negroes, as well as to the white people." "It is difficult," he claimed, "for anyone who has not lived in a slaveholding State to comprehend the relations which exist between the slaves and their masters." Taney was too old to give aid to Maryland's disunionists, but he hoped that the government would allow the South to separate peacefully. His last action as chief justice was his decision in the Merryman case where he opposed Lincoln's attempt to coerce local rights.[13]

John Lee Carroll, great-grandson of Charles Carroll and of Thomas Sim Lee, secretly supported the Southern Confederacy. Carroll was educated at local Catholic schools and at Harvard, and he was a successful Baltimore lawyer. In 1859, he left Maryland to practice law in New York, but he soon returned to the ancestral plantation, Doughoregan Manor in Howard County, due to his father's illness. The perceptive English journalist William Howard Russell found the Carroll family very Southern and very Catholic. The genteel Carrolls had held on to the past, and Russell summed up their arguments for secession as support for "the sovereign independence and right of every state in the Union." The Carrolls resolved to wage war to protect "their institutions and their reputations and honour."[14]

Kentucky's antebellum Catholic elites followed a similar pattern to those of Maryland. After the American Revolution many native Maryland Catholics emigrated there, drawn by the opportunities for rich farm and plantation lands. They built Bardstown, supported the clergy, founded schools and colleges, and, in many cases, became successful planters. One of them, Robert Abell, gained election from the Catholic settlement to the convention that formed the state government. This lawyer and planter served in the state legislature and was prominent in the constitutional convention of 1799.[15]

---

[13]Swisher, *Taney*, p. 458; Baker, *Politics*, pp. 67, 70.

[14]*Biographical Cyclopedia of Representative Men of Maryland and the District of Columbia* (Baltimore, 1879), pp. 441-42; William Howard Russell, *My Diary North and South* (New York, 1863), pp. 183-84.

[15]Mary Ramona Mattingly, *The Catholic Church on the Kentucky Frontier* (Washing-

During the early nineteenth century Kentucky's Catholics shifted from the agricultural region to the merchant-trade community of Louisville. Irish- and German-born settlers soon vied with the Maryland Catholics for positions of political and financial leadership. The Catholics who remained on the land were not large slaveowners. A few elite planters held seats in the legislature, although it is unlikely that the rural Catholic population was large enough to influence their activities.[16]

Perhaps because of the ethnic composition, the advantages of Louisville, and the decline in slaveowners, Kentucky's Catholic leaders rarely supported Southern sectional views. For example, Clement S. Hill, who attended St. Mary's College and practiced law in Louisville, fought the nativists in the state legislature and supported the Union in 1861. Hill had built a political following among Louisville's Catholic population strong enough to send him to Congress.[17]

The career pattern of Kentucky's famous Catholic man of letters, Benedict Webb, divulges the reasons why Kentucky Catholics appeared to have little feeling for the Southern cause. Webb's father Nehemiah had settled in Bardstown around 1800 and had established a mill. Before there were churches in the region, priests said Mass in his home. The brilliant Ben graduated from St. Joseph's College and entered the printing trade. He was foreman of the Louisville *Journal*, worked on local Bardstown papers, and, in 1836, was named publisher of the diocesan *Catholic Advocate*. He moved the paper to Louisville in 1841 to counter anti-Catholic feelings in the city. Webb often wrote against the nativists and vividly described anti-Catholic riots. From 1858 to 1861, he edited the *Guardian*, where he supported the bishop's neutrality on secession, and urged Kentuckians to support the Union. He simply had no business or social relations with what remained of Kentucky's slaveowning community.[18]

---

ton, 1936), pp. 17-36; Benedict J. Webb, *The Centenary of Catholicity in Kentucky* (Louisville, 1884), pp. 45, 49, 60, 67, 74, 102.

[16]Martin J. Spalding, *Sketches of Early Catholic Missions of Kentucky* (Louisville, 1844), pp. 17-26; Josiah Stoddard Johnston, *Memorial History of Louisville*, 2 vols. (Chicago, 1897).

[17]E. Merton Coulter, *Civil War and Reconstruction in Kentucky* (Chapel Hill NC, 1926), pp. 18-56; Webb, *Centenary*, pp. 304, 394, 485.

[18]Madeleine Hooke Rice, *American Catholic Opinion in the Slavery Controversy* (New York, 1944), pp. 74-75; Webb, *Centenary*, p. 497; Benedict J. Webb, *The Catholic Question in Politics* (Louisville, 1856); Eugene P. Willging and Herta Hatzfeld, *Catholic Serials of the Nineteenth Century United States* (Washington, 1966), pp. 6-7.

Except for the French influence, antebellum Missouri largely followed the pattern of Maryland and Kentucky. St. Louis, a fur-trading French Catholic village, attracted Maryland and later Kentucky Catholic settlers when the territory opened around 1800. French-speaking Catholics had already grown wealthy in that frontier community. One of them, Colonel Auguste Chouteau, helped to lay out the site for the nineteenth-century town, while his partner, Bernard Pratte, owned much of the town's best land. When Missouri entered the Union in 1821, a sizable Maryland and Kentucky proslavery element had joined the French to make St. Louis into a commercial center and to construct plantations along the Mississippi and Missouri rivers.[19]

St. Louis soon attracted Irish and German settlers from the urban East and Europe. The richest Irish-born Catholic, John Mullanphy, amassed his large fortune in real estate and used much of his wealth to build churches and St. Louis University. Mullanphy's son, Bryan, was a judge and political leader of the Catholic community and eventually was elected mayor, where he opposed nativism. When he died in 1851, the younger Mullanphy left his fortune to the city's Catholic poor.[20]

Few of Missouri's late antebellum Catholic immigrants succeeded in business or politics. They did not develop many ties to Missouri's Southern Catholic leaders. Most of the farmers were German immigrants who lived near St. Charles County and along the Maries River; few of them owned slaves. In St. Louis a number of immigrant Catholics emerged from poverty into the middle classes through trade and political organizations like the German-Roman Catholic Benevolent Society.[21] Those immigrants did support the pro-Southern Democratic party, largely because it opposed nativism. They were unable or unwilling to support secession, perhaps because they had not adjusted to Southern ways.[22]

---

[19]Eliher Shepard, *The Early History of St. Louis and Missouri* (St. Louis, 1870), p. 80; Perry McCandless, *A History of Missouri, 1820-1860* (Columbia MO, 1972), p. 13; John Rothensteiner, *A History of the Archdiocese of St. Louis*, 2 vols. (St. Louis, 1928), 1:272-74.

[20]Rothensteiner, *Archdiocese of St. Louis*, 1:260, 450; Shepard, *Early History of St. Louis*, pp. 93-113.

[21]Rothensteiner, *Archdiocese of St. Louis*, 2:472, 454-55; Sister Audry Olson, "The Nature of an Immigrant Community: St. Louis Germans, 1850-1920," *Missouri Historical Review* 66 (1972): 342-59.

[22]William Roes, "Secessionist Strength in Missouri," *Missouri Historical Review* 72 (1978): 412-23.

Their leaders—Missouri's Catholic elite planters, lawyers, and urban businessmen—divided in their support for the Union. The Church remained neutral in the sectional struggle, leaving the elites to follow their own interests and values. One typical Catholic leader, Wilson Primm, born in Kentucky and a graduate of St. Joseph's College, was a conservative Whig lawyer from St. Louis, who remained neutral when the war broke out. But the prominent Hannibal lawyer and planter, William Mordecai Cooke, descendant of a rich Virginia family, was a secessionist. As a leader of the Catholic immigrant population, Cooke persuaded many of them to support the Confederacy. Cooke claimed to stand for secession because he identified with the slaveowning values of his Virginia heritage.[23]

Like Maryland's Catholics, Southeastern Catholics date back to the earliest colonial settlements along the Atlantic Coast. But their numbers were always small. Virginia had only 300 Catholic families on the eve of the Revolution; only a few of them had become planters or businessmen. Once the new state of Virginia lifted restrictions on Catholic officeholding, Richard Brent, a nephew of Maryland's Daniel Carroll and the descendant of seventeenth-century Virginia landed wealth, participated in the Revolution. Brent, a lawyer, was elected to a seat in the House of Delegates. He later served as a Republican in both the United States House and Senate. Perhaps because he felt isolated as a Catholic in Virginia, in his last years Brent's business interests took him to Baltimore and Washington. Antebellum Virginia also lost the services of that gifted man's family and relatives, as all of Brent's children moved to Baltimore or Washington, where they could send their children to Catholic schools and have the opportunity to particpate in the commercial growth of those port towns.[24]

Few Catholic elites lived in antebellum Virginia. Most of the Catholic population consisted of working-class immigrants from Richmond and Norfolk. With the migration of Irish and German Catholics into late antebellum Virginia towns, their numbers increased, and by 1860 Catho-

[23]Jasper W. Cross, "The St. Louis Catholic Press and Political Issues, 1845-1861," *Records of the American Catholic Historical Society* 80 (1964): 210-23; William Van Ness Bay, *Reminiscences of the Bench and Bar in Missouri* (St. Louis, 1878).

[24]James S. Easby-Smith, *Georgetown University*, 2 vols. (New York, 1907), 1: 27, 37, 43, 46, 65, 72, 94, 102.

lics made up one-fourth of Richmond's population.[25] Those Catholics who did rise to prominence strongly supported their adopted state's sectional politics. Perhaps they felt the pressure of being outsiders, or their social and business interests were intricately tied to the South.

The most famous of Virginia's antebellum Catholics was the newspaperman-politician, Anthony M. Keiley. Raised in Petersburg, where his father was principal of a Catholic seminary, Keiley was editor of the *South-Side Democrat*. Although his father left the family and the Church, Anthony and his brother Benjamin, who later became bishop of Savannah, remained lifelong Catholics. Anthony entered politics to defend Catholics against the Know-Nothings who had claimed that Catholics opposed slavery. He led the Hibernian Society and, after his removal to Richmond in the mid-1850s, founded another Irish political club. A National Democrat, he supported Stephen A. Douglas for President in 1860. Yet, when Virginia seceded, he followed his state.[26]

Similar to Virginia's Catholic experience, colonial North Carolina's small Catholic population huddled mainly on the coastal region in the village of Newbern. Without a priest, under religious restrictions for officeholding and schooling, and with no native Catholic population to speak of, North Carolina's Catholic elites had little role in the Revolution. One important Catholic Revolutionary, James White, was originally from Philadelphia. White had attended the College of St. Omer, studied medicine at the University of Pennsylvania, and eventually clerked in a Philadelphia law office. He moved to North Carolina to practice law, served in the post-Revolutionary General Assembly, and held office in Congress. But North Carolina was just a way station for White and other ambitious members of that small Catholic community. Named superintendent of Indian affairs in Tennessee, he later held office in the territorial legislature before moving on to Louisiana in 1799. There he was judge of the Attahopac district. His son was a governor of Louisiana and his

---

[25]F. Joseph Magri, *The Catholic Church in the City and Diocese of Richmond* (Richmond, 1906), pp. 46-61, 88-89; Joseph P. O'Grady, "Immigrants and the Politics of Reconstruction in Richmond," *Records of the American Catholic Historical Society* 83 (1972): 87-101; David R. Goldfield, *Urban Growth in the Age of Sectionalism: Virginia, 1847-1861* (Baton Rouge, 1977), pp. 65, 125.

[26]W. Asbury Christian, *Richmond* (Richmond, 1912), pp. 200-50; Joseph P. O'Grady, "Anthony M. Keiley," *Catholic Historical Review* 54 (1968-1969): 613-35.

grandson, Edward Douglas White, became an associate justice and later chief justice of the United States Supreme Court.[27]

Among those Catholic elites who remained, the most eminent post-Revolutionary figure was the lawyer-jurist William Gaston. The first student at Georgetown University and a graduate of Princeton, he studied law under the historian and judge Francis Xavier Martin and began his law practice in Newbern with his brother-in-law, Judge John T. Lewis. From a prominent landed family, the conservative Gaston served as a Federalist in the state house and senate before entering the United States House in 1812. A legalist who felt that laws could protect minorities, Gaston made a speech in the House in which he stated that "the end of regulations in society where a majority governs, is to limit the power of the majority and to secure the few from the oppression of the many."[28] No doubt his experience as a member of a minority made him sensitive to an excess of democracy.

Gaston left political office in 1817 to pursue his legal practice and Catholic philanthropic duties. His 1832 *Address before the Dialectic and Philanthropic Societies* of the University of North Carolina reflected what many of the state's old elites felt about slavery. Gaston spoke of the importance of the work ethic, admonished wealthy youth to understand their roles in public life, and blamed "slavery, which, more than any other cause, keeps us back in the career of improvement."[29] There was anti-Catholic reaction to Gaston's views on slavery, and he was forced to temper his criticisms out of fear of calling attention to his coreligionists. In the state constitutional convention of 1835 he made a "Plea for Toleration" for religious minorities. He concluded, "I am opposed, out and out, to any interference of the State with the *opinion* of its citizens, and more especially with their opinions on Religious subjects."[30] Gaston returned to public life as chief justice of the North Carolina Supreme

---

[27]Henry A. Bullard, *A Discourse on the Life of Francis Xavier Martin* (Philadelphia, 1850); Lewis S. Cassidy, *The Catholic Ancestry of Chief Justice White* (Philadelphia, 1927).

[28]*Annals of Congress* (Washington, 1817), 29:717; Joseph H. Schauinger, *William Gaston, Carolinian* (Milwaukee, 1945), pp. 200-209.

[29]William Gaston, *Address Before the Dialectic and Philanthropic Societies* (Chapel Hill NC, 1832).

[30]William Gaston, *A Plea for Toleration* (Raleigh NC, 1835), p. 5.

Court. All his life he was cautiously critical of his state, but loyal to local rights and to slights against the society to which he belonged.

The judge also believed in the Catholic Church and aided the rising generation of North and South Carolina Catholic elites by providing legal advice and funding for the Church and Catholic youth. A close friend of Bishop John England of Charleston, he entertained traveling priests and helped to build the first Catholic church in Newbern. Along with other prominent Catholics, such as the lawyers John Devereaux and Mathias Manly, he assisted in permanently settling a priest in North Carolina in 1824. Gaston also sent his children and his nephew to Catholic Mount St. Mary's College in Maryland.[31]

If North Carolina had only a few prominent Catholics, colonial South Carolina had a sizable and diverse Catholic population. When Revolutionary South Carolina lifted religious restrictions on officeholding, the sons of Catholic merchants, low country planters, and lawyers took active part in public life. Catholics served in the state assembly and the Continental Congress. They also held important line commands in the state militia during the war. One Catholic Federalist reached the United States Senate, and another became a judge and later a congressman. But the Catholic elites soon decreased in numbers, and many went north or west to pursue their careers in friendlier atmospheres.[32]

The Catholic population stagnated during the national period, although revolutions in Ireland, France, and Santo Domingo brought a number to the state. Many of those immigrants were lost to the Church due to the absence of priests and intermarriage with Protestants. During the 1820s Catholics again began to settle in South Carolina. Bishop John England came to Charleston to minister to the growing Catholic population. He established the *United States Catholic Miscellany* in the 1820s. Not only did England expand the Church, but he also instructed Catholic slaveowners on adequate treatment of slaves, deplored both slavery and abolitionism, and implored Southern Catholics to support their section. England felt the sting of religious prejudice when he was forced to close his school and later made to apologize publicly to the citizenry for

---

[31]Peter K. Guilday, *The Life and Times of John England, First Bishop of Charleston,* 2 vols.(New York, 1927), 1:500-30; Jeremiah J. O'Connell, *Catholicity in the Carolinas and Georgia* (New York, 1879), pp. 405-20.

[32]Charleston *Courier,* 1 August 1816; John Belton O'Neall, *Biographical Sketches of the Bench and Bar of South Carolina,* 2 vols. (Charleston, 1859), 1:35-38.

questioning the place of slavery in Southern life. After that, the bishop turned the magazine toward a defense of slavery.[33]

Only a few of antebellum South Carolina's Catholics managed to rise in public and business life. John Lynch, son of an Irish immigrant and brother of Patrick Lynch, the third bishop of Charleston, was educated in Charleston parochial schools and was a successful Columbia physician. Irish-born William McKenna emigrated to Lancaster disrict, where he acquired a fortune in retail trade, bought slaves, and succeeded as a planter. Thoroughly assimilated to the values of the community, in the state legislature McKenna was a strong Southern rights advocate. Also Irish-born, Thomas J. Coglan settled in Sumter district, where he established a grist mill and iron foundry. He never lost his distinctive accent nor his love for the Church, even as he acquired Southern values. As mayor of Sumter, he provided materiel for the Confederate war effort. Evidently, those up-country elites felt great loyalty to their adopted communities.[34]

Low country South Carolina had a number of prominent converts to the faith. Ellison Keitt, brother of Governor Lawrence M. Keitt, married into a Catholic family and converted. After the wealthy Charlestonian Susan Bellinger converted, she persuaded her brother John and some of her Northrop cousins to join the Church. John Bellinger was an eminent lawyer-businessman and a state legislator. Lucius Bellinger Northrop was the state's most famous Catholic convert. Born into a notable Charleston family, Northrop went to West Point, became a close friend of Jefferson Davis, and retired from the army in 1839. He studied medicine. When the Civil War broke out, he entered Confederate service as President Davis's commissary general.[35]

It appears that Catholic elites, cradle and convert alike, were imbued with the South Carolina secessionist spirit. Bishop Lynch was a virulent secessionist, and he no doubt influenced many of his coreligionists. To read the *Catholic Miscellany* during the late antebellum period is to read a paper thoroughly in the spirit of Southern nationalism. It reflected the

[33]Guilday, *England*, 2:471; Sebastian C. Messmer, ed., *The Works of the Right Reverend John England*, 7 vols. (Cleveland, 1980), 4:318.

[34]O'Connell, *Catholicity in the Carolinas and Georgia*, pp. 135, 240, 297, 304-25.

[35]Thomas R. Hay, "Lucius B. Northrop, Commissary General of the Confederacy," *Civil War History* 9 (1936): 5-23.

Catholic elites' Southern values, their identification with business interests, and their devotion to the life-style of the plantation gentry.

Last of the south Atlantic coast colonies to be settled, Georgia also had few Catholics. After Savannah developed as a commercial center, some Catholics did emigrate to the state. By 1850, there were enough small farmers and urban laborers to establish the diocese of Savannah. One significant Catholic leader was Irish-born Patrick Walsh who attended Georgetown University, and started his career as a journeyman printer. As editor of the diocesan newspaper, he supported Bishop Augustin Verot's defense of Southern rights. Walsh eventually parlayed his talents as editor-publisher and his staunch support for the Confederacy into election to the United States Senate.[36]

Unlike other slaveholding colonies, the Gulf coastal regions of Alabama, Mississippi, and Louisiana did not belong to England and had a dominant French and Spanish colonial culture. Planters and merchants in the port towns, Catholic elites held all political offices and controlled most of the economy during the colonial period. After the American purchase of the territory in 1803, the territories of Alabama and Mississippi experienced an influx of Protestants who rendered the Catholics a minority population. Although the ablest of Mobile's 2,000 antebellum Catholics succeeded in business and attained prominent social places, after the Protestants arrived the old Catholic families declined in public prominence.[37]

One Irish immigrant eventually became mayor of Mobile, while another, Theodore O'Hara, edited a newspaper and wrote poetry. O'Hara's career particularly reveals the role of the Southern Catholic politician-intellectual in the romance of the Old South. Born in Danville, Kentucky, to a father who had escaped Ireland during the conspiracy of 1798, the younger O'Hara doted on his father's exploits. His father, a schoolteacher, married into a prominent Maryland Catholic family, which enabled him to send Theodore to St. Joseph's College in Bards-

[36]O'Connell, *Catholicity in the Carolinas and Georgia*, pp. 577-600; Michael V. Gannon, *Rebel Bishop* (Milwaukee, 1964), pp. 54, 74; [Augustin Verot], *Tract for the Times* (Baltimore, 1861).

[37]Michael Kenny, *Catholic Culture in Alabama* (New York, 1931), pp. 49, 98, 201; William Russell Smith, *Reminiscences of a Long Life* (Washington, 1889); William M. Sweeny, "Theodore O'Hara, Author of 'The Bivouac of the Dead,' " *Journal of the American-Irish Historical Society* 25 (1926): 202.

town. Well connected to the Kentucky elite, young O'Hara clerked in a Louisville law office, where he became the lifelong friend of his fellow clerk, John C. Breckinridge. O'Hara became dissatisfied with the practice of law and volunteered for the Mexican War. During the war he composed "The Bivouac of the Dead," a prime example of Southern romantic martial poetry. O'Hara longed for a more Southern society and shortly moved to Mobile. There he edited a paper and schemed with other Gulf Coast imperialists to spread slavery into the Caribbean and Latin America. In 1860, he supported secession, and he backed up his views by becoming a colonel in the 12th Alabama Regiment.[38]

Raphael Semmes, another upper South Catholic who lived near Mobile, gave great dignity to fellow Catholics because of his naval exploits during the Mexican War. Born into a prominent Charles County, Maryland, planter family, upon his father's death, Semmes was raised by an uncle in Georgetown. Young Raphael entered the navy, rose to important command, and bought a plantation, Prospect Hill, near Mobile. Because he wanted his children to have the benefit of education at the prestigious Spring Hill College in Mobile, and because he could practice law, Semmes moved to Mobile where he rose to the leadership of the Catholic community. Active in church affairs, close to the bishop, Semmes was a major benefactor of Spring Hill College. He regarded Spring Hill, a Catholic institution, as a preparation for leadership for Catholics and Protestants alike.[39]

Like Mobile, the Mississippi port towns of Biloxi and Pass Christian lost their Spanish and French heritage. Without spiritual guidance the Mississippi Catholic community dwindled in numbers. During the early decades of the nineteenth century, however, Catholic families from Ireland and the upper South moved into the upstate river towns of Vicksburg and Natchez. Most of the wealthy Catholics wanted to build churches and encourage the settlement of priests for their towns. But the communities could not support a church until 1841. By 1850, there were over 5,000 Catholics in the diocese of Natchez, made up mostly of poor

---

[38]Sweeny, "Theodore O'Hara," p. 203.

[39]Oscar H. Libscomb, "The Administration of John Quinlan, Second Bishop of Mobile," *Records of the American Catholic Historical Society* 78 (1967): 34-47; Raphael Semmes to William B. Preston, 4 October 1849, Raphael Semmes Letterbook (Library of Congress).

Irish and German workers on the railroads and levees. Few of them managed to rise out of poverty.[40]

Still, some Catholics distinguished themselves in business and public life. For example, Pierre Becker, a poor immigrant, left New Orleans in 1847 to work on the railroad near Brookhaven. Becker soon owned the general merchandise store, assisted many Irish railroad workers, and helped to establish a Catholic church. Francis C. Semmes, a Maryland Catholic, settled in Lauderdale County, where he owned over 1,000 acres and many slaves. The richest antebellum Mississippi Catholic, Hubert Spengler, came from Alsace in 1835 to settle in Jackson. He was senior partner in Spengler and Sons grocery and hotel business. Spengler's sons moved to Vicksburg and joined his brother Armand in the ownership of sawmills, markets, and hotels. Armand's bank and loan association made him the city's wealthiest man. Those Catholic businessmen ably served the need for skilled labor in the community, generally kept out of politics, retained their ethnic ways, and actively supported the Church.[41]

Natchez had the largest number of Mississippi Catholics during the late antebellum period. Catholic businessmen owned town residences and some of them were also large planters. The wealthiest and most powerful was Henry E. Chotard, who came from Brittany around 1808. Like so many who gained status in the region, he served on General Andrew Jackson's staff in the War of 1812. Chotard was a successful town businessman who later settled on a plantation with over 2,000 acres and many slaves. He was active in local religious affairs and assisted in the construction of the church in Natchez. His son, Henry Jr., served in the local militia, which he commanded during the Civil War.[42]

In the interior of those states one seldom found Catholic elites. Only along the rivers was there a recognizable Catholic population. For example, Memphis had 7,000 Catholics in 1860, yet produced no leader. Nor did Tennessee Catholics seem to have any interest in the sectional

---

[40]Gerald M. Capers, *The Biography of a River Town* (Chapel Hill NC, 1939), pp. 106-15; James J. Pillar, *The Catholic Church in Mississippi, 1837-1865* (New Orleans, 1964), pp. 2, 18, 55; William Henry Elder, "Pastoral of the Diocesan Synod of Natchez, April, 1858," *Freeman's Journal*, 13 November 1858.

[41]Pillar, *Catholic Church in Mississippi*, pp. 113-20, 122-23; Richard O. Gerow, comp., *Catholicity in Mississippi* (Natchez MS, 1939), pp. 53, 143, 179, 211.

[42]Dorris C. James, *Antebellum Natchez* (Baton Rouge, 1968), pp. 137, 171-73, 202, 243-44.

conflict, perhaps because so few of them had any financial stake in the community.[43]

Farther west, Arkansas had at least one important antebellum Catholic who rose to public prominence. David W. Carroll had attended Mount St. Mary's College and had moved to Pine Bluff, Arkansas, in 1836, in hopes of succeeding as a planter. Instead, he practiced law, entered the state legislature, and eventually became attorney general of the state. His fortune made, he followed in his ancestors' footsteps by buying a large plantation and settling into the life of a gentleman planter. Perhaps because of his ties to the slaveholding community or his place in Southwestern Democratic politics, Carroll was an outspoken secessionist. It is certain that he had little contact with the Church, so that his Catholicism did not seem to influence his politics.[44]

Texas Catholics were unique in the South because so many of them were Mexican-Americans. None of those Mexican Catholics appeared to rise in either business or politics. But after Texas became a state a large number of Irish and German Catholics settled in the towns. Immigrant Catholics such as James Vance, John Twohig, and Michael Menard profited as merchants in Galveston and San Antonio. All of them began as poor immigrants, devoted much of their effort to build the Anglo-Catholic community, and had little interest in things Southern. At least one Texas Catholic entered public life and was a thorough Southerner in his politics. Nova Scotia-born Thomas J. Devine practiced law in San Antonio and rose in local government as city attorney and later as district judge. While mayor, he helped to disperse a Know-Nothing mob and killed one of its leaders. This endeared him to the Catholic community, and the citizens reelected him mayor in 1856. A staunch Democratic Southern rights advocate, Devine later served in the Confederate Congress.[45]

By contrast to the small number of Catholic elites along the Gulf coast of Alabama and Mississippi and in the southwestern interior, the sugar

---

[43]Victor F. O'Daniel, *The Father of the Church in Tennessee* (New York, 1926), pp. 40-157, 468-525.

[44]George Mackenzie, *Colonial Families of the United States of America*, 7 vols. (Baltimore, 1911), 3:120.

[45]Carlos E. Castañeda, *The Church in Texas Since Independence* (Austin, 1958), pp. 2, 31, 114, 125, 129; Samuel C. Griffin, *History of Galveston, Texas* (Galveston, 1931); Sidney S. Johnson, *Texans Who Wore the Gray* (Tyler TX, 1907), p. 114.

planting region of southern Louisiana, and the great commercial port city of New Orleans produced the Old South's largest Catholic elite as well as most of its Catholic population. Before the American settlement the French and Spanish who lived along the bayous and rivers surrounding New Orleans created a unique culture. The city also attracted a number of Irish immigrants who rose in power before the War of 1812 changed the structure of leadership.

The War of 1812 gave many of the *ancienne* families an opportunity to display their loyalty to their new rulers as well as the chance to rise in public and professional life. Most prominent among the Creoles was Bernard De Marigny, heir to the largest merchant and plantation wealth in the city. Marigny maintained both a large plantation and a New Orleans mansion where he gave lavish parties, which eventually dissipated the family fortune. Unsuccessful in business, he was forced to live off the generosity of friends. In some respects, Marigny's life fits the career pattern some historians have created of a lazy, precapitalistic planter elite. But he ably served at the battle of New Orleans, which paved the way for his own and other Creole political careers during the antebellum period. The new settlers and the Creoles at first shared political power, trading the office of mayor, having a Protestant and a Catholic senator, and rotating the governorship.

Marigny served in the legislature for years and ably participated in the state constitutional conventions of 1812 and 1845. His son married the daughter of the American governor, William C. C. Claiborne, thus symbolically merging the political and financial interests of the wealthy American and Creole families.[46]

Other wealthy Creoles held important government positions. Perhaps the most influential was the sugar planter Jacques P. Villere, whose granddaugher was Pierre Gustave Toutant-Beauregard's first wife. Elected to the constitutional convention of 1812, he helped to assure the state's southern Catholic section a place in the new government. He served as a major general in the War of 1812 and became governor in 1816. As governor, he soothed the friction between the *ancienne* families and the Americans, invited further immigration to the state, and lobbied unsuccessfully for educational reform. Villere and many of his relatives

---

[46]Grace Gardner King, *Creole Families* (New York, 1898), pp. 23-58.

also gained from New Orleans' growth as a commercial port. Like many other Creoles with inherited wealth, he increased his family holdings through shrewd business connections.[47]

During the antebellum period the descendants of those *ancienne* families formed their own ethnic political blocs, eventually gained much political power, and invested wisely in the city's commercial growth. William Howard Russell, the distinguished British journalist, found that those Creoles exhibited the attributes of Southern gentlemen and French aristocrats, yet were shrewd businessmen. One such Catholic leader was Charles J. Villere, grandson of Jacques. After having studied law in a prestigious Creole law firm, he established an excellent practice, and also ran the family sugar plantation in Plaquemines parish. As a member of the state legislature and the secession convention, he supported disunion.[48]

Two other Creoles gained from the city's growth by developing professional skills that allowed them to rise in public prominence in late antebellum Louisiana. They were the cousins Louis and Paul Octave Hebert, members of the old sugar planter aristocracy, who had grown up accustomed to owning slaves, to great wealth, and to the manners of Southern country gentlemen. Louis received an education in New Orleans parochial schools, and graduated third in his class at West Point. Shortly thereafter, he resigned his commission in the Army Corps of Engineers to become a sugar planter. From 1855 to 1859, he served as chief state engineer, where he designed the levee system along the Mississippi River below New Orleans. Paul, also educated in New Orleans parochial schools, graduated first in his class at West Point. He taught at the Academy until his resignation in 1845 to become a state engineer. Honored for his heroics in the Mexican War, he parlayed that recognition into election as governor. An outspoken foe of anti-Catholic nativism, along with his cousin, he was a Southern Democrat and a secessionist. Both men had built their careers on family connections and had gained prominence because of their engineering skills. Both were also very devoted to the Church and were regarded highly by the bishop.[49]

---

[47]Ibid., pp. 133-58, 292.

[48]Ibid., pp. 159-65.

[49]Jon L. Wakelyn, *Biographical Dictionary of the Confederacy* (Westport CT, 1977), pp. 224-25.

Another Creole achieved public importance through his literary career. The descendant of Spanish gentry who had settled in New Orleans in 1760, Charles Gayarré was the son of a wealthy planter. He attended the College of New Orleans, read law, gained election to the state legislature, and served in the United States Congress. An opponent of the Irish and John Slidell, Gayarré defended Creole political power and propriety in his *The School for Politics*. In his book he attacked popular elections and defended conservative leadership principles. But his career changed course at a political gathering in Philadelphia, when he discovered that the Know-Nothing party vehemently opposed Catholics. He turned on them and for the rest of his life he advocated united Catholic politics.[50]

Gayarré also described the Creole life of old New Orleans in his many works of history. His own manners were much like those of the characters he described from history. He was courtly, with a code of honor, a sense of chivalry, and he united his own past with the values of the South. As Clement Eaton says, "he exhibited the best qualities of the Creole planter aristocracy," which, but for its Catholicism, closely resembled the Southern planter. On the eve of secession, Gayarré abandoned plans for a European research trip to remain with his state in the moment of crisis. To the Catholic Congressman John Perkins he wrote in defense of Louisiana's historical right to separate from the Union. He stated that if Napoleon, the hero of all Creole boys, were alive he would support secession. A firm believer in states' rights, Gayarré concluded his letter with this warning: "Sovereignty once acquired can not be lost, except by complete and permanent subjugation, or by voluntary abdication."[51]

The *beau ideal* of Southern manhood was the Catholic Creole Pierre Gustave Toutant-Beauregard—planter, engineer, businessman, and a major military leader during the Civil War. T. Harry Williams has called this cavalier, this ardent Southerner, "the most colorful of all Confederate generals." Certainly he was chivalrous, arrogant, dramatic, and he had that "vague air of romance" about him. Beauregard was born into an aristocratic Creole sugar planting family. He grew up on country life,

---

[50]Charles Gayarré, *The School for Politics* (New York, 1854); Charles Gayarré, *An Address to the People of Louisiana on the State of Parties* (New Orleans, 1855).

[51]Russell, *Diary*, pp. 89-102; Judge Gayarré to Hon John Perkins, Gayarré Papers (Library of Congress).

rode, hunted, and knew slaves intimately. Luxurious living, fine manners, built-in tradition, and honor marked that young man whose father had intended him to be a Frenchman. The family, more French than American, fearful of Americans, and devoted to Paris even more than to New Orleans, sent young Pierre to private Catholic schools in New Orleans, and then on to a French school in New York.

But the young Toutant-Beauregard then carved his own career pattern which built on both his Creole and Southern traditions. With the support of Governor André Roman and Congressman Edward Douglas White he obtained admission to West Point. There he excelled, finishing high enough in his class to enter the Corps of Engineers. He did service along the Gulf Coast and spent considerable time at his Villere in-law's plantation. After the Mexican War he became an ardent Gulf Coast expansionist, and even asked for leave from the service to join William Walker in 1856 on his filibustering trip to Nicaragua. He entered politics as a Democrat and ran for mayor of New Orleans as a conservative against the Know-Nothing candidate. Not much of a churchgoer, Beauregard nevertheless felt Catholic because of his heritage. When the Civil War began, he joined a battalion of Creole aristocrats. He defended slave society, his aristocratic roots, and the Southern view of states' rights. He identified with Louis Napoleon's principle of the right of a nation to choose its own form of government and applied French political ideals to defend the "right of a people to select its own form of Government."[52]

Antebellum New Orleans' cosmopolitanism, its financial opportunities, and Catholic character also attracted many foreigners. Many of them, just like a number of Creoles, never really established permanent residence or identified with Southern life. One of those foreigners who did was the politician Pierre Soulé, who emigrated to New Orleans in the 1830s. This Frenchman soon established himself as a merchant-lawyer, entered local Democratic politics, and rose in public life. Early a states' rights advocate, he became an expansionist and a sectionalist. As President Pierce's minister to Spain, he wrote the Ostend Manifesto, which linked him with those who wanted to expand slavery into Latin America.

---

[52]T. Harry Williams, *Napoleon in Gray* (Baton Rouge, 1955), pp. 7-68; Beauregard to Major J. G. Barnard, 18 March 1861; Beauregard to Lucius P. Walker, 17 April 1861, Beauregard Papers (Library of Congress).

Although he was a National Democrat during the late 1850s, Soulé followed his adopted state out of the Union.[53]

Louisiana's early Irish settlers also produced wealthy and powerful Catholic leaders who competed with the Creoles for local political power. The last Catholic group to rise in business and political life felt keenly the impact of later Irish and German immigration to New Orleans. The most important of those early Irish leaders was Edward Douglas White, Sr. Born in Tennessee, White studied at the University of Nashville, clerked in the law firm of the Irish Protestant Whig politician Alexander Porter, established a successful law practice, and later became a sugar planter. He entered Congress in 1828, and eventually served as Whig governor. Aligned with the powerful old Irish families and the Roman wing of Creole politics, he again entered Congress after his term as governor. White never adjusted to the influx of new Irish and German immigrants, few of whom rose to prominence in the antebellum period.[54] That task he left to his son and to other members of the "New South" Catholic leaders.

After perusal of these Old South elite career patterns it is clear that where they lived, what they did for a living, their political activities, their values and attitudes, and their link to their religion were instrumental in understanding just where they fit into the life of the Old South. Assessment of these patterns should give us an indication of what Catholic elites contributed to the economy, to public life, and to the mind of the South. We also should understand how the Old South influenced their lives.

Catholic elites and most of the Old South's Catholic population lived mainly in the major cities. They clustered in the border South, the Southeast coast, and along the Gulf Coast. A few dwelt in the small towns along the principal rivers, especially those which either connected to the Mississippi River or flowed into the Gulf. The oldest Catholic settlements of Maryland, Kentucky, and Louisiana had some farmers and planters. They continued to own slaves and to plant cash crops. Other

---

[53]*Speech of Mr. Soulé on Intervention* (Washington, 1852). Another important settler to New Orleans was John Perkins, from a wealthy Mississippi planter family; see John Perkins, *The Results of Two Years of Democratic Rule in the Country* (Washington, 1855).

[54]Earl F. Niehaus, *The Irish in New Orleans* (Baton Rouge, 1965), pp. 38, 81, 85, 110, 162; Diedrich Ramke, "Edward Douglas White, Sr.," *Louisiana Historical Quarterly* 19 (1936): 273-327; Robert T. Clarke, Jr., "The German Liberals in New Orleans," *Louisiana Historical Quarterly* 20 (1937): 137, 141.

Catholics, whose major occupations were urban-commercial, bought plantations, perhaps to emulate the patterns of the rural Protestant elite.

Although I have not established quantitative affirmation, from the elites discussed in this essay it appears that an inordinate number had been lawyers at one time in their lives. Because so little is known about professionalism, one hesitates to make assertions, but it seems that the level of elite education and the opportunities in the antebellum period for lawyers may have been attractive to an emerging Catholic elite. Moreover, old, wealthy families with commercial interests wanted a lawyer in the family.[55]

Likewise, Catholics entered urban retail business, in occupations that required contacts, skills, and optimism about the future. For some, this was a way to rise in life; for others, like the Carrolls and Mullanphys, this was a means to add to a fortune and to adjust to economic changes in their society. Occupations such as banking, real estate, and overseas commerce were also attractive to Catholics. A few entered the new scientific professions, mainly as engineers. More of those Catholic businessmen lived in the upper South and in New Orleans rather than along the south Atlantic seaboard. Perhaps this was because those elites with status in the Atlantic South of Charleston and Savannah remained skeptical about business, or because there were fewer Catholics there.

Catholic occupational patterns also seemed ideally suited for those who planned to enter public life. Some of the lawyers parlayed their skills into judgeships, while many others were involved in municipal politics. A few had long and distinguished careers in state and national government. From the republic's beginning they were involved in constitution making, revisions of legal codes, and in making new states. Some took the lead in movements for religious toleration, while others enhanced their careers by opposing the nativists. Most considered themselves conservative defenders of state and local rights.

How they rose in politics was related to time, place of Catholic population, ethnic composition, and geographical location. Early in the republican era Catholic leaders came largely from states with large Catholic populations, primarily from the upper South. By the antebellum period the Catholic population was changing drastically, both in ethnic

---

[55]For a helpful beginning on the question of professionalism, see Burton Bledstein, *The Culture of Professionalism* (New York, 1976), ch. 1.

composition and in geographic dispersal. Antebellum Louisiana, the largest Catholic population center, produced the most elected Catholic officials. But enough Catholics from states with few Catholics, such as South and North Carolina, were elected to public office to call into question the extent to which Catholic voters were instrumental in electing Catholic officeholders. In Louisiana, Maryland, Kentucky, and Missouri, ethnically diverse Catholics divided the religious vote.

One wonders whether those politicians voted as Catholics. Perusal of Catholic leaders' positions on nativism and anti-Catholic politics shows that most of them unsurprisingly were hostile to those groups. Catholic elites also supported religious toleration. Most Gulf Coast Catholic Congressmen favored expansion of the Gulf Coast slave society into Catholic Latin America. John Perkins thought this was in part because of the desire to spread the Catholic population of the United States. Others believed they were protecting Southern interests. Many Catholic leaders called themselves conservative; they supported states' rights and often equivocated over expanding suffrage. They were sensitive to their minority position in antebellum Southern politics and aware of how the Catholic voters had changed in their ethnic composition. Perhaps there is a connection between those changes and the fact that so many lower South Catholic politicians were such outspoken secessionists.[56]

If it is unclear to what extent being Catholic gained them office or influenced their votes, it is perfectly clear how Catholic elites related to their church. They were helpful with funds, expertise, and time in building churches. As the pillars of local benevolent societies, they assisted the Catholic poor. Many were faithful church attenders. In areas where few Catholics lived, some held church services in their homes and paid for circuit riding clergy. Many sent their sons to Catholic schools.

It is most difficult to probe the religious beliefs of those elites, because so few of them left records of their piety. Intermarriage, mobility, the absence of clergy, and bitter battles over lay roles in church affairs no doubt caused lapses from the Church. Perhaps business and social pressures to conform to Protestant religious practice left some equivocal in their Catholic belief. But the pious Catholic William Gaston expounded his theological views in private conversations and correspondence with

---

[56]Ralph Wooster, *The Secession Conventions of the South* (Princeton, 1962), chapter on Louisiana.

Bishop England. The brilliant Charles Carroll often discussed religion with members of his family. Creoles like Gayarré and Beauregard reflected in their writings a close relationship to the heritage of their faith. The hierarchical and institutional loyalty of the Catholic elites observed in this study distinguished them from their Protestant counterparts.

The Church had means to retain the allegiance of its elites through its educational system. Colleges were first founded to educate the priests, but the lay elites soon benefitted from those schools. In the Catholic population centers, primary schools and colleges for the laity soon sprang up. An ordered curriculum, student uniforms, and strict social obedience marked the clergy's control of those schools. The Church also opened its doors to members of the Protestant elite, perhaps to proselytize, but more importantly to preach toleration and to unite elite groups. One priest from Spring Hill College commented, "Spring Hill had succeeded in giving the fraction of Catholics in the South a standing and position in the public mind and civil life far beyond the proportion attained at that point by their Catholic brethren in the North."[57]

Bishops and lay leaders administered and edited the Southern Catholic press, which had an enormous role in perpetuating the Church's power over the laity. The press formed opinion and pointed out the dangers of being part of a religious minority in the South. Articles and editorials showed preoccupation with prejudice shown to Catholics, contained much discussion of bishops' views of local church affairs, and showed a keen sensitivity to the mores of Southern life. Bishop England used the pages of the *Miscellany* to apologize for any slight to Southern life and values. Some of the papers cautioned Catholic slaveowners to the proper treatment and instruction of their slaves, but none opposed slavery. Prominent lay leaders such as Webb in Louisville, O'Hara in Mobile, and Patrick Walsh in Augusta wrote for the religious press. An editorial in the official newspaper of the bishop of New Orleans, *The Catholic Standard*, in January 1856, summed up the lower South Catholic

[57]Kenny, *Catholic Culture in Alabama*, pp. 80, 111-12, 119, 145, 153, 190; Edward J. Power, *Catholic Higher Education in America* (New York, 1972); Walter H. Hill, *Historical Sketch of St. Louis University* (St. Louis, 1879), pp. 37-43.

position on the region: "We have never yet met a Catholic who was not true to his Southern rights."[58]

With its control over the chief tools of propaganda, the schools, and the press, the Southern hierarchy influenced those elites whom it reached. The bishops also from time to time released documents in which they took specific positions on various issues essential to their people. Because they believed so fervently in social order and community loyalty, they often commented on slavery in the life of Southern Catholics. The Southern-born Bishop Elder of Natchez claimed: "Catholic masters of course are taught that it is their duty to furnish their slaves with opportunities for being well instructed and for practicing their religion." In his pastoral letter of 1861 Bishop Augustin Verot of Savannah linked Southern sectional feelings with the need for protection against antislavery activity.[59]

No matter what their private opinions, it is clear that all the border state bishops equivocated on secession and all the lower South bishops supported secession and the Southern Confederacy. Bishop Patrick Lynch of Charleston blamed Northern radicals for causing secession. Bishop John Quinlan of Mobile spoke like a true states' righter when he refused to save the Union for fear that his efforts would violate the rights of citizens of the state. In a pastoral letter of 21 August 1861, Bishop Augustus Martin of Natchitoches proclaimed that he and all the Catholic citizens of Louisiana identified with the values and the beliefs of the state. The bishops supported the South's social and political system, and identified with the romantic, paternalistic, and localistic beliefs of Southern writers. Many of their utterances could have been said by any defender of secession. The bishops' views, if not fully intellectually persuasive, must have given those elites a rationale for action.[60]

The lay Catholic cultural leaders were influenced both by the Church and by the Old South's intellectual climate. Catholics have been part of the intellectual life in every country in which they have resided. Men with

---

[58]*New Orleans Catholic Standard*, January 1856, quoted in Niehaus, *The Irish in New Orleans*, p. 55.

[59]William Henry Elder, "Pastoral of the Diocesan Synod of Natchez"; Gannon, *Rebel Bishop*, pp. 31-39, 61.

[60]Maria Genorino Caravaglios, "A Roman Critique of the Pro-Slavery Views of Bishop Martin of Natchitoches, Louisiana," *Records of the American Catholic Historical Society* 83 (1972): 67-81; William Henry Elder, *Civil War Diary* (Natchez, 1960), pp. 25-125.

international reputations such as the chess player Paul Morphy and the musician and composer Louis Moreau Gottschalk, both of New Orleans, would have distinguished themselves in any society. Others made major contributions to their native section. Writers such as the editor and poet Theodore O'Hara and the novelist-historian Charles Gayarré in their work particularly caught the cadence of Southern romanticism. Catholics too were famous newspapermen. All of those artists felt the anti-intellectual and often patronizing attitudes of most Southern elites bent on improving their fortunes rather than their minds.

Southern Catholics also made important contributions to political thought. The Carrolls assisted in the formation of the federal republic. Conservative to the core, the Federalist Charles Carroll defended a strong federal presence, yet also supported separation of powers which gave the states an equal say in making public policy. William Gaston was an outspoken supporter of religious freedom. In lectures, legal decisions, and essays Gaston defended individual and community rights. Charles Gayarré worried about the common herd, the victims of demagogues. His histories of Louisiana were chauvinistic works portraying the growth of Southern nationalism. An outspoken secessionist, Gayarré wanted Louisianans to free themselves from the illegal hold of the evil and corrupt American republic.

Catholic intellectuals usually subscribed to the bishops' defense of slavery. Charles Carroll and William Gaston wanted to end slavery and belonged to various colonization schemes but wondered what would happen to freedmen. Justice Taney opposed slavery, yet he also made strong defense of personal property. By the 1830s, Catholic elites strongly supported slave society. The Southern expansionists, who lectured and wrote so eloquently about the "dream" of a Southern empire in the Caribbean, believed that possession of Latin America would assure the perpetuation of the plantation slave society they valued so highly.[61]

To look at the behavior, the ideals and values, and the writings of Catholic elites is to see what Clement Eaton has called the "mind of the Old South." Acculturated Catholic elites had a strong sense of personal honor, practiced the cult of the gentleman, had a profound religious orthodoxy, were intensely localistic, had strong feelings for the family,

---

[61]Rollin G. Osterweis, *Romanticism and Nationalism in the Old South* (New Haven, 1949), pp. 155-85.

were extremely conservative, and had strong racial feelings. Old Catholic families, after all, had been born into and were an integral part of the region that became the Old South. Creole Catholics refined and expanded the duel, the epitome of honor and gentlemanliness. Catholic immigrants to the lower South either brought Southern values with them from the upper South or soon acquired the sentiments and characteristics of their fellow Protestant elites. Most of the Catholics wanted to perpetuate their family name, and their correspondence is filled with references to close business and personal ties with members of their families. Catholic elite political thought was staunchly conservative. If Catholic elites did not subscribe to a fundamentalist Protestant religious orthodoxy, they had their own hierarchical rigidity. Certainly they wer intolerant of Yankees, of Catholic ethnics, and of the lower classes in general. The prime example of the Catholic Southern aristocrat was Beauregard, who was quick to anger over any slight, a conservative scion of landed slaveowning wealth, and the model of the cult of the gentleman.[62] But for their Catholicism they resembled in activities, beliefs, and interests their fellow Protestant elites.

Of course, the final test of those Catholic elites' Southernness was whether they were Confederates. Some of the Catholic elites who resided in the South did not support the Confederacy; they were mainly from the upper South, or they were lower South residents who regarded themselves as citizens of Europe. The vast majority, however, did go along with their region. Their church leaders, their own business interests, their acquired and historical belief in the Southern way of life, and even the fear of being outside the mainstream of class and societal interests, no doubt all contributed to make their position on secession. At the last, it is clear that, like their Protestant counterparts, most Catholic elites felt that there was too much to lose if the North prevailed in the sectional struggle.

---

[62]Clement Eaton, *The Mind of the Old South* (Baton Rouge, 1964), pp. 241-42.

AFTERWORD

by Jon L. Wakelyn

Southern Catholics fought in large numbers for the Confederacy. Members of old and new elite families held major line commands and important government positions. A few of their lives became synomymous with the ideals of the Confederacy, and their names live on in the legends of the Old South. But their Catholicism seems lost to the historians of that great struggle. Sturdy sons of immigrants served in the ranks, often in special Catholic brigades. Irish and German alike fought across the lines from their Northern counterparts. Others worked at home in the factories which provided materiel for the war effort. Priests and bishops sent the boys off to war with their blessings, urged on the war effort with morally uplifting sermons, and served as battlefield chaplains and as orderlies in the camp hospitals. Nuns took care of the sick and the dying in those hospitals. These clerics' activities also are stories without a modern historian.

Catholics who lived in the South also lost much during the war, and the war's aftermath devastated many others. Farms and plantations were burned, stores were sacked, and families lost sons. The Northern press and government attacked Church leaders and even imprisoned two bishops for a time. Shortly after the war, Bishop Augustin Verot called for Catholics to educate and employ the newly freed black work force. But the Church had as little success in recruiting ex-slaves as it had had with the slaves themselves. As Gary Mills has shown, the free colored Catholics also found that the white society refused to make distinctions between colored and freed blacks. A devastated and wasted South also hurt the Church's efforts to grow and to maintain influence over its laity. Many of the poorer urban Catholics left the South, while immigrant Catholics with no hope of employment were discouraged from coming there. Lay leaders, like some of their fellow Southerners, lapsed into the bemused reveries of the lost cause. The historians Alfred Roman and Charles Gayarré attempted to preserve the old Catholic population's past and to long for the mythological Old South.

By their contributions to the Confederacy and the extent of their war losses, Southern Catholics appeared to have had an important place in that region's life. The object of this collection of essays has been to describe and to understand that place. To understand Catholic life as a minority in a section becoming increasingly conscious of its minority status in the Union is not only to tell us about one Southern group but also to learn more about that society known as the Old South. The book should also provoke other questions and topics for analysis about Catholic life and its place in the Old South. This afterword is to suggest possible areas for future study and expansion on the topics of this volume.

Southern Catholic activities before the sectional crisis show a people adjusting to the post-Revolutionary expanse of new land and influx of new migration. Catholics sought to carve out a place for themselves in the new nation, and many found that through family heritage and inheritance they could thrive in a slaveholding society. Open lands, the thrust of commerce along great waterways, and the many jobs that came with an expanding society lured poor Catholic immigrants to what would become the South. By the 1830s, Catholic leaders who had questioned slavery (many upper South planters had belonged to the American Colonization Society) were forced into silence. To speak out against their community was to invite retaliation in the form of the religious bigotry which so haunted much of the antebellum United States. As suggested in these essays, much can be learned about the entire South by looking at when and how minorities responded to the heightened self-consciousness and defensiveness that made those from the slaveholding states identify with the peculiarities of their region.

There were many Souths in the antebellum period. Richard Duncan shows in his essay on the upper South that as the border state South lost slaves and developed large urban complexes with commercial ties to the North it slowly drifted from Southern interests and values. Catholics in those border state cities, many of them recent immigrants, had few ties to the South. Although small in numbers, old elite families from southern Maryland, the Kentucky bluegrass, and the upper Mississippi River were thoroughly imbued with a plantation ethic. If the lower South supported the slave economy and proslavery values, it often differed on just how to protect those interests. These studies have pointed out that Catholics in those regions also differed in social characteristics and economic interests. Numbers, concentration, and Church outreach all influenced the ways Catholics related to their sections. Those regional differences among Catholics suggest the possibilities of more sensitive appraisal of subregionalism in the larger South.

Just as Catholics in the South's regions may have differed over economic and social interests, they also differed, as Dennis Clark suggests, in ethnic composition. The old Anglo-American Catholics whom Professor Duncan discusses and the New Orleans Creole families described by Randall Miller confronted the New Irish and later German Catholics who moved into their regions. Unlike the experiences of their fellow Southerners, except perhaps for the eighteenth-century Charlestonians, ethnic differences affected class and status as well as political and social development of the Catholic community. Although much work has been done on the Irish and on the Germans, we still know little about the activities of those immigrants as they sought to adjust in their Southern communities. Through the essays in this volume we now understand how many generational changes buffeted the Catholic community. These contributions suggest that the various ways Catholic ethnic subgroups responded to changes in Southern society could tell us why Catholics themselves were so divided. Even the controversial Know-Nothing party, which recent scholars have tried to deemphasize in political importance, can be placed in historical focus in the South with clearer understanding of the class and ethnic bases of Catholic life.

Catholic political life, too, has drawn attention in this volume. It has been studied through the actions of the Catholic elite and in Professor Miller's analysis of the New Orleans tensions between new Catholic immigrants and the older established Catholics. But further study should be made of how old Catholic families came to use religiously based political organizations to exploit the new Catholic vote. We should quantify Southern Catholic voting just as scholars have looked at ethnic voting patterns in the North. Conventional wisdom and much political study claim that Catholics were mainly Democrats, but certainly this was not true among the elites. Many began as Federalists and later became Whigs. Others only joined the Democratic party after they associated the Whigs with anti-Catholic feelings. Recent scholarly research shows that the Democratic party became the party of slave protection, which suggests that the Catholic minority may have become Democratic in order to conform to societal pressure. Whatever the case for party affiliation, it is clear that much can still be learned about Southern Catholics by scrutinizing their political behavior.

If Southern Catholic politics are complicated, so is the question of occupation and its relationship to regional loyalty and the rise of professionalism in the so-called backward South. The different jobs that a successful plantation economy created relate to the modernization arguments for professionalism. Catholics have been described as either having been planters and farmers or as immigrant workers on the docks, in railroad construction, and in building the levees along the Mississippi and the Gulf. But the elites seemed to have had professional jobs in larger proportion than their numbers might have warranted. Not only did Catholics hold many merchant and other business positions, but they entered the legal profession in great numbers. For men like Roger B. Taney, William Gaston, and Edward Douglas White, the law may have been a means of achieving status as well as a livelihood. Catholics also were journalists, working for the large city newspapers and the diocesan press. Often Catholics who succeeded in the professions bought plantations, owned slaves, and apparently aspired to the status of rural potentates. We must have more analysis of occupation as it relates to economic and social changes in Southern society because business, the professions, and status could reveal much about how and whether Catholics or any group were assimilated in the Southern culture and to what extent work patterns influenced where they stood on secession.

Still other members of the work force require study to place Catholics into perspective. Sister Frances Jerome Woods's account of Catholic nuns not only tells us much about women at work, but also gives us an understanding of women's place in Southern society. Questions about recruitment and conversion and the dangers of both in that society are herein handled with delicacy. Her essay suggests how we might find out more about lay women, especially from the poorer immigrant families, to see how they fit into Southern life. Catholic women no doubt intermarried with Protestants, and vice versa. Just how intermarriage influenced assimilation remains to be seen. As women's history grows into its own, the place of Southern Catholic women in that society may tell us more about the South. Sr. Frances has made an excellent beginning. She has avoided letting elites speak for all of womanhood and has introduced the question of how another minority adjusted to life in that minority section.

As one would expect, Catholic slaves and free blacks have much concerned our essayists. Not only have the authors discussed slaveholding among Catholics, but they have sought to look afresh at important questions relating to slave life. Professor Mills's detailed study of the free colored community has added to our growing knowledge of free blacks. Professor Miller's careful look at the sensitive issue of why the Church did not attract slaves tells us much about the religious needs of slaves and also gives us some idea of the difficulties which that institutional and hierarchical Church faced in a Protestant-dominated society. If we are to continue to test the Elkins thesis of Catholics as benevolent masters, then we need many more local and community studies using the models provided by Professors Mills and Miller.

All of these essays point to the importance of the Church in the Old South. When the editors first discussed this study they believed that the Church as institution had been overworked. Raymond Schmandt's overview and Professor Miller's speculation as to how the Church managed in that Protestant society changed all these assurances. For the Church's problems of adjusting to the South, living in that prejudiced world, and above all, trying to mediate among the many different types of Catholics, point up that if we are to know more about Catholic life we must begin anew with the Church. We should distinguish between the different orders in their adjustment to the South and use priests' memoirs to look at everyday social and political life as well as the problems foreign priests faced. As Father R. Emmett Curran demonstrates, we can also expand our understanding of the Church in its capacity as slaveholder.

It is evident that the institutional Church also provided Catholic lay theorists with political views, thus sharpening their defense of their section. For when the bishops took a stand in favor of the Confederacy, they affected the behavior of the lay Catholic population. We know that the Church in Rome stressed regional loyalties and support for the existing social organization wherever the Church happened to be. Recent work which accuses the Southern bishops of complicity in defense of slavery and support for radical states' rights theory neglects the setting, the cultural and geographical background of many of the bishops, and the ideology of the institutional Church. We are just now beginning to understand the outside pressures on these Church leaders.

In addition, little is known about Church benevolent societies in the South, except in their concern for infectious diseases and the horrors of fire and nature. But the Church founded excellent schools that educated many Catholic Confederate leaders as well as offered schooling to prominent Protestants such as Jefferson Davis. What role these benevolent societies and schools played in the politics, the culture, and the way Southern Catholics were either assimilated or remained aloof from the Protestant culture could well be a key to understanding both the Protestant acceptance of and distrust of that minority.

The Church, then, became a force for lay support of Southern institutions, values, and the social system. Perhaps Church leaders even encouraged assimilation into the dominant Protestant community. But, at the same time, as Professors Miller and Schmandt show, the Church strongly maintained the distinctiveness of Catholic life through religious belief. To know whether the Catholics who lived in the South had become Southern, one needs to ask whether the Church leaders, despite the structural and organizational dissimilarities within, adopted the attitudes and the beliefs molded by a separate Southern history, a separate labor force, and a vigorous fundamentalist religion. Here again, the position of the hierarchy and the activities of the everyday priests must be reviewed to see if we have a Church divided against itself or a Church in search of meaning and survival in that often hostile religious environment.

We have thus attempted to describe and to ask questions about many aspects of the life of one segment of a minority society. The key issues continue to be those of what it meant to be Catholic, Southern, and to live in the South. How Catholics who lived in the South held on to their faith and the extent to which their faith influenced their various activities is essential to understanding how they lived in the South. How they identified as Catholic and the dissension among various Catholics, too, reveal their relationship to Southern society. How they became and whether they behaved as Southerners certainly contribute to deciphering life in the Old South. The foregoing queries also point to the necessity of fusing the many components of Southern Catholic life. The Church as religious institution and purveyor of distinct yet assimilated culture; the Catholic power elite, how it thrived, and who led it; the ordinary people and how they survived; and the colored Catholics, slave and free—all require uniting into one story. This volume has begun that process. We hope that those who follow build upon these efforts to understand that community.

CONTRIBUTORS

DENNIS CLARK is the Executive Director of the Samuel S. Fels Fund in Philadelphia. He has written numerous articles and several books on American ethnicity and urban affairs. Among his books is the widely acclaimed, *The Irish in Philadelphia: Ten Generations of Urban Experience* (Temple University Press, 1973).

R. EMMETT CURRAN, S.J. is Associate Professor of History and chairman of the Department of History at Georgetown University. He has written several important articles on American Catholicism.

RICHARD R. DUNCAN is Professor of History at Georgetown University and a former editor of the *Maryland Historical Magazine*. Dr. Duncan has published many articles on the upper South and on Civil War history.

RANDALL M. MILLER is Professor of History at Saint Joseph's University in Philadelphia. He has published numerous articles and written or edited seven books on aspects of Southern, religious, or ethnic history, including *"Dear Master": Letters of a Slave Family* (Cornell University Press, 1978); and *Immigrants and Religion in Urban America* (Temple University Press, 1977), coedited with Thomas D. Marzik.

GARY B. MILLS is Associate Professor of History at the University of Alabama. He is the author of numerous articles on Southern and black history. Among his books are *The Forgotten People: Cane River's Creoles of Color* (Louisiana State University Press, 1977), which won the Louisiana Literary Award for Nonfiction in 1978; and *Of Men and Rivers: The Story of the Vicksburg District, United States Army Corps of Engineers* (Government Printing Office, 1978), which won the Mississippi Historical Association's Award of Merit in 1979.

RAYMOND H. SCHMANDT is Professor of History at Saint Joseph's University in Philadelphia and former editor of the *Records of the American Catholic Historical Society*. Dr. Schmandt is a leading authority on the Catholic Church. He has published widely on American Catholicism, medieval history, and theories of war. His text on the Catholic Church remains standard in many schools.

JON L. WAKELYN is Professor of History at The Catholic University of America and editor of the American History series for Greenwood Press. Dr. Wakelyn has written several important articles on Southern history and written or edited several books on Southern history. Among his books are *The Politics of a Literary Man: William Gilmore Simms* (Greenwood Press, 1973); *A Biographical Dictionary of the Confederacy* (Greenwood Press, 1977); and coeditor, *The Southern Common People: Studies in Nineteenth-Century Social History* (Greenwood Press, 1980). Dr. Wakelyn is at work on a book on higher education in the Old South.

SISTER FRANCES JEROME WOODS, C.D.P. is Professor of Sociology at Our Lady of the Lake University in San Antonio. She has written widely about ethnicity, religion, urban affairs, and sociology. Among her works is the much celebrated book, *Marginality and Identity: A Colored Creole Family Through Ten Generations* (Louisiana State University Press, 1972).

INDEX

Abell, Robert, 217

Acadians, 44

Alabama: Catholic Church growth in, 63-64; Catholic elites in, 225-26; colored Creoles in, 172. *See also* individual towns and cities

American party. *See* Know-Nothing party

American Republican party, 94

American Revolution: Catholics and, 78, 86, 93

Anti-Catholicism. *See* Nativism

Anwander, Thaddeus, 111

Appalachian Mountains: Irish culture in, 196-97

Architecture: of churches, 26-27

Arkansas: Catholic Church growth in, 66, 202; Catholic elite in, 228

Badin, Stephen T.: and education of slaves, 51; and lay-trusteeism, 84; as slaveholder, 90; mentioned, 61

Baltimore, Maryland: Catholic colleges in, 73; cholera in, 118; ethnic rivalries in, 83; founding of Catholic diocese of, 55; immigrants in, 91, 92; nativism in, 93, 116; riots in, 97

Baptists: freedmen as, 168, 188; slaves as, 166-67

Bardstown, Kentucky: Catholic cathedral in, 80; Catholic colleges in, 72-73; Catholic life in, 61; founding of Catholic diocese of, 60

Barron, Edward, 89

Barry, John, Bp., 67

Beauregard, Pierre Gustave Toutant de: biography of, 231-32; mentioned, 236, 239

Becker, Pierre, 227

Bedini, Gaetano, Abp., 24, 95

Bellinger, John, 224

Bellinger, Susan, 224

Blacks. *See* Creole (colored); Free blacks; Slaves

Blanc, Antoine, Abp.: and blacks, 37; episcopal administration of, 43, 58-59; and lay-trusteeism, 36, 73; and recruitment of priests, 34n

CATHOLICS IN THE OLD SOUTH

Designed by Haywood Ellis

Composition by Omni Composition Services, Macon, Georgia
    The text was scanned by Joan McCord, "read" by a Hendrix Typereader II OCR Scanner,
    formatted by Janet Middlebrooks on an Addressograph/Multigraph Comp/Set
    5404 Phototypesetter, then paginated on an A/M Comp/Set 4510.

Text paper—60 pound Warren's Olde Style

Printing (offset lithography) was by Omnipress, Inc., Macon, Georgia
Binding by John H. Dekker and Sons, Grand Rapids, Michigan